D0400798

2ND EDITION

GUERRILLA PUBLICITY

Hundreds of Sure-Fire Tactics to Get Maximum Sales for Minimum Dollars

JAY CONRAD LEVINSON, RICK FRISHMAN, AND JILL LUBLIN
WITH MARK STEISEL

AVON, MASSACHUSETTS

Copyright © 2008, 2002 by Jay Conrad Levinson, Rick Frishman, and Jill Lublin.
All rights reserved.
This book, or parts thereof, may not be reproduced in any
form without permission from the publisher; exceptions are
made for brief excerpts used in published reviews.

Published by Adams Business, an imprint of
Adams Media, an F+W Publications Company
57 Littlefield Street, Avon, MA 02322. U.S.A.
www.adamsmedia.com

ISBN 10: 1-59869-845-1
ISBN 13: 978-1-59869-845-9

Printed in the United States of America.

J I H G F E D C B A

Library of Congress Cataloging-in-Publication Data
is available from the publisher.

This publication is designed to provide accurate and authoritative information with regard to the subject matter covered. It is sold with the understanding that the publisher is not engaged in rendering legal, accounting, or other professional advice. If legal advice or other expert assistance is required, the services of a competent professional person should be sought.

—From a *Declaration of Principles* jointly adopted by a Committee of the American Bar Association and a Committee of Publishers and Associations

Many of the designations used by manufacturers and sellers to distinguish their product are claimed as trademarks. Where those designations appear in this book and Adams Media was aware of a trademark claim, the designations have been printed with initial capital letters.

This book is available at quantity discounts for bulk purchases.
For information, please call 1-800-289-0963.

To God, who makes my life and light possible. May I always spread great messages to make a difference in the world. I am grateful for all your blessings.

—Jill Lublin

To my wife Robbi, with love and thanks.

—Rick Frishman

ACKNOWLEDGMENTS

We want to extend our heartfelt appreciation to the following people who generously shared their expertise with us. Each of these individuals is an acknowledged expert who helped us immeasurably in the writing of this book. Thank you for your knowledge and your time and for sharing them with us. We are extremely grateful! They are:

Denise Bach
Darren Ballegeer
Alex Carroll
Jody Colvard
Jennifer Gerinomo
Randy Gilbert
Beth Gissenger
Tia Graham
Bill Harrison
Steve Harrison
Steve Lillo
Alex Mandosian
Elena Miranda
Jeff Nordquist
Michelle Price
Joel Roberts
Penny C. Sansevieri
Jess Todtfeld
Bob Witeck
Cecilia Zamora

From Jill: I so appreciate my coauthors—Rick Frishman, a wonderful colleague, and Jay Levinson, always a kind and loyal supporter. I acknowledge with deep appreciation the efforts and superb work of Mark Steisel, who is a master in every way and dynamite at his craft.

Thanks to the super people at Adams Media—Andrea Norville, our patient and terrific editor, and Laura Daly. Thank you for making this happen! Thanks also to Michael Larsen and Elizabeth Pomada, whose friendship and literary services have been invaluable in my career.

Steve Lillo—a partner beyond my dreams—your continuous, unending, unconditional love and support provide a rock solid foundation for my life.

I also want to acknowledge the varied contributions of so many colleagues, mentors, and friends. Thank you one and all:

- Bill and Donna Bauman, founders for the Center for Soulful Living (*www.aboutcsl.com*). Your wisdom and teaching have greatly influenced my life.
- The circle of angels, friends, and colleagues—particularly, Lynn Dohrmann and Berny Dohrmann, two visionaries committed to growing dreams and businesses (*www.ceospace.net*).
- Mark LeBlanc, whose unwavering brilliant advice and sweet heart has contributed greatly to my life and success (*www.smallbusinesssuccess.com*).
- Michelle Rochwarger—a dear friend whose profound business advice and friendship has meant the world (*www.strategicresourcesalliance.com*).
- My amazing friends and family who bring such support, heart, joy, direction, advice, spirit, and sweetness into my life: Seymour Lublin, Rose Sugerman, Randy Peyser, Gloria Wilcox, Michelle Price, Reggie and Andrea Henkart, Jeff Herzbach, Hollis Polk, Jessica Heller Frank, Steve Lublin and family, Jack Lublin, Lynn Fox and family, Marci Shimoff, Russell Feingold, Cheri Hill, Eric Lofholm, Tiana Contedubs, Les Hewitt, T.Harv Eker, Natashia Halikowski, Patricia and Vern McDade, John Assaraf, Sue McKinney, Tim Smith, Ann Evanston , Jeanne-Marie Grumet, Carol Heller Frank , Marie Cooke, David and Andrea Lieberstein, Loral Langemeier, Ana Amour , Charles Peri, Jessa Rank, Carol Kramer, Camille Kurtz, and all my other angels, both visible and invisible.

—JILL LUBLIN

From Rick: The first thank-you goes to my wonderful coauthors, Jay and Jill. Mark Steisel, your help and wisdom have been invaluable. Working with all of you has been a joy.

Thank you to our super editor at Adams Media, Andrea Norville, and to Laura Daly, Beth Gissinger, and all the wonderful Adams gang who helped in making this book. And to my friends and agents Michael Larsen and Elizabeth Pomada—thank you for all of your help.

I have to acknowledge Mike (Manny) Levine, who founded Planned Television Arts in 1962 and was my mentor, and partner, for over eighteen years. Mike taught me that work has to be fun and meaningful, and then the profits will follow.

To my exceptional management team at PTA—David Hahn, Deb Kohan, Paul Schwartz, Brian Feinblum, Sandy Trupp, Kristin Clifford and Sharon Farnell, your professionalism, loyalty and friendship mean more to me than you will ever know. To Hillary Rivman, and David Thalberg, who helped build PTA and are still affiliates and friends of our company. To Bob Unterman, you are always there when I need you and are truly a best friend. To the staff of PTA, you are the best in the business.

To my friends Mark Victor Hansen and Jack Canfield. Making the journey with the two of you has been incredible, and your friendship and advice have been invaluable. To Harvey Mackay, for the lessons about networking and for your amazing support. You are in a class of your own. And to my brother Scott, who has always been there to support me in whatever I do. To my children, Adam, Rachel, and Stephanie. Watching you grow into fine young individuals has been the highlight of my life. And to my wife, Robbi—you are my strength.

—Rick Frishman

CONTENTS

INTRODUCTION

When the original version of this book was published, we were overwhelmed by the reception it received. Who would have known? When readers told us how much they liked our book and how helpful it was, we felt great. When people continued to praise the book and kept asking us when we would write a new and updated version, we were delighted to comply. So here it is.

Over the last six years, a lot has happened in publicity, but then again, much has remained the same. In *Guerrilla Publicity, 2nd Edition,* we've tried to build on the solid foundation of our original book and teach you what's new. First, we reviewed the entire book, updated it, and retained the basics upon which solid publicity campaigns must be built. Then we added ten new chapters, nearly one-third more, to the original edition. These new chapters cover campaign timelines, utilizing specialized groups, media training, public speaking, and radio; they get into the emerging technical areas of teleseminars and virtual tours, blogs, podcasting, e-mail campaigns, and other online options. These new additions will give you many concrete ways to build and enhance your publicity campaigns.

The impact of technology has made publicity more accessible to more people because the Internet provides so much information and has such a broad reach. Publicity may be more accessible, but it remains the most overlooked marketing tool, even though it can be the:

- » Least expensive,
- » Least risky,
- » Most effective, and
- » Easiest to use . . . *when you understand how to use it.*

Most people don't know the value publicity adds to their businesses or how to implement it. *Guerrilla Publicity, 2nd Edition* will show you the light!

THE *GUERRILLA* APPROACH

What we mean by the term *guerrilla* has not changed from the first edition. Guerrillas are business operators who use their time, energy, and imagination instead of their money to build their businesses. And unlike traditional marketing, which is geared to big businesses, guerrilla publicity is targeted at smaller businesses which have big dreams rather than big bankrolls. Guerrillas place primary importance on how many relationships they build, not on how many dollars they take in. Guerrilla entrepreneurs know the importance of the journey and they are not inclined to rush toward a goal.

Guerrilla publicity works best for small- to mid-level businesses and provides the widest exposure at the lowest price; it costs far less than advertising and can produce better results. Publicity lets you tell your story in greater depth than advertising, which is crucial for new and unique enterprises. You also gain credibility sooner with publicity because people believe information that is reported as news. Since the tools and techniques covered in this volume are relatively inexpensive, they offer you plenty of help to effectively launch your campaign at low cost.

Ironically, larger corporations are adopting many of the low-cost techniques at the heart of guerrilla publicity. Principles such as the importance of building relationships and promoting within communities are now being more widely recognized. This basic belief is at the center of powerful, new developments in new media and Web 2.0—viral marketing, blogs, podcasts, and social networking—areas that we have included in this volume.

Guerrillas have always been efficiency and cost conscious. The first edition of *Guerrilla Publicity* helped destroy the myth that using publicity was too expensive, too complicated, too time consuming, and that it required special expertise, staff, and resources. Now, this edition goes even further. It explains many exciting new approaches that guerrillas can inexpensively and efficiently incorporate into their arsenals to get their stories told and stay on the cutting edge.

PUBLICITY, PUBLIC RELATIONS, AND ADVERTISING

For the purposes of this book, *publicity* is getting free or inexpensive exposure for your product or service, and building favorable interest in it. It's creating a buzz, an identity, and name recognition, and getting your message across. However, publicity is just a part of public relations.

Public relations (PR) is the overall planning, approach, and strategy for dealing with the media in general. While PR encompasses publicity, it goes beyond merely publicizing what you are selling. It includes a variety of other specialties such as reputation management, communication with investors, and crises control.

Public relations is human relations. It isn't merely getting your name in the paper or appearing on radio or TV; it's how you interact with and represent yourself to the world. PR begins as soon as you meet or are seen by others. It's about how you treat your clients, employees, and suppliers. It's virtually a full-time job that starts the moment you walk out your door each morning and continues until you say your last "good-byes" each night. It's everything from how your receptionist answers the phone to how your staff presents themselves.

Advertising is a typically more expensive alternative to publicity. Publicity and PR utilize relationships to build support for your products and services, while advertising builds interest by paying for it. As the old adage says: "With advertising, you pay for it; with publicity, you pray for it." Advertising can also get you publicity, but advertising will cost your company money.

TECHNOLOGY

Technology has become the publicist's major tool and is vital in promoting your product or service. Teleseminars, virtual tours, blogs, e-mail, podcasting, and other Internet tools are now crucial to getting great publicity. Therefore, in writing this book, we consulted with leading experts in these technical fields and devoted a number of chapters to the role they play in getting publicity today.

In the past, most technology-based publicity innovations were expensive and difficult for the average user to employ. Now, that's completely changed. Blogging, podcasting, social networking, and other Internet approaches can be started inexpensively and without a degree from MIT. These *new media*, communication technologies that use computers, are user friendly and will help you launch a successful guerrilla publicity campaign. In this book we cover these various Web 2.0 tools—blogs, podcasts, social networking sites—and other Internet applications, and discuss how you can use them to build the base of your guerilla publicity.

LET US KNOW

Publicity can change your life. And it can certainly change your business. So, sit back and enjoy this book. When you've finished it, please feel free to contact us at our Web site *www.guerrillapublicity.com* with your comments and suggestions, and tell us about your personal experiences with guerrilla publicity.

Thanks!

CHAPTER 1

PUT YOURSELF ON THE MAP

"A terrible thing happens without publicity . . . NOTHING!"
—*Master showman P.T. Barnum*

A subtle, but important change has taken place in publicity since the first edition of this book was published in 2002. Instead of trying to promote individuals, businesses, and their products and services, the focus has shifted to making connections with smaller communities, building relationships with their members, and using these networks as a base to promote their goods. Although guerrillas have always focused on such relationships—larger, more mainstream businesses have recently followed suit. And the ways in which these relationships form and grow has changed.

At the forefront of this change is the new media, which disseminates information through blogs, podcasts, social networking sites, and other online means. The new media focuses on reaching communities: groups of people with shared values, interests, and beliefs. These communities are built on trust. Their members regularly read blogs, listen to podcasts, instant message, visit social network sites, and participate in other online activities.

In order to relate to these people and develop relationships within their communities, you need to be able to take advantage of the new media. Community members are loyal: they follow bloggers' and podcasters' advice, attend the events they recommend, try the goods and services they endorse, and adopt the positions they advocate. As Internet marketing expert Penny C. Sansevieri points out, "Consumers don't buy from ads, they buy from other consumers."

In the new media, information is distributed by *viral marketing*. That means that when it is introduced into a community, members comment on it, which causes it to spread from person-to-person and to other communities like a medical virus. Some believe that the new media's viral marketing makes traditional publicity concepts obsolete. We disagree. Although the impact of these new innovations is great and continues to play an increasing role, publicity is still based on established concepts that have withstood the test of time.

Throughout the book, we will give you the whole package: the tried and tested as well as the modern and cutting edge, the traditional along with the new media. We will also tell you how to use established approaches differently. We want to give you all the options; to arm you with an arsenal of different weapons that you can use to address any situation and conduct any publicity campaign.

PUBLICITY BASICS

So as you know, publicity is the art of stirring up interest to promote you or your product or service. It's convincing others to sing your praises, to blare from the rooftops:

» Who you are,
» What you do, and
» Why it's important.

Publicity will put you on the map because it:

» Builds your identity.
» Increases your visibility.
» Generates name recognition.
» Gets your message across.
» Compels people to buy, invest, and do business with you.

Publicity is the art of putting yourself in the spotlight. As you know, spotlights are narrowly focused—they don't shine on everyone. To capture the spotlight, place yourself in the proper position; work your way onto center stage.

Positioning is an intricate process that takes time, trial and error, endless patience and persistence. It's more than a one- or two-shot effort that produces wonders overnight, it's a coordinated series of actions that requires explicit planning, devotion to detail, and endless follow up . . . that's why they call them publicity *campaigns*. And in this book, we'll explain just how they work.

GUERRILLA TACTICS

In publicity, rule number one is *blow your own horn*, but do it melodically, musically so you don't scare people away. If you don't let the world know how great you are, no one else will. And if you don't assert yourself, those who are more aggressive than you will cut in front of you, block your path, and you'll end up stuck in the same old place . . . you'll never get ahead. So *toot, toot, toot* to everyone you speak with, write, or meet. Become a one-person advertising agency. Tell them all who you are, exactly what you have to offer, and precisely how it can benefit them. If the public doesn't hear about you, your product, or your service, as Barnum pointed out, *nothing* will happen.

YOU ARE THE PRODUCT

Guerrillas know that regardless of what product you produce or service you provide, *you are the product*! You are your own brand and you must always sell yourself. And selling yourself is a full-time job. When you repeatedly sell yourself, you build name recognition, which will increase your business because consumers are drawn to those with familiar names. So, make yourself known; build name recognition and sales.

Become a recognizable brand; it will put you on the map. Brand names have status and prestige. They give you a big edge in business because name recognition translates into hard currency, greenbacks, moolah, *lots of money*. Publicity is a time-tested method of making you stand out.

People trust the familiar. They find the familiar safer than the unknown, and yearn to be associated with the familiar. When your name first appears in the papers, on TV, or on the Internet, the public starts to take notice and becomes aware of you. It's the "*I've Heard of Her Somewhere*" syndrome. People become curious. "Who is she? What does she do? Why do I always hear her name?" As they get answers, you become familiar and gain name recognition.

Name recognition isn't simply people knowing who you are; it's also their knowing what you do. It's associating your name with your product or service. When you gain name recognition, the public thinks of you when they want your product or service, they will stand in line to do business with you. For example, if you need to ship a package overnight, companies like FedEx or UPS immediately come to mind because they have created name recognition.

GUERRILLA TACTICS

To get on the map, start modestly. Don't immediately think hemispheres! First, start on your street, and when it's saturated, branch out to your neighborhood, then to your district, city, county, state, country, your continent, and finally the world. Spread the word. Tell everyone you know, everyone you come in contact with, who you are, what you do, and how your goods or services can benefit them. Don't overlook anyone, you never know who might help. Approach those closest to you, your family, friends, and neighbors. Then speak with the folks who run the pharmacy, the tailor shop, and the car wash. If they can't use your product or service, ask them who they know who could.

To expand your contacts, join clubs and organizations. Increase your visibility by volunteering, teaching, coaching, and serving on committees. Write articles or submit items about your business or interests to local publications such as free weekly newspapers, advertisers, newsletters, or Web sites. Write and publish a blog or a newsletter, organize and lead a workshop. Discover what the media is covering and cultivate journalists, editors, and radio and TV producers.

POSITION YOURSELF AS AN EXPERT

You're an expert, even though you may not think you are. If you operate a business, you're probably an expert in your field. Professional expertise simply means that you know what you're doing. It doesn't necessarily mean that you're the world's foremost authority. It also doesn't mean that you know absolutely everything about your field . . . no one does!

GUERRILLA INTELLIGENCE

Expertise has a way of sneaking up on us. We start with little and before we realize it, we've acquired a storehouse of knowledge and know-how. Mastering your interests is one of life's great satisfactions. Think for a moment about how much you know about what you do, how long it has taken you to learn it, and how helpful it is to others. It's a significant accomplishment, one that not everyone attains. Let's call this achievement "professional expertise."

Besides your professional expertise, you're also an expert in a number of other areas. For example, being a single mother, part of a married couple, or a PTA member; growing roses, researching on the Internet, or canoeing; yodeling, taking photographs, or canning peaches. Whatever it is—it's your "personal expertise."

In most cases, professional expertise is what you're selling; it's your basic product. However, your *personal* expertise enhances your *professional* expertise by adding special flavors that make it unique. Your personal expertise places your special stamp on your work. The combination creates the perspective that makes approaches special, original, and insightful.

Let your personal expertise shine through. That's what people want. They want *your* unique vision, *your* particular understanding, and *your* distinctive form of expression, creation, and implementation. When you build on your professional expertise with your personal expertise, it distinguishes you and you deliver something special.

Let others know you're an expert. Declare that you have knowledge and/or skills that others can use and tell them why it's special. Establish your expertise by:

- ❑ Writing articles
- ❑ Giving talks
- ❑ Holding demonstrations
- ❑ Starting a Web site
- ❑ Writing a blog
- ❑ Making a podcast
- ❑ Participating in conferences, workshops, panel discussions
- ❑ Creating a presence on social networking sites
- ❑ Volunteering your services

Write or talk about tasks that you've performed a thousand times: how to bid at auctions, create word processing shortcuts, or invest in art online. Demonstrate it and teach others, step by step, how to do it.

GUERRILLA TALE: When your professional expertise is in a specialized niche, inform the media. A therapist who specialized in issues with people over age forty became a media darling after he submitted an article on midlife crises to a local TV station. The station aired a feature on him and began consulting him when it needed information on the over-forty generation. Soon major TV news organizations came calling; he became a TV fixture and a national authority.

TESTIMONIALS

Use testimonials from your customers to your advantage. They help build your credibility, so compile a testimonial file. Ask everyone you work with for written endorsements; leave no stone unturned!

> **GUERRILLA TALE:** After hearing a new artist's recording, a consumer wrote the record company, "This is what my heart would sound like if it was a symphony." *Voilà!* The company pounced on the phrase and plastered it on all its materials for a promotional campaign that helped the recording go platinum.

Guidelines for Securing Testimonials

- » Get in the habit of asking *every* client or customer for letters of praise.
- » Ask them to state how great your work was and how much they enjoyed working with you. You'll be surprised how highly they extol you and how wonderfully they express it.
- » Ask for endorsements during the first thirty to sixty days or as soon as short-term projects are complete.
- » Have your clients/customers write their testimonials on their letterhead and limit them to one or two paragraphs.
- » Explain to clients/customers that you plan to post the testimonials on your newsletter, blog, and Web site, and use them in promotional materials.
- » Point out to your clients/customers that the testimonials could help *them* by increasing *their* visibility.
- » Offer to prepare drafts for their approval if clients hesitate to write them themselves.

When you begin receiving testimonials, update your Web site regularly to add recent praise and delete that which is dated. However, you may want to continue to run a few older testimonials because they attest that you've got a long track record delivering customer satisfaction.

SWITCHING GEARS

GUERRILLA TACTICS Successful salespeople lug around a ton of products in their sample cases. If one item doesn't sell, they move on to the next. When you pitch, have backups, and if your targets don't bite on the first item you pitch, move on to item number two. If they show any interest in number two, three, or four, go with it, give them what they want. Then after you've built a more solid relationship, go back and pitch your initial item.

If media organizations aren't interested in covering your business-writing service, switch gears to get their attention. Pitch the fact that you build replicas of famous buildings out of toothpicks, that you can simultaneously play three string instruments with your toes, or that you were a Navy SEAL. Show them something that will get their attention—even if it's not your primary product or service. Then, when you have their attention, work in information on the main thing you want to promote: your business writing.

When it comes to publicity, the fact that the media is interested in you is more important than the reason for their interest. So, don't get lofty if a reporter's reason for interviewing you is not exactly what you want. Make the most of it and—as much as it may hurt—grin and bear it. Publicity can be humbling, but it's still publicity that can work to your advantage.

When the media seizes upon angles that you're not pushing, it's usually better to adjust and be their resource than to fight for your own agenda. Many roads can lead to your destination. It is important to get whatever publicity you can or else you may find yourself alienating the press and ending up with nothing. Go along with the media, but try to get them to include what you primarily want to promote.

GUERRILLA TALE: A cancer survivor's press releases promoted her new clothing line. The media that picked up her story concentrated on her medical triumph rather than on her designs. Instead of throwing in the towel when her clothing line wasn't featured, the designer adjusted. To remain in the limelight, she kept in contact with the media as a cancer survival expert. She kept them posted on her developments, sent them information, and when questions arose, quickly responded. She also actively promoted her clothing line, always mentioning it. Within a few months, the media began referring to her as the cancer-surviving clothing designer and soon it was running separate features on her design business.

REMEMBER

Create your own promotional opportunities. Since you're the product, blow your own horn. It will build name recognition, and get you in the public sphere as an expert in your field. You have the knowledge that people can use, and let customers' and clients' testimonials explain to them why that expertise is special.

CHAPTER 2

INTRODUCE YOURSELF WITH A SOUND BITE

"The short words are best,
and the old words are the best of all."
—*Winston Churchill*

In our busy world, no one has time for the full story—they want a synopsis, a digest, a capsule that takes only seconds to deliver, is easy to swallow, and resonates in their minds. And it must contain everything they need to know. Since publicity is about getting your message across, brevity is a must. You must create a short introductory message that will cut through the din and draw attention to who you are, what you do, and the benefit it will provide. We call these messages sound bites.

If you want to get your message across, you need a great sound bite that will immediately capture the attention of busy people. When you get an opening to deliver your sound bite, you better make it good! You must deliver your sound bite *quickly*, *clearly*, and *compellingly*. The more briefly you say it, the better it is.

The media is especially impatient and wants information fast. When you watch TV or listen to the radio, notice how quickly everything moves. Most news stories are delivered in ten seconds or less and most TV segments run for three minutes. Since the media moves so fast, you must deliver information to them fast.

The purpose of a sound bite is to turn listeners on; it's a verbal business card that you can deliver when you're introduced to new people. It's your "elevator speech": a snappy, self-description that you can rattle off in the time it takes an elevator to rise from the lobby to the fifth floor.

GUERRILLA TACTICS Create a sound bite. Make sure it includes your name, the product or service you provide, and how it will help your consumer. Create your sound bite in two stages: first, create a message that you can deliver in less than thirty seconds; then cut it down to ten or fifteen seconds for the media. Radio news segments come in ten-second increments so "if you can't express what you want and why it's newsworthy in ten seconds, you're off the phone," advised a news director for a major NBC affiliate.

As theatrical impresario David Belasco said, "If you can't write your idea on the back of my calling card, you don't have a clear idea." A sound bite is the foundation on which to build a forceful and memorable public persona. It's the first impression you make, an attention-grabbing device that will get you and your message noticed. Think of it as an investment with an immediate return because every time you use it, someone considers paying you.

Writing a sound bite forces you to sharpen your focus and examine your approach. It makes you identify your audiences, clarify who you are addressing, and focus on what you hope to receive from them. When you narrow these fields, it's easier to promote yourself.

THE ABCS OF SOUND BITES

Your sound bite must be a grabber—a memorable message that makes listeners want to buy your products, champion your causes, and fight your wars. If it's short and gets their attention, it buys you more time to sell. Your sound bite must be:

INTERESTING enough to attract immediate **ATTENTION**,
POWERFUL enough to be **REMEMBERED**, and
CONVINCING enough to stir overloaded listeners into **ACTION**.

Examples of a variety of effective sound bites are:

» "I used to weigh over 300 pounds. Now, I'm a size 8. I can teach you how to lose weight and keep it off."—*Diet book author*
» "My name is ______. My free tips on ______.com make investors rich from Internet stocks."—*Investment broker*
» "I teach people to look rich, even if they aren't."—*Fashion advisor*
» "I'm a ghost writer. I turn your experiences, adventures, and ideas into bestselling books."—*Freelance writer*
» "My name is ______. I free folks from financial worry. Give me a call at ______ and I'll do the same for you."—*Financial consultant*

Most people aren't accustomed to promoting themselves. So when it's time to blow their own horns, they don't know what to say or they tend to over do it. However, in business, with so many competitors vying for the same dollars, you must distinguish yourself from the crowd. The best way to start is with a sound bite.

GUERRILLA INTELLIGENCE

If you can't give your sound bite quickly and powerfully, you don't know your material well enough or have not perfected your delivery. Go back to the drawing board. Rethink it, rewrite it, and practice reciting until it feels just right. Then test it on your friends and family to see how well it plays.

SOUND BITE CHECKLIST

Be creative, speak like a star, and make your product or service sound groundbreaking. Write a sound bite that captivates media people, showing them your star potential and making them want to move mountains to advance your career. In our celebrity-obsessed society, the media is desperately seeking new faces to promote and help launch to fame.

Learn from those who have come before you and research recent publicity masters. Study those who constantly receive media attention. Ask yourself, what keeps drawing the media to Donald Trump, Richard Branson, and Martha Stewart? Identify the elements that constantly keep these people in the public eye. Isolate the techniques they use, what they project, and have in common, and which parts of their approaches could work for you. Then weave those pieces into your sound bite.

Before creating your sound bite, ask yourself the following:

- What's most interesting or unusual about you and your work? What makes it memorable?
- How did you get into this career?
- What excites you most about your career?
- What are your strengths?
- What is special about what you provide to your clients/ customers?
- How do you satisfy your clients/customers?
- What motivates you?
- What's on your drawing board? When do you see these plans being enacted?
- What interests people most when they first meet you? What are their first questions?
- What about you makes people stop, listen, and say "wow"?

While drafting your sound bite, think about your answers. List the reasons why your product or service is unique and/or unusual and why your target audience can't do without it. Identify what's special about your work and come up with the most colorful words to describe it.

HOW TO WRITE YOUR SOUND BITE

Start by writing whatever comes to mind without worrying about how long it runs. Be honest and truthful, but remain positive. Take your time, this isn't a race. When you finish your rough draft:

1. Circle every descriptive word that you've written.
2. List each circled word on a separate sheet of paper.
3. Question whether the words you selected are the most descriptive and colorful words available. If not, add or substitute more hard-hitting words.
4. Place the words you've listed in the order of importance.
5. Draft a new sound bite consisting of one or two sentences, using the most important words on your list.

Read the completed sound bite aloud several times and change whatever sounds awkward. Trust your ear. Although your sound bite should cleverly communicate your message, clarity is paramount. *Don't sacrifice clarity for cleverness.*

Recite the sound bite out loud until you believe it and feel comfortable delivering it. *When you believe your sound bite, others will too.* You'll also sound more confident and convincing. Read your sound bite to others, get their input and consider making the changes they suggest.

Time how long your revised sound bite runs. If it's more than thirty seconds, cut it down to 30 seconds or less. After you've whittled it to less than thirty seconds, try to cut another ten to fifteen seconds without weakening the message. Don't memorize your sound bite; instead picture key words and reel them off in order as if you're descending a ladder. When you know the key points you have to cover, you can state them in different ways, which helps your sound bite seem more spontaneous and less rehearsed.

HOW TO DELIVER YOUR MESSAGE

Practice your sound bite in front of the mirror, in your car, in the shower. Audio and video tape yourself reciting it. Concentrate on looking sincere, enthusiastic, and confident, but don't overdo it. Don't act or be dramatic. Speak conversationally and with sincerity. Don't be a ham or a clown, be professional. When you deliver your sound bite, imagine that you're meeting the President or the Pope or Oprah—and that your business depends on your being booked on her show.

When you give your sound bite, maintain eye contact and smile softly. Not some big, silly grin, but a warm smile that conveys confidence and conviction. Show listeners that you're happy to deliver your message and that you believe in yourself and your message.

Project that you're an expert by speaking with *authority*, *excitement*, and *passion*. Your audiences will sense your conviction, feed off it, and want to share their feelings with others. Football immortal Vince Lombardi reportedly said, "If you're not fired with enthusiasm, you'll be fired with enthusiasm!"

Remember, your sound bite serves as your verbal calling card. Work it into letters, mailers, announcements, e-mail blasts, brochures, ads, Internet chat rooms, questionnaires, blog introductions, and applications. You want to use your sound bite at every opportunity.

Also, always have lots of printed business cards on hand to distribute when you deliver your sound bite. If you have brochures or other business materials, hand them out liberally. Think of them as emissaries that will spread your message. Repetition reinforces name recognition, brand identity, and it builds confidence.

GUERRILLA TACTICS

Customize your sound bite for specific audiences and situations. For example, if you're at an auto dealers' meeting, sprinkle in terms that relate to that industry like "on all cylinders," "out of gas," or "cruise control." Speaking their language breaks down barriers, lightens the mood, and makes groups feel that you're targeting them directly. In doing so, you become one of them, at least for the time you're together.

HAVE A BACKUP PLAN

Prepare a backup sound bite. Be ready to ditch your standard spiel if it's inappropriate, if someone else in the group has a strikingly similar pitch, or if your sound bite doesn't seem to be going over well. If your pitch is not working, use prewritten "ad libs." Add something about the weather, the traffic or your companion's business. You can throw them in to sound spontaneous—even though you've already written them. Your main objective is to get your message across, so if altering your sound bite improves your chances, be sure to go for it.

Always trust your instincts. You'll quickly learn how and when to alter your sound bite and become adept at making changes based upon your instincts and observations. Work in references to hot news items, scandals, or events that will make your sound bite more relevant and up to date.

REMEMBER

Creating a memorable sound bite will make people take immediate notice. Be sure to practice it until you can recite it naturally and with confidence. Customize your sound bite for special occasions and vary your pitch so that it seems to be spontaneous. And always deliver your message with authority, excitement, and passion.

CHAPTER 3

YOUR CAMPAIGN STARTS WITH YOU

"It takes a person who is wide awake
to make his dreams come true."

—Roger Babson, investment banker, author, and educator

People want you to be authentic. They want to know that what you say is true, that you will deliver as promised, and that your product or service will work as advertised. If you hope to garner great publicity, your campaign must be authentic as well. It has to come from within and reflect what you truly believe and how you actually perform. Never promise what you can't provide and make sure whatever you are putting out there is the truth.

Publicity never sleeps—it's an ongoing, 24/7 battle—so you can't sleep either. You have to fight for it night and day, and really, truly want it. Since you're the product, you're also your best marketing tool. So to be successful, you must honestly believe in what you are promoting. You can't fake it.

GUERRILLA INTELLIGENCE

In business, results are the bottom line. Glamorous, exciting individuals may initially get ink, but even high-profile people cannot succeed in business if they do not consistently get the job done. If the word gets out that you don't deliver as promised, doors will slam in your face and it will become increasingly difficult, if not impossible, to sell yourself.

If you claim that you're an expert, you'd better be one. Know what it takes to get the job done—and make sure people are aware that you get it done right.

SING YOUR OWN PRAISES

Your publicity campaign starts with you, so it's your job to prove your expertise to people. The most obvious signs of expertise are that your customers or clients keep coming back and recommend you to others, and that your peers consult you for advice and assistance. Make this information known. You can capitalize on your achievements by singing your own praises.

Self-promotion is essential. You can't be shy, embarrassed, or rely on others to champion your cause. Even when you hire marketing or promotion professionals, you're still responsible for your own publicity. Look at the successful people you know. They quickly let everyone know who they are, what they do, and how important it is. Follow their lead. With practice, extolling your own virtues will become easier. And before you know it, it will be fun.

Jim McCann, a client of Rick's, has had extraordinary success as the TV spokesman for his company, 1-800-FLOWERS. Audiences sense that McCann believes, from his core, that 1-800-FLOWERS will deliver all he promises. They believe that he's more than just a petal pusher; they see him as a true believer—and consumers are more likely to listen to true believers and to buy what they're selling. This sort of name recognition requires repetition. Repetition makes the unfamiliar familiar. When your name and message become familiar, you gain credibility and become a known commodity.

Self-promotion, when done well, is extremely beneficial, but when done poorly, it is offensive. It can be the difference between success and failure. While it's important to trumpet your triumphs, no one wants to listen to obnoxious, self-serving boasting. It scares folks away.

GUERRILLA INTELLIGENCE

After years of being bombarded by a relentless stream of pitchmen making promise after promise after promise, the public has become selective. They want authenticity. They insist on seeing results in order to believe the pitch. Today's audiences may be entertained by hucksters, but they will seldom buy what doesn't ring true to them. And if they buy it, and it doesn't work, they'll remember who sold it to them.

It's not enough to tell others that you're an expert; you have to specifically explain how you can benefit them. "Hi, I'm Computer Cal and I can save you hundreds of dollars on the ideal system that is custom-built just for you." A strong, grounded pitch will deliver your qualifications, without any hint of arrogance.

CAPITALIZE ON EVERY OPPORTUNITY

In order to run a successful publicity campaign, position yourself for opportunities by joining clubs, groups, and organizations where you can meet people. Attend their meetings, take part in their events, become a member of their social networking sites, and tell them who you are, what you do, and how it can help them. Go to bars, cafés, and online venues where people in your industry, the media, or those who might be interested in your product or service meet.

Learn to spot promotional opportunities and take advantage of them. Always be alert for openings that can work in your favor. At first, it may feel strained, uncomfortable, awkward, pushy, or overly aggressive, but before long, you'll develop a knack for when to jump in and when to back off.

When it's time to jump in you should tell that person who you are and what you do, and speak with conviction. Consumers buy products because of the seller's passion and excitement. Your enthusiasm and belief become their cause. In order to tell them how your product or service can help them and properly answer their questions, you must believe that what you are promoting will change the world and you must express this flawlessly.

GUERRILLA TACTICS Train yourself to spot opportunities and, when you see openings, pounce. Opportunities don't find you; you have to find them—and make them happen! Have you ever wondered how some people can always be so witty? It's because of their focus. Witty people are continually looking for the humor in every situation. They constantly search for openings for clever comments, observations, and jibes . . . they know how to turn every situation into a joke. Top salespeople and publicity professionals possess a similar talent. They focus on weaving information about their products and services into the most remote, unrelated subjects. And they pounce . . . they know how to turn every situation into a sales or promotional opportunity.

ALWAYS BE PREPARED

Unexpected opportunities can occur any time and at any place—so be prepared to capitalize on them. You might be walking your dog, riding on the bus, or sitting in a restaurant when you run into a reporter, a writer, a producer, or another person of influence. You never know when opportunity might strike and it's your job to be prepared to promote your product. Coauthor Jill Lublin tells clients, "V8 publicity (*I should have done my publicity today*) doesn't work. You can't be half hearted. A successful publicity campaign works on volume. It takes repeated efforts, over the long haul, to spread your message and tell the world who you are."

If you deal in a product, carry it with you. Take it everywhere, not simply obvious places like trade shows, conferences, and business meetings. Bring it when you go to the store, to concerts, even to church. If it's too big to lug around, carry pictures that you can easily show.

Even if it's a pain, always carry your products, brochures, or samples with you. Make it a habit. Stuff them in your pockets, purses, or briefcases. Never miss a chance to show them, explain them, and respond to all questions and comments.

GUERRILLA TALE: On a flight from New York to Washington, DC, Rick Frishman's client Kurt Eichenwald was holding in plain sight a copy of his book *Serpent of the Rock: Crime, Betrayal, and the Terrible Secrets of Prudential-Bache*. Seated next to Kurt was a producer from *60 Minutes*. They quickly struck up a conversation, the producer asked about Kurt's book and *bingo*! *60 Minutes* ran a full segment on Kurt and his book. Carrying a copy with him on his flight—that's all it took.

REMEMBER

Publicity is a full-time, 24/7 job. It never stops! Continually tell the world that you're an expert and how you can help them. Good self-promotion can inspire, excite, and energize your prospective customers and clients as long as you believe in it. Become a walking self-advertisement. Learn to spot opportunities to toot your own horn and always be prepared to seize upon them.

CHAPTER 4

BUILD RELATIONSHIPS TO BUILD EMPIRES

"My pappy told me never to bet my bladder against a brewery or get into an argument with people who buy ink by the barrel."

—Lane Kirkland, former President of the AFL-CIO

The term "public relations" consists of two words, "public" and "relations." Relations with the public are publicists' inventories. Relationships are the most valuable assets in publicists' portfolios. The most valuable relationships are those with the media because they in turn produce relationships with the greater public. And by media we mean both the traditional media—print and television news reporters—as well as the new media—bloggers, podcasters, and social networkers.

Generally, you won't see immediate results because these types of relationships must be nurtured. It's a slow, deliberate process like erecting a brick wall: firmly and precisely placing, aligning, adjusting, and mortaring one brick at a time, row after row, until the wall is completed. However, unlike a brick wall, your relationship with the media is never complete—you must always continue building.

Every contact is important—even calls that are intercepted by voice mail and aren't returned. Repeatedly leaving your message builds name recognition; it places you on your target's radar screen. After a few messages, strangers, who once never knew that you existed, know who you are and why you're calling. And if down the road they need what you have, they will call on you.

Media relationships should be mutually beneficial. You look to the media to publicize your product or service and they look to you for stories. Let's be honest, if you didn't want publicity, you'd probably never bother with the media and visa versa. Essentially, it's a simple exchange, giving in order to receive. However, it isn't exactly an equal relationship. Sometimes you do all the work and nothing happens. The media has a monopoly over the means of distribution. While you may have the raw materials—the stories—the media controls the delivery. Without the media, your stories wouldn't get to many people.

GUERRILLA INTELLIGENCE

What we're talking about is building and maintaining long-term, ongoing relationships. Think in terms of:

CAMPAIGNS as opposed to **ADS;**

CAREERS instead of **JOBS;**

DECADES rather than **DAYS, MONTHS, OR YEARS.**

Remember that you're in business for the duration, not simply for a one-shot quickie. Develop media contacts that you can grow with, contacts that will evolve into invaluable sources down the line.

THE RULES

You can't win the publicity game if you don't know the rules. Only fools play high-stakes poker without knowing whether a flush beats a straight. Yet that's precisely what you're doing when you don't know the rules that govern relationships with the media. Since the media holds all the cards, they make the rules. If you want to play at their table, you have to adhere to their rules. Ironically, there are only three rules and they're alarmingly simple:

1. You are a resource for the media.
2. It's never personal. It's always about the story and its impact.

3. The media can always change its mind, but you can't. At any time, it can revise, cut, postpone, or even kill a story it agreed to run.

By adhering to their rules, the media will consider you a professional, someone they can rely on and with whom they'll do business.

DEAL WITH CHANGE

Remember rule number three? When it suits its purposes, the media will change what it agreed on—count on it. Actually, it can change more than that; it can change everything. Your story or appearance can be edited, rewritten, revised, chopped, bumped, postponed, or even canceled. However, be alert to the direction in which they may be taking you. If you think that direction could ultimately be harmful, stop them in their tracks—even if it costs you great publicity.

Even though you're fuming inside, be professional. Mildly express your displeasure, take it in stride, and behave as though you understand because, frankly in most cases, there's nothing you can do about it.

Instead of wasting time and energy arguing, salvage the relationship so that it will benefit you in the future. Use the word "disappointed" rather than "angry" or "frustrated." Make your point once and then drop it. Resume being a team player.

Never show anger or threaten. Instead, immediately focus on finding bargaining chips to position yourself for the future. When you capitulate, gently slip in "OK, you owe me one" and make sure they get the message. During subsequent contacts, plant subtle reminders by asking how the matter turned out.

POSITION YOURSELF AS A HELPER

The media feeds on information. It devours massive amounts of content that must continually be replenished. It's a never-ending cycle. However, the media can't possibly generate all that content itself, so it relies on others to provide leads to new stories.

Become a source for the media, proactively providing information to your various media contacts. Don't wait to be asked: volunteer all you can offer. By offering your help, you can ease their burden, earn their gratitude, and, before long, they'll rely on you, be obligated to you, and help you.

GUERRILLA TACTICS Since the media considers you its resource, it's wiser to accommodate your contacts than to try to convince them otherwise. Their only interest in you is what you can do for them or their audience. That's the reality of this relationship. But it can work to your advantage.

Take the *concierge approach*: When you speak with your media contacts, ask what they're working on and see if you have information or associates that might help. Alert them not only to items you want publicized, but also to items in which you have no stake. Convey the impression that you're looking out for their interests.

If you're able to help when the media calls, it may pay off down the road. If you don't help them out, someone else will—and it may pay off for them instead.

The best way to generate buzz—to get more articles and blog entries written about you or to be invited on more programs and podcasts—is to help your targets reach their goals. If a journalist or a producer is working on a story about nursing homes, give him or her the name of the last nursing home director you met at a seminar and offer to set up an interview.

Ask media contacts for a list of the projects on their editorial calendars for the next 30, 60, or 90 days. Inquire into and be sure you understand exactly what they need to complete their story. Then try to get it for them. Make an indelible impression by exceeding their expectations, by going beyond what's required and beyond what others will do. In addition to referring them to your sources in those fields, you can send your media contacts an article that they could use. Or you can recommend Web sites that deal with the issue they are covering. Become their researcher, investigator, contact person, and colleague.

STAY ON THEIR RADAR

With the media, the saying "out of sight is out of mind" is a truism. So remain in their minds. Besides helping them with other projects, make sure you remain a constant presence in your media contacts' professional lives.

Few things are appreciated more than small considerate gestures that aren't required or even expected. These can be as basic as a thank-you or congratulatory telephone call, e-mail, note, post card, or even a small gift. Before you give gifts, check with the organization to see if they have rules that prohibit or limit gifts. Remember, *it actually is the thought that counts* . . . so keep it simple.

After making a new contact, send a handwritten "nice-to-meet you" note. In our world of busy schedules and brief e-mails, the fact that you went to the trouble of sending a handwritten note will distinguish you. To make a grander statement, send flowers, a box of candy, a book, or a bottle of wine to show your appreciation. Or if you're marketing an inexpensive product, send the product with a short handwritten note. Send "thank-you" notes for business referrals and offer to take them to lunch or to an event of mutual interest. Act promptly or the full impact of your gesture might be lost.

In addition to sending cards or gifts as a follow-up, you can also follow writers' careers and note what they're writing and where they're working. If a certain article, interview, or piece strikes you in particular, write a short note or e-mail telling them it did. Track producers as well and see what type of programs they're running and subjects they're covering. Send a quick note on a piece of theirs you enjoyed. You can also mail handwritten congratulatory notes whenever they get promotions, awards, or a new job.

Don't go overboard. Small efforts usually pay big dividends by:

- Keeping you and your product or service in your contact's mind
- Portraying you as pleasant, considerate, and smart
- Producing more referrals
- Tightening your relationship

Remaining in contact with your various associates in the media industry will help you in the long run. By doing just a few of these simple things, your chances for publicity will grow.

HANDLE REJECTION PROPERLY

Even if you've helped your media contact and remained close with them, rejections are inevitable. You may be trying to sell flounder to a chef who needs turnips. So, make the most of them.

GUERRILLA TALE: A few years ago, coauthor Jill Lublin pitched an idea to a producer for a nationally syndicated cooking show, but the producer didn't buy Jill's idea. After the rejection, Jill continued to call the producer every month, even though she didn't have anything to pitch. She simply called to say hello and find out what the producer was working on. Most of the time, Jill got the producer's voice mail and just said "Hi, this is Jill Lublin of Promising Promotion. I'm just calling to say hello. Hope all is well." About a year and a half later, a client hired Jill to promote a video called "Cooking for Busy People." Jill immediately contacted the producer who loved the idea and booked Jill's client on the spot. After Jill's client appeared on the show, the orders for her video poured in. Sales went through the roof and her single appearance launched a thriving business . . . all because of Jill's persistence and repeated calls to develop an invaluable media contact.

Rejections can be opportunities. They can form the basis for future successes and can be building blocks for long-term relationships; use them to make a favorable impression. If you do, those who turned you down may remember your name, your courtesy, and professionalism. They may even remember where to turn if they need flounder.

REMEMBER

Although media relationships should be mutually beneficial, they aren't equal: the media holds the upper hand. However, there are ways you can use your relationships with media contacts to your advantage. Even if you have been rejected, stay in touch with that contact. Offer to help with leads on other stories and remain on his or her radar by sending follow-up notes. Try to turn even your rejections into solid, long-term relationships.

CHAPTER 5

ZERO IN ON YOUR MARKET—SAVE TIME, MONEY, AND AGGRAVATION

"All distances are the same for those who don't meet."

—Penelope Fitzgerald, Booker Prize–winning author

How often do you get lost because you don't really know where you are going? You end up stuck some place you don't want to be and in order to find your way you often must go back to where you started. Frequently, you don't know how to get back because you don't know which route to take, and in the process get even more lost. And if you do get back, you may be too exhausted to start again. Be careful—this can happen to your publicity campaign!

GUERRILLA INTELLIGENCE

When a publicity campaign veers in the wrong direction it's usually fatal; the campaign is finished. You may not detect your mistake until it's too late. And, by the time you do, you may not have the resources to get back on track or begin again. You may have spent all your capital and have nothing left. Every publicity campaign needs a direction; it needs a target. The hardest job is identifying your target and remaining focused on it. In other words:

» Know where you're going *before* deciding how to get there.

» Identify your destination.

» Then map your route.

When you know the destination, the route often is clear.

TWO AUDIENCES

Publicity is a unique marketing tool because it forces you to identify and reach two separate audiences:

1. The buying audience—those who pay you for your products or services
2. The media audience—members of the press and electronic media who could publicize your products or services

The Buying Audience

The key to publicity is identifying your potential customers. Ask who will buy what you sell? Your buying audience could be universal, or split into smaller specialty groups like farmers, pet owners, or overweight people.

Define your buying audience as narrowly as possible so you can find the best ways to reach it. Also identify various segments of that audience because you may find that different promotional efforts work better with particular segments.

The Media Audience

When you've identified your buying audience, try to determine which specific media outlets would be the most effective for your publicity efforts. Distinguish between those outlets that reach the most people and those that reach the most buyers. Don't delude yourself into thinking think that the entire world is your buying audience—it's not! Campaigns are usually more successful when they focus on smaller, more specific audiences.

When you've broken down your buying audience, it's easier to identify your ideal media audience. PR professionals excel at knowing which media outlets will most effectively reach which markets. For example, if the buying audience is senior citizens, they could target *Modern Maturity*, the magazine of AARP. For clients hoping to sell apparel to new mothers, they would pitch *Parenting* magazine.

Sources to find the best media outlets include:

- Broadcasting & Cable yearbook:
  www.bowker.com
- Cision MediaList Online:
  www.medialistsonline.com
- Media Finder:
  www.mediafinder.com
- National Directory of Magazines:
  www.oxbridge.com/NDMCluster/theNDM.asp
- Online Public Relations:
  www.online-pr.com
- Standard Periodical Directory:
  www.oxbridge.com/SPDCluster/theSPD.asp

These are all great resources for you to use in order to find publications that will reach your buying audience.

SET YOUR TARGET

Before you get started on your campaign, make sure that your plan is achievable. Be certain that the goals you set are realistic, or you could wind up not getting the results you want.

Be Realistic

Set achievable goals. If your dream is to conquer the world, don't try to conquer it in one swoop. It's like trying to devour an entire pie in one gulp. You'll make a mess, choke, get sick, disgust others, and probably lose your taste for pies. Not to mention, you'll never get the whole thing down.

Set modest, attainable goals; meet them and then take on bigger, more ambitious targets. Move slowly and build steadily. If you miss modest goals, it's relatively easy to regroup and begin again. However, when large, unrealistic goals are unmet it can be impossible to get back on your feet.

Be Specific

Quantify your goals. Instead of merely trying to increase your sales, set precise dollar targets. The more precise your goals, the easier it will be to track your progress. If you set specific benchmarks, like gross sales of $100,000 in three months, $300,000 in six months, and $750,000 for the first year, you will know exactly how you are doing throughout—and what you need to do if you are falling behind.

GUERRILLA TACTICS

Research your target. Before you approach an editor or a producer, know his or her work inside out. Read, watch, or listen to whatever they have put out. Know it cold. Don't pitch Oprah stories related to cooking or cookbooks; she avoids those pieces. Instead, focus on the self-betterment, human redemption features she prefers. No matter how fascinating your family, friends, and coworkers may find your story, it may not interest certain editors. Find out what they want before approaching them.

1. Listen to their programs, read their articles, and check out their Web sites, podcasts, and blogs.
2. Keep a list of what kinds of features they run, the slants they take, and the type of audience they attract.
3. Contact them and ask what would interest them.
4. Shape your presentation and pitch stories to fit what they want. But don't try to force a square peg into a round hole.

The bottom line for editors and producers is what your story can do for them and their audience. If you want to be their resource, prove to them that you know what they want, understand their needs, and can deliver items that fill those needs. Once they see that you understand what they want, and can deliver it, they'll shoot you right to the top of their list of reliable resources.

BE PREPARED

When you're bumped—and you will be—roll with the punches. Your main job now is to remain on your media contacts' radar screens. Invite producers, editors, and bloggers to call you at the last minute if they incur problems, if features fall apart, or guests cancel. Show them that you know how to play the game. If they feel that you're a real professional, they'll call you to fill in or when news breaks in your area of expertise.

Since producers and editors may call you at a moment's notice, be prepared to promote yourself and your product or service with little warning. Practice your act and get it down pat. Even though you won't have a lot of time to prepare for these last-minute appearances, you still need to be engaging, entertaining, informative, and easy to work with—a producer's dream. Make the media fall in love with you and be eager to book you again.

GUERRILLA INTELLIGENCE

Everything in the media is always in a state of flux and constantly subject to change. Major decisions are frequently made at the last moment. Features scheduled months ago get postponed or canceled for something newer, trendier, flashier, funnier, or sexier. Pieces are routinely canceled and replaced because of late-breaking news, guests becoming sick or testing poorly, or when features don't successfully materialize. Magazine covers and stories are frequently dropped at the eleventh hour when editors decide that replacements will sell more magazines. These changes mean opportunities for you.

Always stay ready. Producers, editors, and writers have "fall-back lists," sources whom they will call to appear at the very last moment. Get yourself on that list. Inform producers and editors that you can be available at short notice. Make yourself their go-to resource in short-notice situations.

GUERRILLA TALE: *The Oprah Winfrey Show* was interested in Rick's client, Dr. C. P. Chambers, the author of *Are Bald Men Sexier?*, but never got around to booking him. One Wednesday morning, nearly a year after the show first contacted Dr. Chambers, a producer called Rick to book the author for a feature on bald men that was scheduled for the coming Friday . . . just two days later! Naturally, Dr. Chambers dropped everything and immediately flew to Chicago. The following day, Oprah's staff again called Rick and explained that while interviewing Dr. Chambers they mentioned that the second half of the show was a segment on short men and they needed more guests. Dr. Chambers recommended Rick and, *voilà*, both Rick and Dr. Chambers appeared on Oprah's Friday program . . . suddenly, at the last minute, and when they least expected it.

REMEMBER

Identify your market and don't forget that you have two audiences: consumers and the media. Set realistic and specific monetary goals. Research your target media by listening to their programs, reading their articles, and visiting their Web sites. Be prepared for change because *everything* always changes.

CHAPTER 6

PRESS RELEASES: GRAB 'EM FAST AND DON'T LET GO

"Many attempts to communicate
are nullified by saying too much."

—Robert Greenleaf, founder of the Servant Leadership movement

Recently, the value of sending press releases has been questioned. Many feel that they are ineffective and a waste of time. Then again, all it takes is for just one press release to slip through and catch the eye of someone who then runs with your story. It happens all the time!

The truth is that every day, the media is flooded with press releases. Most radio and TV producers don't read press releases. At best, they glance at them, set aside the few that look interesting, and toss out the rest. Producers rarely receive a press release, read it, jump on it, and begin developing it as a feature.

Compared to radio and TV, print journalists generally pay more attention to press releases. However, they also have enormous demands on their time and short attention spans. So, your press release needs to grab them and grab them fast!

WARNING: Mass-e-mailed press releases can be considered spam. If you're going to send press releases, be selective. Send them to specific media targets, post them on your Web site, and consider sending them directly to consumers.

WHY SEND PRESS RELEASES?

Good question. Some people believe that press releases are obsolete and that no one actually reads them. True—most press releases are not read thoroughly, but they are scanned. People glance at headlines and bullet points and give most releases a quick once over at the very least. So there's always the chance that yours will grab their attention as long as yours has strong headlines and easily accessible information. If something in your press release does catch someone's eye, it may cause him or her to contact you and say, "Hey, what you sent is really interesting. Tell me more about it." Press releases are intended to stir up interest and generate follow-up calls.

GUERRILLA INTELLIGENCE

Ironically, media personnel expect and want press releases, even though they won't thoroughly read them. They are addicted to information; they can't get enough of it and never want to miss something that could be newsworthy. The media loves to sniff out stories and find needles in haystacks. So, sending press releases is a cost of playing the game.

TARGET YOUR PRESS RELEASE

Press releases should be targeted at the specific audience you want to reach. Releases sent to the print media should differ from those directed to radio and television producers. And releases directed at the consumer vary from those sent to the media. All press releases should provide information quickly, be easy to read, and clearly state the who, what, where, why, and how of your story.

Print Media

The print media can publish press releases, or parts of them with limited changes, and their job is done. They will often augment press releases with quotes and information from their own sources, or even extract key points from your release to use as the basis of their own pieces. Occasionally, because of pressing deadlines, journalists will run well-written press releases verbatim.

GUERRILLA TACTICS For the print media, the first paragraph of your press release is vital. The first paragraph should run no more than four or five sentences and set forth all the main points covered in your release. Don't complicate your opening paragraph with too much detail. The press doesn't care about every trivial point, and extraneous details can deaden the impact of your more important main points. If you insist on including details, back-load them at the end of your release or place them in a separate, more comprehensive article that you send as a part of your media kit.

After the first paragraph, amplify your story. The first paragraph is intended to alert readers to what you're promoting; the subsequent paragraphs are meant to further explain your intentions. Provide background information and extra details and specifics, as well as quotes or endorsements to get your point across. Since you are writing for the print media, mimic the style of printed articles—start with a strong lead and deliver your points in descending order of importance, beginning with the lead.

WARNING: Avoid repeatedly sending the same press release to the same contacts. A single, well-written press release for each contact is fine—it's all you need. Don't send out the same press release every thirty days; it's a waste. Receiving the same thing over and over again can turn off sources that you hope to cultivate.

It can be effective to send different press releases every week or two. You don't have to completely rewrite each subsequent release, but each should be significantly different. Change it by revising your headline and lead paragraph, bulleting different information or providing new facts, statistics, quotes, or anecdotes.

Repeatedly sending press releases builds name recognition. Before long the recipients think of you as an expert and may contact you when they need help in your area of expertise or if they spot interesting new information in one of your press releases.

Radio and TV

Radio and TV producers react differently to press releases than their print counterparts do. Therefore, you should send them a different version of the release. These types of professionals rarely read through press releases; instead, they quickly scan the headlines and read over bullets. Unlike print journalists, radio and TV producers can't simply run your press release. They're interested in building features around the key points of your story. Therefore you need to highlight them in an accessible fashion by creating a strong headline, equally strong subheads, and condensed bulleted lists.

GUERRILLA INTELLIGENCE

This may seem like a no-brainer, but always be sure to include your contact information. You should run your name, the name of your company, your telephone number, and e-mail address at the top and bottom of each page.

Direct-to-Consumer

In the past, press releases were sent primarily to the media in the hope that they would run items and create a buzz. Since the media controlled the distribution of news, they were the only game in town. Recently, however, the media has become less of a force and the Internet has opened up new distribution channels for news and information. As a result, creating press releases for consumers can pay off.

Millions of people constantly use the Internet's various search engines. So increase the odds that they will find you. Run searches to find the keywords related to your items that receive the most hits. Note the keywords most frequently searched for and include them in your headlines and the copy of your press release. Then post the press release on your site so it can be picked up by search engines. And since media professionals are always browsing the Web, they might come across your press release as well.

Besides including as many popular keywords as possible in your copy, make sure you write it so it appeals to potential buyers. Stress the benefits your product or service will provide and include incentives such as free trials, discounts, or special offers to sweeten the deal. Offering incentives can help you build loyal customers.

While it's important to integrate consumer-directed press releases into your publicity campaign, don't neglect the media. Keep sending press releases to selected media contacts.

GUERRILLA TALE: A client of Jill's developed a newsletter for sexually abused women—a tough, uncomfortable subject. When the newsletter featured Jill's client's poetry, readers responded strongly. So Jill put her poetry in a press release and the impact was hard-hitting, heartfelt, and dramatic. Her client's story was widely covered: first in one of the San Francisco area's largest newspapers and then in national syndication. *USA Today* also picked it up and listed Jill's client in the same list of resources that Oprah Winfrey is on for women who have been victims of abuse.

STRUCTURE YOUR PRESS RELEASE

Now that you have identified your press release's audience, it's time to pull them in to your story. Headlines are critical. Think of them as nuggets, small but valuable pieces that catch peoples' eyes. Headlines are the first, and often only, thing people read. Headlines must immediately grab the reader's attention or your release will go straight in the trash (see Chapter 18 to learn how to write a great headline).

If your headline grabs the media's attention, it will buy you another twenty seconds to explain yourself further in the first paragraph and in bulleted subheadings. These bulleted subheadings are like headlines within the release, intended to attract further attention and quickly provide information.

Rules for Press Release Bulleted Subheadings

» Bullets should be placed in the order of their importance—most readers don't usually make it through the entire list.
» Include no more than five to seven bullets.
» Hold each bullet to no more than two concise sentences. One sentence is preferable.
» Aim each bullet at the reader for maximum impact.

The structure of your press release is very important. You should have a strong headline and follow up with subheads that are just as strong. If you are able to pull readers in with your headline and then get them invested with your subheads, your press release has done its job.

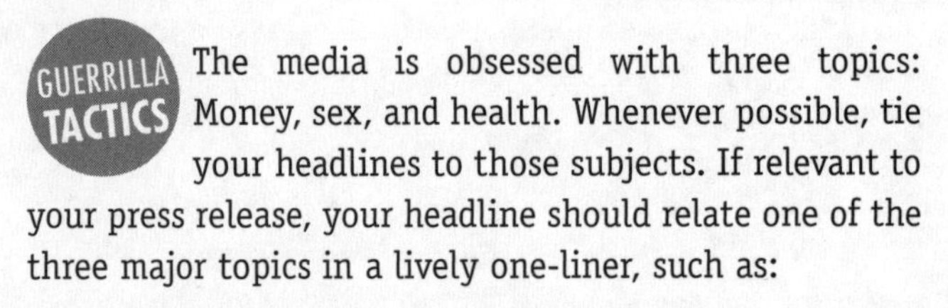

The media is obsessed with three topics: Money, sex, and health. Whenever possible, tie your headlines to those subjects. If relevant to your press release, your headline should relate one of the three major topics in a lively one-liner, such as:

» "Five Ways to a Free College Education"
» "How to Have Ten Orgasms a Day"
» "Get Immunity from Mad Cow Disease"

You should always optimize your headlines. You will get more hits by relating the most popular topics in your headlines and the content of your releases.

LEARN FROM THE MEDIA

The purpose of your press release is to attract the interest of those whose job it is to attract the public's interest. They are the authority on grabbing attention, so you should learn from them.

Study the anchors on news and entertainment shows. Listen to how they introduce stories, phrase teasers, and promote upcoming programs. Identify how they try to interest audiences and the precise words they use.

Read newspapers and magazines. Make a list of headlines that attract your interest. Note what those stories were about, how the headlines were worded, and why they caught your eye. Then try your hand by writing your own headlines for the same stories. As you're writing, try to develop a feel for the rhythm, the use of language, and the impact they create.

Visit Web sites. Entries on the first screens are often in headline form, so study their techniques. When you view the opening pages on sites like Yahoo!, MSNBC, and AOL, you're reading headlines. Print out those screens and circle the headlines that you like. Compile a list of colorful, descriptive words. Then write your headlines and bullets using those words and techniques.

As you're reading through the various headlines and listening to the newscasts, establish a "Who Gives a Damn?" meter. Determine:

1. Who would specifically care about this piece?
2. Why would they care?
3. How are they targeting that specific audience?

After you finish reviewing how the media manages to make people care, write your own headlines and bulleted subheads with the "Who Gives a Damn?" meter in mind. Ask yourself what's newsworthy about your product or service. Identify what's new, what people didn't know, and draft your headline accordingly. Try and find an interesting, unusual slant in order to grab the media's attention. Provide the pertinent information under each subhead with your unique slant in mind.

CREATE A ONE-SHEET

Now that you've crafted a strong headline, structured the press release with bulleted subheads, and supplied the reader with information they will care about, cut away all the fat and even trim some of the meat. Condense your press release to a single page, or a *one-sheet*. People don't have much time to read so they only want the facts. They want to know why they should care about your story, what problems it will solve, and how it will benefit them. Answer these concerns in your one-sheet.

Every time you create a one-sheet make sure it answers what your audience wants to know. The media wants to make sure there is a dynamic story behind your product or service, and consumers are interested in how it will help their lives. Spell out your answer with bulleted points. For example, if you're trying to sell a car to a consumer, explain that "Your new automobile will:

- Make you feel like a million bucks.
- Impress your friends, neighbors, and business associates.
- Save you money by providing years of warranted service."

By cutting down your story to a one-sheet, you are sure to deliver the most pertinent information, the best way possible. Your audience will be hooked by its strong headline, reeled in by the subheads, and able to digest your condensed information. You will have them interested in your story—hook, line, and sinker.

REMEMBER

Media people are information junkies who want to receive press releases. You can also generate consumer interest with a press release by writing tight, compelling copy that contains searchable keywords and a promise to the consumer. No matter whether your intended audience is the media or your consumers, your information should be written clearly, and have a strong headline and bulleted information.

CHAPTER 7

MEDIA LISTS: PLAY THE NUMBERS GAME

"Publicity is easy to get. Make yourself so successful that you don't need it, and then you'll get it."

—*Anonymous*

Generating publicity is a cumulative process that is built by developing relationships. Your promotional efforts involve many of the same players, so it's essential to create and maintain a record of them all. This is your *media list*.

Media lists are databases containing the names and information about people and organizations that can help promote your product or service. They're your address book or Rolodex. They're the roster of your network.

When it comes to media lists, collect as many names as possible. The more names included on your media list, the greater your chances of getting your story told. It's simple mathematics: if you send a press release to 200 media contacts, it's more likely that your story will be picked up than if it just goes out to 20 contacts. It's the old theory of throwing it against the wall and seeing what sticks. You never know who will be interested in your story. So it's better to throw it out there to as many people as possible, and see who picks it up.

GUERRILLA INTELLIGENCE

Direct mailings usually yield a 1 to 2 percent response. Although some of those responding may immediately agree to air your story, the majority usually just want more information. Since the percentage of those who ultimately end up publicizing your story is so low, sending larger mailings increases your chances for success. However, as we previously stressed, large, unfocused e-mail distributions can be considered spam, which can alienate recipients. Therefore, target your e-mails to those who you think will be interested in receiving them.

MEDIA LIST CHECKLIST

Start compiling your media list by including the names of all your contacts who might conceivably publicize, or help promote, your product or service. Don't be overly selective. Sometimes, the most unlikely contacts will fall in love with your story and go to great lengths to promote it. Your media list should contain the contacts:

» Name
» Their media outlet
» Street address
» E-mail address
» Telephone number
» Backup telephone numbers
» Fax number
» Specialty areas and interests
» Information on how you know the source (such as how you got his or her name, how and where you met, and friends or associates in common)
» Miscellaneous historical and personal information (such as projects pitched to him or her, projects bought, dates you last spoke, and the results)

» The contact's hobbies, family information, schools attended, background, and hometown

Include as much personal information as possible because it could come in handy. If you try to contact a member of the media, you can add a bit of personal information that might break the ice or generate interest in you and your story.

HOW TO COMPILE YOUR MEDIA LIST

It's never too soon to start building a media list. A media list is always a work in progress; it's never a finished product. It's added to, updated, and revised constantly.

GUERRILLA TACTICS Begin creating a media list *now*, even though you may not even have the idea for a product or service. Jot down the names of members of the media and interesting people and how they might help. Form the habit of making notes and collecting names. At all times, carry something to record information: a small notebook, a PDA, or a Blackberry.

List the names of whoever might remotely help: writers, reporters, editors, radio and TV producers, and publicists. Study the media to discover who's covering your field and add them to your list. Collect the names of and information on bloggers, podcasters, and influential online people. Ask your friends, family, and business associates for names to add to your list.

Call local newspapers, magazines, and radio and TV stations; e-mail online publications for the names of editors, reporters, and producers who cover areas that could help you.

Ask everyone you meet for their business cards. Keep all your notebook entries and business cards in a certain area—a bowl, a shoe-box, or a file drawer. Then set aside a specific time each week (for example, every Monday at 9:00 A.M.) to add these new entries to your list. Insert comments on how you met, your mutual friends or contacts, and any other information that might break the ice when you contact them.

EMPLOY SERVICES FOR HELP

You can subscribe to services that give the names and contact information for people in the media. They include:

- Cision MediaList Online—*www.medialistsonline.com*
- Media Finder—*www.mediafinder.com*
- Online Public Relations—*www.online-pr.com*

Online services are updated regularly and are usually more reliable than print directories. Books of media lists are basically out of date the moment they're published because media people move around constantly. Sure, the main listing for the *Chicago Tribune* will be the same and even the managing editor may remain unchanged, but associate editors and producers won't be because they're always changing jobs. If you simply send blanket mailings to names listed in directories, you'll end up sending press releases to people who left months ago.

CASH—CLEAN UP, ASK, SEND, AND HANDLE

Update your list on an ongoing basis. Review the entire list from top to bottom at least once every three months, since the turnover at media companies is huge. Unless you keep your list current, you'll end up wasting time and energy trying to contact people who have long been gone.

Clean Up Constantly

Whenever you hear of a change, note it and update your list. Staying current is time consuming, but it's essential and it keeps you up on changes in the industry that you depend upon.

A quick and inexpensive way to update your media list is to mail a post card to everyone on it. Be sure to include a return address. And if cards are returned undelivered, update your list with the new address provided on the returned mail or delete the entry if no new address is provided. Although these mailings will help remove dead leads, they're not always accurate and don't identify that person's current position. You'll have to do that yourself.

GUERRILLA TACTICS The best approach for thoroughly cleaning up your media list takes work. It entails calling each newspaper, radio, and TV station and asking "Is Zara DeMatran still the Lifestyles editor?" If she isn't, find out who her replacement is and ask to speak with him or her. Also, get the replacement's direct phone number and e-mail address. Find out where Zara went and try to get her new phone number and mailing or e-mail address because she still could be a valuable contact. If Zara is still with the paper ask to speak with her.

Ask

If either Zara or her replacement picks up the phone, introduce yourself and say, "I only want to take thirty seconds of your time. Is it OK if I send you a media kit for my latest product? Please take a fast look at it. I think it's great and I'm sure you'll like it, but I just wanted to let you know that it's coming." If you get her voice mail, recite your sound bite and ask her to return your call. Be sure to end each conversation with the fact that you understand and respect how pressed your contacts are for time.

Send

As soon as you get off the phone, send the package to Zara or her replacement by next-day delivery. Addressing your package to a specific person by name—in this case Zara or her replacement—rather than an unknown editor gives you a clear advantage. They know who you are, that you're sending a package, and have a general idea what it contains. Advanced warning increases the chances that your package will be opened. If nothing else, this approach shows that you're courteous and considerate, which people remember.

Handle

The day after your package is scheduled to arrive call Zara or her replacement. Don't wait more than a day because if you do your package will probably be buried in her in-box. Tell Zara, her replacement, or the answering machine: "I'm calling to make sure that you got the media kit. I know it probably just arrived and that you have 10,000 things on your desk, but I just wanted to make sure that it got into your hands. Thanks."

Call again every week or ten days thereafter. Say that you're just checking in. Ask if anything is happening with your kit and whether there is anything that she needs from you. Don't pester, or push—*gently nudge*. If she has no interest in your kit, politely accept the rejection, thank her for her time, and let her know you will be in contact about your next project.

PRIORITIZE YOUR MEDIA LIST

If you compile a beefy media list, you won't always want to contact everyone on the list. For example, if you're trying to pitch your new catering service, focus on the media that is involved with food. So prioritize the entries on your list into three groups, as discussed below.

A List

These are the media contacts that provide the biggest bang for your buck. Usually, this is the national media or national trade/industry media. Your A List is your most important media targets, the ones you want to land and to hold on to. Examples of A List media include *The Oprah Winfrey Show*, *Entertainment Tonight*, the *New York Times*, the *Today* show, *USA Today*, the *Wall Street Journal*, and national trade/industry publications.

B List

Although a notch below the A List, your B List is still important. It includes less popular national media and dominant media in large metropolitan areas that can put you on the map. While entries on your B List may lack the size and clout of the A List members, frequent coverage by media in this group can be the equivalent of A List coverage. Try to turn B List contacts into As and treat them like As. B List media includes large-city newspapers like the *Atlanta Journal-Constitution, Chicago Tribune, San Francisco Chronicle,* and *Boston Globe*, daytime talk shows like *The Tyra Banks Show* and *Montel*, and major market morning shows.

C List

Your C List should be made up of local media in both urban and rural areas. C List media are often ideal for local promotions. Since media on this list provide less coverage, you have to send more mailings and place more follow-up phone calls. However, it may be easier to get local C List coverage, which could possibly be picked up by larger media outlets. C List media includes: local newspapers like the *Yakima News*, *Marin Independent Journal*, and the *Jersey Journal*, small radio stations, and local cable and network news programs. C List media could be the easiest and best approach for you.

REMEMBER

Your media list is the roster of your network. By creating a large list filled with names and contact information that you constantly update, you will stay on top of all your available media contacts. Be sure to prioritize your list so your publicity campaigns can be as effective as possible.

CHAPTER 8

MEDIA KITS—GUERRILLA STYLE

"If you have a great press release, you have a great press kit."

—Jill Lublin

Less is often more and that's especially true with media kits. Traditionally, publicists would blanket the media with bulging, elaborate media kits (also called press kits) in the hope that a few members of the press might bite. The costs were great and the responses were slim, which helps explain why PR was used primarily by large corporations and the exceptionally rich.

GUERRILLA INTELLIGENCE

Forget the mustard, hold the catsup and mayo, never mind the relish, lettuce, tomato, onions, pickles, bacon, cheese—or even the buns. The media only wants the beef. All they want is your story, told clearly and concisely. If the media wants more information, they'll ask. The beef in your guerrilla media kit is a juicy press release (see Chapter 6). Unlike traditional media kits, a guerrilla kit should be a scaled-down package built around a killer one-page press release. The release can be supplemented by a few selected supporting documents including articles about you, but be careful not to include too much. Too many supporting documents can kill the impact of a great press release.

Well, things have changed—drastically. Even if guerrillas could afford to send lavish media packages, we question whether they're worth the cost and whether they still work. Today's media no longer wants to be showered with reams of promotional materials, no matter how beautifully they're written, designed, or packaged. They've seen every gorgeous presentation and read through all kinds of hype. They don't have the time, or the inclination, to fight through stacks of paper to uncover possible gems.

MEDIA KIT TOOLBOX

To create an effective media kit you can use the following tools to build a great publicity package for your product or service.

- Press release
- Company history
- Personal biography
- List of suggested questions
- List of articles and appearances
- Brochures
- Copies of articles
- Your photograph
- Your business card
- Endorsements and testimonials
- An expansive article
- Quiz, trivia, and anecdotes
- Giveaways

Press Release

A media kit needs a terrific one-sheet. The press release is the necessary centerpiece of any media kit. Everything else is gravy. Without a great press release, your package will usually be ignored. Your press release deserves prominence. It should be the first item seen when your kit is opened. If you put your media kit in a two-pocket folder or envelope, make the press release the first item in the left-hand pocket.

Company History

In three or four paragraphs that run no more than one page, tell your story: how you started your company in your parents' garage, spun it off from UNICEF, or began by selling fat-free muffins door to door. Then, track your company's growth through product developments, mergers and acquisitions, and expansion. Describe your financial growth, goals, and projections for the future.

In writing your company history, build on the human-interest angle: how you rose from rags to riches, overcame adversity, or found a new niche that everyone else overlooked. Stress ideas, vision, innovation, commitment, and long, hard, dedicated work. Write a narrative that the press can run without changing. Avoid technical language. Just tell your company's story, don't pat yourself on the back—let the media do that.

Sparingly weave general financial information about your company into the narrative to show its growth and potential. Give general figures, not detailed numbers. If you wish to provide more in-depth financial information, include such documents as financial statements, annual reports, and projections on separate sheets.

Personal Biography

Your personal bio charts your background. It can supplement the human-interest angle of your company's history; however, your bio should focus on you as an individual and your personal accomplishments. Make its tone light and personable; your bio should be used to blow your own horn, but in a way that does not make you seem arrogant or conceited. It is intended to document that you're an expert who merits media coverage.

Keep your personal bio succinct; limit it to one page. It is a place for information, not prose, so be to the point, not wordy. Include only factual information that readers can scan for items of interest. It should outline your training, experience, and achievements in chronological order as well as list your hobbies, interests, and charitable, civic, social and athletic activities.

List of Suggested Questions

Send radio and TV producers a list of suggested questions, but don't suggest questions to print journalists unless you obtain their consent. Print journalists may resent your questions because they believe they should ask their own questions—not yours. Determine their preference and note their responses in your media list records.

Radio and TV hosts seldom read media kits or examine products or services beforehand. They only read what producers put in front of them and they probably won't read that until moments before they're on the air. Therefore, many producers will rely on your suggested questions. They may rewrite them or change their order, but they usually won't stray far from their basic meanings.

List a minimum of five questions on four separate topics. Review prior interviews that the writers or hosts conducted, study their questioning patterns and approaches, and draft questions that fit their style. Prepare answers to these questions so you are ready to reel them off during interviews.

Media kits are no longer necessary for most initial mailings, but ideal for follow-ups. When a media contact requests more information, send your entire media kit. When additional information is requested, you can't overdo it.

List of Articles and Appearances

People in the media move cautiously. They're paid to produce lively, entertaining shows and articles. Dull or bad subjects are deadly and can cost them their jobs. Therefore, they want to see your track record. If you've been interviewed by the *New York Times, Fortune,* or *Wired,* or appeared on *Oprah*, *Larry King,* or *The Today Show*, radio and TV producers will assume that you're a good interview.

But not too many people have had such big media exposure. So let them know what you *have* done. If you've been on or featured in teleseminars, tours, blogs, or podcasts, list them.

Writers and editors like to read pieces that others have written about you. They may take or rework material from earlier features. Prior articles may let them avoid what others have covered or help them come up with a unique angle or spin.

When listing an article, provide the publication's name and the date the piece ran. In listing appearances on radio and TV shows, blogs, and podcasts include the names, dates you were featured, and favorable quotes about you from the audience, producers, or hosts.

Brochures

If you have a brochure on your product or service, include it in your media kit. In most cases, it's not necessary to create a special brochure for your media kit; just include the brochure that you usually distribute. Make sure it looks professionally written, designed, and printed.

Brochures in media kits are more than throw-ins because they convey credibility. They show that you are a legitimate entrepreneur and are an example of how you've decided to promote yourself to the public.

Copies of Articles

Include two or three copies of articles about you and/or your business written by others. Remember, the press likes to see how others covered you and your business. Articles by others also support statements in your brochure and enhance your credibility—with both the public and the media—because people tend to believe what they read.

If articles about you have not been written, try to get some written and published. Contact your local paper and see if they are interested in writing about your product or service. It's not hard to convince hometown papers to run a feature on you because they like to spotlight local businesses. But it may take persistence. If you run into a brick wall, write an article yourself, or have one written for you, and submit it to a local paper.

Don't disregard older articles that were written about you, but supplement them with current pieces that tout changes or developments in your business. Older pieces show you have staying power, that you were news then and that you are still news now.

If available, include reviews on anything you've previously released—books, products, services—or mentions of your previously released product or service in "Best Bet" sections.

Your Photograph

Pictures give stories a human face. Both the media and the public like to see what you look like; it adds to the story. After seeing your picture, a producer may recognize you from a PTA meeting, the gym, or a local charity event, and decide to help out a neighbor. Five-by-seven-inch black and white shots are fine for media kits. Color and larger images can get costly especially if you're sending a lot of kits.

Think about your pose, clothing, and setting. How do you want to be perceived? If you want to appear professorial, go for the glasses, tweed sport coat, and a library or classroom setting. When you're promoting your home repair service, pose in your overalls in front of your truck.

Make sure that the photographs you send are flattering and professional looking—not like they were shot with your cell phone. Your photos can be circulated in cyberspace and their quality may fade as they are reproduced, so make sure that the ones you submit are clear and of a high quality and resolution.

Your Business Card

Throw a few of your business cards in your media kit. Many envelopes and folders come precut to hold standard-sized business cards. If your card is not standard sized, attach or clip it to the left-hand pocket. Members of the media will often file your card separately and hang on to it long after they've discarded your media kit.

Endorsements and Testimonials

Including praise from your actual clients and customers will help establish your credibility with the media. You should collect the best testimonials from the most recognizable names and make them a part of your media kit.

An Expansive Article

If you feel that you must tell the press more than you can fit in a one-page press release, write a more expansive article. Use the article to fully tell your story with all the details. The press often picks up such articles and runs them as is or may use them as the basis for their own pieces.

Don't waste time sending more-detailed articles to radio and TV producers because they won't read them.

Quiz, Trivia, and Anecdotes

Create quizzes or games, such as anagrams and crossword puzzles for your media kit. Audiences love them and they keep your message in the public eye. Producers and editors may even use them in on-air interviews or run them as sidebars or box stories with print articles. Quiz takers invariably repeat questions to others, which helps to spread the word even further.

People are fascinated by, and usually repeat, interesting tidbits and lesser-known facts about you, your product, service, and industry. Trivia creates memorable links that the public will continue to associate with you.

Anecdotes are memorable and are frequently retained. They also provide context and turn abstract ideas and theories into more understandable stories, which are great for getting your point across. Verbal anecdotes are usually more effective because people generally prefer to listen rather than read, but reading can deliver a more indelible message.

Giveaways

Everyone loves freebies. It's amazing what people will take and keep when it's free. They may not need it, they may never use it, but they'll take it and hold on to it.

Small inexpensive promotional items such as calendars, tipping percentage cards, pens, pencils, or keychain flashlights can be included in your media kit. If an item relates to your business, better yet.

Millions of items can be imprinted with your name, logo, or motto. Try to send something useful or that makes you stand out. Although people are usually flooded with these promotional items, your calendar may be the one an editor decides to actually hang.

HOW TO PACKAGE YOUR KIT

Place all media kit materials in a two-pocket envelope or folder. Folder prices range according to their quality. The cheapest envelopes work, but don't look great. Find a happy medium; choose something that doesn't look too cheesy, but don't blow your budget on packaging that will probably be thrown away.

Print your logo or a photograph of you or your product along with your contact information on the cover of the media kit folder. For example, to promote a book, use the book cover image as the media kit cover. If printing a graphic on your folder will cause a financial crunch, simply paste a label with your product or service name, your name, and your contact information on the media kit cover.

Use bright or unusually colored media kit folders. Color code and layer various sections of your kit. For example, run your press release on light blue paper, your biography on green, and suggested questions on pink.

DISTRIBUTION OF YOUR KIT

After you've gone to all the trouble of creating and sending your media kit, let's hope people open it. Your package will be competing with lots of other materials recipients receive so take steps to make them want to read it.

When the media requests information, send it overnight. Strike while they are still interested. Also send media kits overnight to small, targeted distributions.

GUERRILLA TACTICS

The best way to get your package opened is by sending it through a mailing service like Federal Express, UPS, or DHL. People usually open these types of packages—that doesn't mean that they'll necessarily read what's inside, but they will open them.

Overnight packages convey the impression that their content is important. They show that you value what you're shipping and that you incurred expense to assure that your media kit was promptly delivered. However, the proliferation of overnight delivery has removed some of the luster and the cost runs high, especially for large mailings.

In lieu of overnight delivery, call attention to your package by using unusually colored envelopes or by placing brightly colored stickers or labels on plain envelopes. Also consider stamping clever or provocative statements or teases about the content on envelopes. For example, a brightly colored yellow or orange sticker could state "Enclosed—Your Ticket to Tomorrow," "How to Beat the IRS," or "Your Prayers Are Answered Inside."

REMEMBER

Don't overload your media kit with tons of slickly produced materials. Instead, include only the most pertinent information. Essentially, the media only wants your story, told clearly and concisely. With a great, one-page press release at its center, your media kit should grab people's attention. And one way of making sure your kit is seen is by sending it via overnight delivery.

CHAPTER 9

FOLLOW UP, FOLLOW UP, FOLLOW UP

"What is promotion without the pro? Just motion.
The pros follow up, follow up, follow up."

—*Rick Frishman*

Guerrillas take the initiative! After they get things rolling, guerrillas strike quickly and often. They don't take the attitude of "My work's done" because they know it isn't. They know much of their work has just begun. Guerrillas don't sit around and wait for things to happen, they make things happen.

The only magic formula for getting publicity is the 3 Fs: follow up, follow up, follow up. As we've previously said—and can't stress enough—people in the media are swamped with work and have to juggle tons of publicity requests. Plus, they surround themselves with electronic fences so they're hard to reach. Securing a booking or getting an article about your product or service published can take ages because when hot stories break, the media frequently drops what it's working on. It's simply how the business operates.

KEEP THE DOOR OPEN

A lack of response isn't the worst thing that can happen. *Rejection* is. If your pitch is rejected, it means your media contact isn't interested. So, try to avoid outright rejections. Your job is to keep the door open and nurse the media until your story is told, which usually takes time. Be patient and understanding, but also be persistent and keep gently reminding them about your story.

GUERRILLA TACTICS Whenever you get an outright rejection, ask, "Who else can I call?" Then use the name of the person who rejected your pitch with the new contact. For example, if Mike Smith gave you Betty Greene's name, tell or leave a message with Ms. Greene that Mike Smith of the *Washington Post* suggested that you contact her.

After you make the initial contact, you can't wait for the media to respond and you can't leave anything to chance. If you do, all your hard work, all those endless hours and mounting expenses, can wash straight down the drain. At every stage of the game, be persistent, tenacious, and determined. Don't assume that good things will just happen—make them happen.

GUERRILLA TALE: Georgia, a financial planner, took all the right steps to get her publicity campaign off to a flying start. She wrote a snappy sound bite that usually elicited positive responses; she identified thirty radio, TV, and newspaper contacts and sent a photo and professional-looking media kit to each. When she was done, she sat back, concentrated on her planning business and waited. Three weeks later, her mailings produced just one response—and that response ended up being a dead end. Meanwhile, a few weeks before the publication date of his book, Stan sent query letters to magazines asking if they were interested in publishing excerpts from it. A few days later, before he received any responses, Stan telephoned each magazine. He asked the editors if they received his letter and if they were interested in running an excerpt. After a steady stream of rejections, Stan finally got through to an editor who said that the magazine was on deadline and was short one story. Stan immediately faxed an excerpt and FedExed a copy of his book, bio, and photo to the editor. The excerpt from Stan's book ran two weeks later.

Expect rejection, but do your best to avoid it. Despite how hard you try, you will be rejected—count on it—but don't let it stop you. Think of a publicity campaign as a marathon, not as a sprint: it requires more than one short burst of speed. In a marathon, the objective is to cross the finish line. Stay in the race and continue to run, determinedly, mile by mile until you reach your goal.

Had Stan given up, or just sat back and waited for editors to respond to his queries, the magazine probably would have published another story, one from their slush pile. Sure, luck was with Stan. He happened to hit the magazine when it needed just what Stan was offering—but *guerrillas make their own luck*. His diligent follow-up improved his odds. The bottom line is that if Stan had not followed up and ignored the rejections, his excerpt would not have been published.

GUERRILLA INTELLIGENCE

Following up is not simply a short-term strategy; it's a critical element of every publicity campaign. Following up is making sure that tasks have been accomplished, done well, and delivered on time. It's a time-tested method for laying a foundation, building for the future, and completing the marathon. Following up broadens your contacts, sharpens your skills, and shows your professionalism, talent, and dedication. It's an essential step in building networks, which will dissolve if they're not maintained.

BE PERSISTENT—NOT A PEST

Following up puts you on a slippery slope between being persistent and being too pushy. You must be persistent, but it's essential to stay in your contacts' good graces if you hope to sell your story. When you e-mail or call people, be warm, friendly, and not aggressive or forceful. Approach them with *gentle, little nudges*.

Let them know that you understand and sympathize with their plight. Be patient because if you're too insistent, they might give you a quick rejection to get you off their backs, which is the last thing you want.

Tell those you contact straight out to let you know when you become a pain. Say something like, "Look, I know that when I'm pitching a story I can get to be a real pain in the butt, so tell me if I'm getting out of line." Ironically, when they see you as a potential pain, they tend to treat you better. Rehearse exactly what you plan to say and get it down. You want to be subtle, to get your message across without sounding threatening or obnoxious. As a general rule, we recommend that you go by the following timetable:

» If you're pitching national media, follow up within one week. Then follow up every third or fourth day for as long as your story is fresh.
» If you're after local or regional media, bloggers, or podcasters, contact them within three days. Follow up every second or third day.
» If you sent information by e-mail, follow up in a day or two. Send follow-up e-mails every other day for a couple of weeks.

Depending on your relationship with the contact, your timetable can shift.

HOW TO FOLLOW UP

Initially, many people find it hard to follow up. Some are shy, or feel like they're being a nuisance or groveling. Others simply don't know how to go about it. In the beginning, following up may feel awkward, uncomfortable, or unpleasant, but you'll adjust to it. It won't take long, but it will take some planning.

Follow-up must be an integral part of your operation! It's essential if you hope to succeed.

Set aside a regular time each day to follow up. Make following up a part of your daily routine, schedule it like an appointment, and enter it on your calendar. Allot a set amount of time to follow up with media contacts, prospects, customers, friends, and anyone else who can help your business.

Don't overly worry about being a nuisance. Media people are always busy and they understand that following up is a part of the business. Usually, their failure to respond is due more to lack of time than lack of interest in you or your story. So, think of your following up as doing your contacts a favor, like a hotel wake-up call, which can be jarring at first, but becomes appreciated in time.

Follow up promptly. Media people can't wait around. Most of them are on tight schedules, with plenty of appointments and deadlines. Try to get to them early by placing follow-up calls as soon as they receive your information. Generally, follow up no later than three days after you've mailed your package.

On your follow-up call, your first sentence should state your name. Identify who you are, and clearly, but briefly, say why you're calling. And begin the conversation with questions, so your contact does the talking. For example:

JANE: "Hi, this is Jane Doe of Flexibility Plus. I sent you information on my foolproof system to build strength, flexibility, and endurance. Did you receive it?"

MEDIA: "Yes."

JANE: "What did you think of the idea? Is there anything that you didn't understand? Would you like to set up an interview?"

Put your pitch first. It will provide context for who you are, why you're calling, and give you a place to begin the conversation.

Do not just call to confirm that they received your package. Ask if they understood everything and if they need any further information. If your contact doesn't recall receiving your package, ask, "May I send you another?" Follow that with your sound bite, so they remember who you are. And suggest faxing or e-mailing the information so they will receive it more quickly. This will also help you update your media list with their most up-to-date contact information. However, if they would prefer to receive the information by regular mail, send it out as soon as you hang up.

Send e-mail with a return receipt request in order to verify that it has been received. Also program your e-mail to contain a signature that automatically gives your contact information—name, business, address, telephone number, fax number, Web address, and business motto—at the end of the message. For faxes, use a fax cover sheet that includes the same information.

Follow up your faxes and e-mails by telephone no later than the next day. If you send it by regular mail, wait until you know it has arrived to call. If a follow-up call goes to your contact's voice mail, leave a brief message. In the message, spell your name, give your phone number, your sound bite, and repeat your phone number. Remember to speak clearly, briefly, and politely—put a smile on your telephone voice. Continue to call until you get a response.

Don't get discouraged—it can take a dozen phone calls to secure an interview with a major media outlet. The media is used to persistent callers; you have to get used to being one. If your contacts are abrupt, don't take it personally. They may be on a deadline, in the middle of another story, having a bad day, or otherwise involved. They may also refer you to a colleague who can help, and your next call may hit the jackpot.

GUERRILLA INTELLIGENCE

Professional, prompt, and repeated follow-up isn't just good business, it's necessary to succeed in business. Following up is as important as any other business task—such as attracting clients or customers, satisfying their needs, and fulfilling orders. But most people don't approach it systematically. They follow up only when they can steal time from other tasks that they consider more important or in order to breathe new life into efforts that seem likely to fail.

Pin down a specific day and time if a journalist or producer shows interest. Find out if there's anything additional you can send or do until you hear from them. If they don't call at the appointed time, which is likely, call them with a gentle reminder.

Be specific about what you want. Let them know if you want an interview, an article in a particular section or time slot, a review, or a photo placement. But also be reasonable. Don't sacrifice a tangible commitment by pushing for more, especially with new contacts. For example, if a contact agrees to give you a listing in "Best Bets," don't demand a feature story. With closer contacts, try to up the ante, but don't get greedy.

If you're asked not to call again—don't call again. On occasion, you may not be the right fit for your contact. So, when you're flat-out rejected, stop following up. Try to salvage something positive from rejections by thanking contacts for their time, asking them what other stories might appeal to them, requesting names of others who might be interested in your story, and inquiring if you can contact them on future projects.

Explore all alternatives. For example, when a newspaper's features editor wasn't interested in a story on a designer's furniture, the designer contacted the paper's Sunday Magazine section editor, who gave him a three-page spread with photos.

Changing the angle of your pitch could generate renewed interest or expand your potential markets.

Seize upon breaking news developments related to you or your business and make the most of them.

GUERRILLA TALE: For a while, a group of disabled comics successfully promoted its performances. Eventually, its publicity campaign started to slow down. However, when the Americans with Disabilities Act was enacted, the troupe quickly capitalized on it. They followed up with media contacts from their earlier campaign, and a radio personality invited a group member to appear on his show to speak about the new law. Other media soon followed. By recognizing their special opportunity, the troupe enjoyed an extended period of free publicity and was able to raise their price-per-appearance.

Maintain records of your follow-up efforts and place them in the project file. Refer to your records before placing follow-up calls. On your record, log in the date of each follow-up attempt, the time, who you contacted, the subject of the contact, the method of contact (e-mail, telephone, press release, letter, face-to-face meeting, etc.), and the outcome.

SAMPLE FOLLOW-UP LOG

Date/Time	*Contact*	*Subject*	*Type*	*Outcome*
1/17/08 at 10:40 A.M.	Petra DeMatran, *DeStijl*	Podcasts	E-mail	No go
1/17/08 at 11:20 A.M.	Josh Jonas, *Newsday*	Article	E-mail	Follow up on 1/22
1/17/08 at 11:30 A.M.	Stephanie Frishman, *Jersey Journal*	New Blog	Telephone	May consider; send more info
1/17/08 at 11:50 A.M.	Matt Kent, *Promising Promotion*	Web links	E-mail	Will appear on 2/4

CONTACT WITH PROSPECTS AND CUSTOMERS

At meetings, conferences, or other networking events, do you collect business cards only to misplace them? If so, you're wasting important opportunities.

Treat business cards like receipts.

When you collect business cards at an event, organize the data when you return home. If you have contact-management software, enter the information and schedule a time to call. If you don't have such software, write the name of the event on the back of each card with other pertinent information about the contact, and file them in a specific place.

If you promised to call certain people, place their cards in a separate stack and make sure to call each one within the next three days. By calling promptly, you can build on the excitement generated at the event and the time you spent together. Prompt calls also make it less likely that they'll have forgotten you.

Capitalize on news developments to follow up with prospects and clients. When you come across items related to a prospect you've discussed with a client or something new with their business, contact them. Ask how they are, what they think about the development, how it impacts them, and even to explain it to you from their perspective. Show interest and concern, but don't try to sell them. Simply try to plant positive thoughts about you and build for the future.

Dedicate a portion of your daily follow-up time to renew contacts with prospective clients and customers. They merit as much of your attention as the media.

IT GETS EASIER

After a while, following up becomes easier. With practice, it becomes routine—even fun. People in the media, even those who repeatedly reject you, can become friends and professional associates. Before long, following up becomes a skill that you've mastered, perfected, and made your own.

As for the discouragement of rejection, focus on our version of the Rule of Seven: it typically takes seven calls or e-mails to actually get a booking. Expect six No's before you get a Yes. Or, after seven unanswered contact attempts, it may be time to move on.

Following up enhances other parts of your life. It teaches you patience, understanding, and persistence. It shows you how to plan, position yourself, wait your turn, be professional, and seize opportunities. Plus, it can help you make lots of money!

GUERRILLA INTELLIGENCE

Create a solid plan, believe in it, and stick to it. Think positively. When you're trying to get a booking, don't think of every roadblock or rejection as a defeat; see it as putting you closer to your goal. Be flexible. When they tell you "No," pursue other options that will get someone to say "Yes." Most importantly, don't become overwhelmed or upset. Don't give up, keep plugging! It *will* pay off handsomely. Getting publicity takes patience and persistence. It may seem repetitive, but it seldom gets dull.

REMEMBER

Follow up, follow up, follow up! Following up is critical to every publicity campaign. It's making sure that each element of the campaign is done correctly and on time. When you follow up with the media be patient, polite, and understanding, but persistent. Gently nudge the media to remind them about your story, but don't be a pest. Make sure to follow up on every lead, and keep track of each time you do.

CHAPTER 10

FIFTEEN THINGS THE MEDIA LOVES—AND FIFTEEN THINGS IT HATES

"Reporters are like alligators. You don't have to love them, you don't even have to like them. But you do have to feed them."

—*Anonymous*

This chapter sets the record straight on what you can do to become friends with the media—and what will make you its enemy. Use each set of fifteen points wisely. Do what they like; don't do what they dislike. It is that simple.

WHAT THE MEDIA LOVES

1. News

Above all else, the media wants newsworthy items. The first thing they ask is, "Will our audience care about this?" News is what affects people's lives, what they discuss at the dinner table and around the water cooler. For the media, news is not just about delivering information; it's about entertaining first and educating or selling second. So, provide your information in an entertaining fashion.

2. The Big Three: Sex, Money, and Health

Stories that involve sex, money, or health attract attention. The media believes that the public is obsessed with sex, money, and health, and if you link your story to one or more of them, it will increase its media appeal.

3. Brevity

Save everyone time and effort by sending short, concise messages, preferably by e-mail. Cut to the chase—be direct and without subterfuge. State what you're pitching and how it will help the intended audience. Long missives often go unread.

> WARNING: Faxes can be unreliable. Some newsrooms, stations, and offices have only one fax machine, or one per floor. In large organizations, faxes are often undelivered or delivered to the wrong person. If you send a fax, follow up with an e-mail to be sure it is received.

4. Targeted Pitches

Every story isn't for every outlet. Research the audience you wish to reach and identify which outlets best target that audience. Before making your pitch, study each media outlet: read its articles, watch and listen to its programs, and visit its Web sites. Customize your pitch to stress how it will benefit each outlet's specific audience. Send business stories to business reporters, not to lifestyle reporters, unless the story has a lifestyle angle.

5. Relationships

Media people like to deal with people who build relationships rather than merely try to sell a story. Although individual stories are important, people in the media know that careers are built by forging strong relationships. To the media, professionals build relationships and they prefer to work with professionals in their network rather than one-shot wonders.

6. Preparation

Do your homework. The media likes to work with people who have their act together and can deliver what is needed. Focus on making the media's job easier. Know your subject inside and out and have written materials completed and on hand to send upon request. With products, send three copies of the product to the media. Being prepared shows commitment and that you're a dedicated professional.

7. Broad Appeal

The story behind your product or service should be able to reach a wide variety of individuals. You want something that makes audiences say, "I know someone who could use that." The media looks for stories that people will identify with. Search for broad themes that deliver some punch.

8. Tie-ins

The media wants stories that feed into larger items such as breaking news or trends. It looks for topics that will spawn families of stories. For example, during mining disasters they go for stories about safety, corporate greed, the closeness and tradition of mining communities, handling grief, treating trauma, technical and scientific advances, and the environment.

9. Experience

Reporters, editors, and bloggers like to see how others have covered your story; send articles that others have written about you or your product or service. Producers and podcasters want to know how you came off on camera or interviews; give them a list of shows you've appeared on and offer to supply tapes for review.

10. Visualization

The media loves stories that they can picture. In your written materials, use visual terms to create images and tell stories that illustrate your main points. The better the media can visualize your story, the better it can visualize its audience visualizing your story.

11. Celebrity Connections

Explain how your product or service is linked to well-known personalities. The public craves information about celebrities and products related to them get plenty of ink.

12. Prompt Response

Since the media works tight deadlines, time is always of the essence. Respond promptly to requests. Send requested material by the fastest route: hand delivery or overnight express. Delays can cause postponements or cancellations. You're always in a race with the clock.

13. Courtesy

Be respectful to everyone you come in contact with, especially those who answer the phones. Before speaking with media contacts, learn the proper pronunciation of their names. Butchering a media contact's name will get you off to a rocky start; it will put you in a hole before you begin.

14. Visual Aids

A picture is worth 10,000 words. Send charts, graphs, photographs, illustrations, and other graphic aids that reporters can stick under their editors' noses to show why your story merits telling.

15. Send Warnings

Before sending unsolicited material, notify your media contacts that it is coming with a quick call or e-mail. If they tell you not to send it, respect their wishes.

AND WHAT THE MEDIA HATES

Now that you know what to do in order to solicit a positive response—here's what to avoid:

1. Not Taking "No" for an Answer

Persistence is an admirable trait, but there comes a point when you must accept defeat. Most people won't build relationships with insistent callers who phone 500 times after they're told "No." When someone says "No," accept it. Walk away before you destroy a potentially valuable connection.

2. Long Press Releases

One killer page is all you need. If the media wants more, they'll ask for it. Come up with a great headline, state the major points in a strong first paragraph, and bullet everything you want to stress. Include secondary information in a background or follow-up release.

3. Lying, Misrepresentation, and Hype

Don't be dishonest or unreasonable. The truth will always emerge, and when stories aren't based on facts, the media usually ends up holding the bag. Most people, especially those in the media, won't forget who got them burned and will not give you the chance to do it again. Media pros know a good story when they see one and they can cut through the hype.

4. Pitches That Don't Fit

Know exactly what the specific contact wants. Don't approach reporters or producers with stories that fall outside their areas of interest. Pitching a story to the wrong outlet shows that you haven't done your research. It wastes everyone's time.

5. Small Talk

Get right to the point—be clear and brief. Don't confuse chit-chat with courtesy. Assume that the people you contact are busy and don't have time for small talk. Needless chatting borders on rudeness, it holds people hostage and keeps them from attending to business. It's thinly veiled manipulation that rarely works.

6. Links That Don't Work

Little is more frustrating than to click on a link that doesn't work. When people go to your site or blog, they don't have time to waste on dead links. If they can't easily access the information they want, they will probably exit your site and move on to something else.

7. Overkill

Media kits that weigh as much as your cocker spaniel are a turnoff. Less is more. When in doubt, leave it out. Most recipients resent bulging kits, consider them wasteful, and won't read them. The last thing they want is more stuff. If you must send tomes, bind them securely because it's maddening to watch papers falling out and scattering in every direction when an envelope is opened.

8. Cold Calls

Unsolicited phone calls are intrusions—verbal spam. They interrupt busy people while they're working. E-mail first to warn them that you plan on calling. Similarly, don't send unrequested attachments—they won't be opened—and unsolicited videotapes won't be watched. Unless you receive express permission, *never* call the media at home!

9. Bribes

Avoid offering free tickets to events and other bribes. Many media outlets prohibit gifts altogether, some bar presents over a fixed dollar amount (often $25) and others require gifts to be shared or donated to charity. Generally, the media wants good stories, not free T-shirts or coffee mugs.

GUERRILLA INTELLIGENCE

Food is often welcome. Many who man late-night newsrooms and stations love receiving free food and will publicly express their appreciation. Clever packaging, such as your picture on a pizza box, can produce positive responses. While free food may build goodwill, it won't guarantee you publicity.

10. Name-dropping

Nobody likes name-droppers. Name-dropping often indicates that a story is weak. In most cases, if connections to celebrated names are tenuous, they seldom change the story's value. While name-dropping may work with friends, it will hurt you with media professionals.

11. Lack of Appeal

Your discovery of a foolproof method of pickling pimentos may be the biggest thing in your life, but it's probably of little or no interest to the rest of the world. If you want your story covered by the media, it must have audience appeal.

12. Unnecessary Confirmation Calls

Unrequested calls made simply to check on whether faxes or packages have arrived draw mixed responses at best. Some media pros see them as helpful reminders for keeping track of items on their plates. Others resent them as pestering. Your best bet is to send a quick e-mail, rather than call, to check on the delivery of faxes and packages.

13. Gimmicks

If you use a gimmick, it better be sensational and the reason you're using it must be clear. That said, the vast majority falls flat. Never assume that the media will get the point you're trying to make. Most media people prefer conventional approaches. A reporter for a big-city newspaper told us that a woman who appeared outside his office clad in a bikini and blowing a trumpet provided a good laugh, but she didn't get the publicity she wanted because she never mentioned why she was there.

14. Not Following Up on Requests

Everybody hates people who send press releases, call, or fax, but then don't follow up with additional information when it is requested. If you say, or even imply, that you're going to do something, do it and do it promptly. Otherwise, you will be considered unreliable and unprofessional. If you don't respond promptly it may be too late. You can't expect folks to wait for you.

15. Recycling Ideas

Don't repeatedly send the same idea no matter how cleverly you repackage it. Writers, producers, and bloggers recognize and resent old dogs dolled up in new duds. "A lump of coal is still a lump of coal and no matter how you package it, it's not a diamond," a producer once explained.

REMEMBER

It's important to stay on the media's good side. If you follow the advice in this chapter and remain aware of what the media loves—and what it hates—you will have a good shot at staying in its good graces. The more the media likes you, the more publicity you can generate for your product or service.

CHAPTER 11

FIND YOUR UNIQUENESS AND CAPITALIZE ON IT

"All progress is initiated by challenging current conceptions, and executed by supplanting existing institutions."

—George Bernard Shaw

Each of us is unique. We have different backgrounds, experiences, and skill sets. Even if you do the same thing as someone else, the way you go about accomplishing it is different. What about you and your approach makes you different?

Take inventory. Find out what's unique about you. What distinguishes you and your product or service from the crowd? What sort of special insights have your experiences given you? In what ways is your voice unique? Compile a list and then come up with clever, interesting, and unusual ways to tell the world about what makes you *you*.

Are you unusually tall, strong, old, young, athletic, talented or accomplished in music, art, crafts or cooking? Are you a member of a minority, are you handicapped or a man/woman performing work typically done by members of the other sex? Have you overcome adversity? Have you lived outside the country, in a car, a commune, a refugee camp, a leper colony? Explain how you're unique, and how your uniqueness can help them.

GUERRILLA INTELLIGENCE

Self-appraisal is tricky. Often, we're completely unaware of which of our qualities others find most appealing. What we think they may be, sometimes isn't so. If we asked our friends and neighbors to complete a questionnaire on our uniqueness, the results would be startling. If you question yourself using the mindset of someone else, you're more likely to find out the truth. What do people normally ask you about when you first meet them? What do they notice? What do they compliment you on?

COMPLETE A PERSONAL CHECKLIST

For a more in-depth analysis, complete this checklist. It deals with you specifically; a checklist that covers your business is in the following section. Be sure to write full, narrative answers. Include as much information as possible, whatever comes to mind, without editing yourself.

PERSONAL CHECKLIST
Your information:
Name:
Age:
Place of birth:
Current address:
Spouse's name, age, and occupation:
Children's names, ages, and occupations:
Parents' names, ages, and occupations:

PERSONAL CHECKLIST
Siblings' names, ages, and occupations:
Well-known and accomplished relatives:
Your previous addresses (cities, states, countries only):
Educational institutions attended and degrees achieved:
Your present occupation:
Your licenses and certifications:
Reasons for entering your current field:
Your previous careers:
Your accomplishments and awards:
Your well-known teachers or business associates:
Your interests, hobbies, and special skills:

EXAMINE YOUR BUSINESS

After you've examined yourself, turn to your business. What's special about your market? Does it involve trade secrets, unusual processes, or ways of doing business? Does it require advanced equipment or exotic materials? Must you have expert knowledge of products or customs in other countries or cultures? Is your service the fastest; the best value; the most inexpensive, experienced, reliable, creative or efficient? Do you offer the best service, warranty, or references? Are you the only one licensed, certified, approved, affiliated, endorsed, or recommended?

Complete the following business checklist. As you write each answer, focus on how it benefits your customers.

BUSINESS CHECKLIST
Business name:
Business address:
Years in business:
Business history:
Your role in the business:
Special knowledge, training, or skills required:
Special formulas, processes, copyrights, or patents:

Your major competitors:
Difference between your business and your competition:
Describe your business plans:
Explain the reasons for your business' success:

GUERRILLA TACTICS

Complete both checklists and then:

- ❑ Reread each answer, but do not make any changes.
- ❑ Circle all the words or phrases you've written that denote anything unique, special, or particular to you or your business.
- ❑ On a separate sheet, list all the circled words and phrases, and explore how these unique items could be used to promote you and your business.
- ❑ Ask your customers and clients what they think you do best. You may be surprised by their answers. Consider their feedback and add some of their keywords and phrases to your list.
- ❑ Every six months, review and update the answers to your personal checklist and explore how you could capitalize on them to promote your business.

CAPITALIZE ON YOUR UNIQUENESS

After you've identified what makes you and your business unique, get creative. Find a hook, a link, or a device to capitalize on that specialness, something that will capture the media's interest. Since the media is under severe time restraints, they may simply go with the slant you took in your press release. However, be prepared for them to spin it in other directions.

GUERRILLA INTELLIGENCE

The media only cares about items that will benefit *their* audiences. What you're promoting may be inventive, it may even be groundbreaking, but if it doesn't relate directly to that outlet's target audience, you won't get much ink—if any at all.

It's not enough to claim that your product or service is special; you must convince the media that your product or service is special in relation to its audience. Each outlet wants stories about new, creative, or unusual things that they think its readers, listeners, or viewers will enjoy. They want to be able to tell their audiences that you can help them.

Review your checklists and highlight all the benefits you can provide your potential customers, for example, your location, low cost, business experience, or special training. Make sure you relate these points to your media contacts, so they can see what you can do for their audience.

Positioning is essential. To help the media recognize your value to its audience, follow these four steps:

- ❑ **Address customers.** Understand what your target customers want from your product or service. Ask current customers what they like best about your product or service and why they do business with you instead of your competitors. Build your identity around your ability to delight your customers. Get written testimonials attesting to your customers' satisfaction.

- ❑ **Address the competition.** Learn how your competitors represent themselves in the market place. What do they claim, what do they promise, and do they deliver? Look at their Web sites and brochures. Ask vendors, suppliers, and subcontractors what they like most about the competitive product or service, and what they like least. Distinguish yourself by going a notch higher—deliver more, or faster, or less expensively, or more reliably. Use your competitors as a standard for improvement.
- ❑ **Address the public's perceptions.** Find out how the public feels about your industry. Accept generalizations as truths and bill yourself as the exception to the rule. If businesses in your industry are considered unreliable, promote yourself as always being dependable and responsible. Advertise as the pain-free dentist, the courier that protects fragile cargo, or the dry cleaner that never breaks buttons. Spin how your industry is perceived in your favor by marketing yourself as the exception to the norm.
- ❑ **Address potential customers.** Prepare media materials that emphasize the benefits potential customers will receive. State, without hype, exactly what you will deliver. Spell out concrete benefits that potential customers will receive such as good health, more leisure time, less stress, or increased financial savings.

REMEMBER

Take inventory. Complete the checklists to identify what makes you and your business unique. Capitalize on these special qualities to gain the media's interest. Focus on what consumers want, your competitors' claims, and perceptions about your business. Use this information to position yourself for success.

CHAPTER 12

PROMOTE EARLY, FORCEFULLY, AND FAST

"You can get much farther with a kind word and a gun than you can with a kind word alone."

—*Al Capone*

Years ago, publicists were called "advance men." The term was coined because their job was to travel around and drum up public interest before a product or service was introduced. Although the term isn't widely used today, the basic concept remains unchanged: in order to mount an effective publicity campaign, you must begin early and lay the ground work well in advance of your product or service's introduction.

GUERRILLA TACTICS

As a general rule, if you're running a promotional event, send out your press release or media kit six weeks prior to the scheduled date. The press, particularly television reporters and producers, won't even talk to you until the week of the event. The print media will usually publicize an event a day or two before it's scheduled to take place.

If you send your press package six weeks before the event, e-mail or call the media during the following week and every week thereafter. Say that you're calling about your package and make sure they understood what it was, ask if they have any questions or would they like further information, and if they have entered your event on their calendar.

It's critical to list your events on media calendars in newspapers, newsletters, Web sites, and bulletin boards. However, some hosts won't list items that charge more than a set amount, usually $25 to $50. So, check ceiling amounts.

However, an effective way to get around ceilings is to schedule a free introductory evening the night before the event. For example, if you're charging $500 for a weekend seminar, list the free introductory evening, not the seminar itself. Then promote the seminar at the free introductory session and try to convince the media to run a feature promoting you as an expert and lauding the benefits of your seminar.

BE THE FIRST

Try to be the first in your field to get the media's attention. Ideally, they'd recognize the sheer innovative genius of your product or service and beat down your door to do features on it. But this isn't always an ideal world, so you'll have to generate interest yourself—and the best way of doing that is by being the first.

Find an angle for your product or service that makes it the first in the market. If you can't position it as the first, make yourself the first. Get in touch with your media contacts and see what they're working on. If you're the first local dietitian to provide comments for a reporter's weight loss program exposé, you could find yourself quoted in subsequent articles. By being the first on the scene, you are getting your name out there and subsequently the name of your product or service.

START EARLY

Begin your publicity campaign as soon as you get the idea for your new product or service. If you put your PR wheels in motion at the time of your idea's inception, the whole campaign will benefit. You will have more time to brainstorm and prepare the necessary materials, get your name out there and build relationships, and put a detailed plan in place.

Another advantage to beginning early is that you'll have time to implement an alternative approach if your first isn't meeting your goals. The more time you have to switch your promotion methods, the better.

GUERRILLA INTELLIGENCE

Writers, editors, and producers seldom have time to talk with you on the phone. Usually, they're so busy that even the briefest conversation takes them away from pressing projects. So every second counts!

In the first ten seconds, seasoned news people know whether they're interested in your pitch. You have to grab their interest, appeal to their needs, and make them want more.

When you pitch a busy editor or producer, it's not a social occasion, so don't waste their time. Minimize the pleasantries and introductions. Hit them hard and hit them fast—or they'll turn you off.

COMMUNICATE FORCEFULLY AND FAST

Delivering your message forcefully makes your pitch convincing and conveys your enthusiasm. Conviction and enthusiasm are contagious. If others believe you are stirred up with passion, they'll follow you and work their butts off to help you, which is exactly what you want. Come off lukewarm about your product or service and expect the media to do the same.

The media is impatient and won't waste time drawing out information or promoting weak spokespersons. Your objective is to get your message across, to be fully understood. So, speak plain English—unless you're dealing with a special subculture and must prove that you know the lingo—and say it simply, clearly, and fast.

GUERRILLA INTELLIGENCE

You only have ten seconds—that's it. If you can't deliver a convincing message in ten seconds, the media won't listen. The first ten seconds will buy you another twenty seconds, so your follow-up must also be strong. Think of your opening as your ace pitcher and your follow-up as your star closer. If you can't interest the media after thirty seconds, they'll either think your story's weak, you don't know it well enough, or you're not prepared. Whichever way, you're out.

REMEMBER

To mount a successful publicity campaign, you must begin early and lay the groundwork well in advance of the product or service's introduction. Send the press package six weeks prior to the scheduled date and then call or e-mail to see if your event is scheduled and if they have questions. Deliver your message forcefully to convey enthusiasm and passion.

CHAPTER 13

SET A CAMPAIGN BUDGET AND TIMELINE

"The only reason for time is so that everything doesn't happen at once."

—Albert Einstein

From the moment you decide to go into business, think publicity. When writing your business or marketing plan you should always include a publicity component. Smart investors know the value of publicity and expect a blueprint of all the tactics you intend to implement. They like to see that you understand the advantages of publicity and that it's a part of your plans.

Besides satisfying investors, a publicity component in your marketing plan helps sharpen your focus. A publicity plan:

» Serves as a checklist for justifying every element and expenditure in your publicity proposal
» Helps you come up with a realistic budget
» Forces you to confine yourself to approaches that fit both your needs and bankroll
» Allows you to schedule sufficient time to develop, conduct, and finance an effective publicity campaign
» Helps you plan for the future and ways to grow

Whether you're launching a new business, product, or service or reestablishing your plan for what you already have on the market, outlining your strategy for publicity helps everyone involved.

STRUCTURE THE CAMPAIGN

You can create the most amazingly brilliant publicity campaign, but it won't do you any good unless all of its parts are coordinated, timed, and executed perfectly. Think of your campaign as if it were a play with a number of actors in different roles. Each actor must enter, convincingly deliver his or her lines, and exit at precisely the right time. All of the actors must coordinate and play off each other or the performance won't make sense.

Like plays, publicity consists of a number of parts or tactics that play specific roles. Campaigns are not successful by accident. Those that work are designed to the last tiny detail. Then each stage and every tactic is implemented with great care. Nothing is left to chance. All tactics must flow flawlessly if your campaign is to be a success.

When you have designed your campaign, identify all the tactics that will be involved: press releases, demonstrations, articles, and kickoff events. Then create a timeline that details exactly when you will run every facet of your campaign. Here's what to do:

- Set a publicity budget.
- Break each tactic down into its component parts.
- Decide which people will be involved in each step.
- Identify the necessary materials and how long it will take to create them.
- Estimate how long it will take for each component to be up and running.
- Calculate the cost of each tactic and apply those costs to the total budget.
- Work backwards from the product's or service's launch to identify the time when each tactic must start.
- Set the date when each tactic will start.

By deciding what's needed for your campaign and then working back from the launch date, you will ensure each tactic is prepared for thoroughly and enacted in plenty of time.

SET A PUBLICITY BUDGET

The central question in any publicity campaign is always: "How much are you going to spend on publicity?"

Start your budget by including identifiable, fixed expenditures, for example:

- » A three-quarter-page ad in *Radio/TV Interview Report*
- » A listing in the *Yearbook of Experts*
- » A subscription to *ProfNet* and the *PR Newswire*

Figuring out these costs early on and working them into your budget is helpful, but whatever you think it's going to take in total—double it. That also applies to time and stress. It's going to be harder than you think and take longer than you think. At the least, marketing should be 10 percent of your annual budget and a good chunk of that should go to publicity. In preparing your budget, include the cost of implementing a media plan.

GUERRILLA INTELLIGENCE

While your timeline should be handled like a set of blueprints, you need to be prepared to make necessary adjustments along the way. Regardless of how thoroughly you planned, changes and developments will occur that may require you to alter your plans. Be flexible and focus on your main objective.

TIME YOUR PROMOTION PLAN

Decide on the specific strategies you will employ in your campaign. For example, writing a press release, giving a series of product demonstrations, holding a number of product giveaways, prewriting articles for the press, and throwing product launch parties or events.

Give yourself sufficient time to think through and plan each element. Examine what you need and estimate how long it will take. Some parts of your campaign may take a great deal of investigation and some of the people you want may not be available when you need them. Examine each strategy and find out the answers to the following:

- How will it work?
- Will it be good for your campaign?
- How long will it take?
- How much will it cost?
- What help will you need?
- When should you start?

Figuring out each tactic's cost, effectiveness, and schedule beforehand will create a stronger promotional plan. So take the time to look carefully at each component.

WORK BACKWARDS

Once you have decided on all the strategies you plan to use, separate them out and determine how long each will take to prepare. Then you can use your target launch date as a starting point and work backwards to figure out when each step of each initiative should begin.

For example, if you want to give six product demonstrations and hold each a week apart, all of the demonstrations will take six weeks to complete. If it will take another six weeks to write scripts, hire and train the personnel who will conduct the demonstrations, order all the items you need for the demonstrations, and have them delivered to the demonstration sites, factor that in.

You will need to start work on the demonstrations twelve weeks from the date the last demonstration is scheduled, or six weeks before the date of your first demonstration. So if your first demonstrations will be held on February 21st, you should begin work in early January.

When you are planning your schedule, try and play it safe by giving yourself a cushion of at least another week or two. Problems always arise, delays occur, and things go wrong when you're setting up publicity events. So build in extra time. Plus, you can always use the added time to refine and polish other aspects of your campaign.

First, work on the strategies with the earliest target dates and those that will be the most difficult or complex to run. Again, expect everything to take longer than you anticipate especially if it will involve the efforts of people you can't control. Constantly keep on top of all phases of the project to make sure that it is proceeding on time and on course.

A SAMPLE PLAN

The plan outlined below is fictitious. It's provided as a guide for reference purposes only. It's intended to illustrate the scope and depth a promotion plan requires. It outlines tasks you can implement at different intervals starting nine months before the formal introduction of your product or service and running through the time when the introduction has been made.

Remember that this outline is only a suggestion, a guide. Prepare your plan to meet the specific needs of your campaign. Since all the activities included below will be appropriate for all campaigns, you may be able to come up with creative ideas that will work specifically for your campaign.

As Soon as You Decide to Promote

The first promotional step you should take when you launch a campaign for a new product or service, or relaunch an established one, is to create a Web site. Before you do anything, you need to reserve a URL. Register a domain under the name of your product or service name, or a variation of its name if it has already been taken. You will also want to purchase the domain names that are close misspellings of your new URL as well. This way, visitors who have mistakenly typed in your domain name will still reach your site.

Once you finish registering for your URL you can begin creating your site. This is covered indepth in Chapter 28: Grow Your

Business with a Web Site. You want to make sure your site has at least a welcome page with your product, service, or business description, history, and release date when you launch. As you go, you can add on a variety of other elements such as testimonials, your sound bite, a blog, and podcasts.

Nine Months Before Introduction

Even though your release date is still almost a year away, you can begin work promoting your product or service. The following strategies will start building awareness, without the danger of burning out people's interest.

» Be sure your Web site has adequate blogging and podcasting capabilities.
» Write and distribute articles for five industry newsletters, blogs, and podcasts.
» Write and distribute articles for three industry Web sites.
» Design point-of-purchase graphic displays for retail outlets.
» Write articles, handouts, and ordering cards to distribute at speaking engagements.
» Solicit preorders.

The main point of this stage is to get your name out there and prepare for later stages of the campaign. The more work you do early on—soliciting, designing, writing—the easier it will be as you go along.

Six Months Before Introduction

Now that you are within half a year of the release date, complete the following to continue your momentum.

» Update your blog and podcasts.
» Distribute camera-ready articles to editors at top magazines (including *Inc.*, *Entrepreneur*, and *Income Opportunities*) and the editors of forty national and major newspapers' business, lifestyle, and specialty sections.

» Post a press release on your Web site and link to it from your blog.
» Send press releases to the sites that will reach your target audience.
» Send press releases to generate articles and coverage by media that focus on business (for example, *CNN Financial News*, the *Wall Street Journal*, *Portfolio*, *Fast Company* and *Wired*).
» Send press releases to syndicated radio and TV shows that focus on business.
» Send out a press release via the PR Newswire, which reaches over 25,000 media outlets.
» Establish an 800-telephone number to receive orders.
» Schedule fifteen talks and workshops at which handouts will be available.
» Solicit client and customer endorsements.
» Place articles and press releases in newsletters and e-zines, and on Web sites for organizations such as Action Plan Marketing (*www.actionplan.com*), Get Clients Now (*www.getclientsnow.com*), the U.S. Small Business Administration and its Small Business Development Centers (*www.sba.gov*), the U.S. Chamber of Commerce (*www.uschamber.com*), and local Chambers of Commerce (*www.chamberofcommerce.com*).
» Create flyers for preintroduction orders.
» Prepare 1,000 preorder postcards for distribution to national organizations such as the National Speakers Association, the National Association of Women Business Owners, Publishers' Marketing Association, and the U.S. Chamber of Commerce.

The above will give you a good start as you head into the core of your campaign. The more you prepare at this point, the more you can focus on making necessary connections and building important relationships down the road.

Three Months Before Introduction

Now that you are getting closer to the release date you should begin approaching media contacts with information about your product or service. Make sure that your timing is precise, so your media hits correspond with your launch.

» Update your blog and podcasts.
» Update the press releases on your Web site and blog, as well as those you sent to the media and sites that will reach your target audience.
» Begin your e-mail campaign by lining up your strategic partners, drafting offer e-mails, and setting your offer date or dates.
» Start to arrange your teleseminar, virtual tour, or blog tour.
» Write and distribute your media (press) kits. The content for media kits are discussed in detail in Chapter 8. Customize separate media kits for business groups, educational institutions, and nonprofit organizations. Items that your media kits for each campaign should contain include:
    - Your logo on the kit package
    - A press release on you and your product or service
    - A list of interview questions and answers
    - A fact sheet about you and your product or service
    - Endorsements or testimonials praising your products or services
    - A photo of the product or service
    - Your photo
    - Your biography
    - Reviews and articles about you and your product or service
    - Your contact information
    - A product sample if feasible

Providing as much information as possible about you and your product or service is key. If your media kit can grab the media's attention, your publicity campaign will really take off.

Thirty Days Before Introduction

Now that you are in the homestretch of your publicity campaign, complete the following list of tasks to make your target audience aware of your product or service's upcoming release and to generate a buzz.

- » Update your blog and podcasts with specific dates.
- » Update the press releases on your Web site and blog, as well as those you sent to the media and sites that will reach your target audience.
- » Send e-mail offers to promote your campaign.
- » E-mail announcements of your teleseminar, virtual tour, or blog tour.
- » Prepare national contest soliciting stories on the wackiest publicity ideas for your product or service.
- » Forge alliances with people who could promote you and your product or service.
- » Print 1,000 three-fold brochures (that you designed nine months prior to the release) containing ten tips, your toll-free number, and Web address. Mail the brochures to your clients and those on your media list, and distribute them at speaking engagements and in response to telephone and Web site inquiries.
- » E-mail the first issue of your newsletter.
- » Place thirty telephone calls daily to secure media interviews with the aim of having daily media interviews run before, at, and after publication.
- » Place articles in newsletters and periodicals like the one for National Association of Women Business Owners, *Working Mother*, *Bulldog Reporter*, and *Bottom Line*.
- » Mail 100 initial press release packets with testimonials, flyers, and reply postcards.
- » Update and maintain your Web site to include current information on publicity, speaking engagements, preorders, and events.

Now, the months of preparation pay will position you to have a successful launch.

Upon Introduction

The day has arrived! It's time for your product or service to be released to the world. However, it does not mean your promotion can stop. Continue your campaign with the following activities:

» Announce the release on your blog and podcasts.
» Place new press releases on your Web site and blog and send out updated versions to the media contacts and sites that will reach your target consumers.
» Launch your e-mail campaign.
» Launch your teleseminar, virtual tour, or blog tour.
» Launch publicity contest.
» Do a Morning Drive Radio Tour, which consists of eighteen back-to-back radio interviews all in one morning.
» Give a one-hour Teleprint Press Conference with fifteen print reporters.
» Send samples of the product to:
  - 300 Chambers of Commerce throughout United States to support speaking engagements
  - 300 people and groups that might invite you to present workshops
  - 200 members of the national media
  - 100 business-course professors at colleges and entrepreneurial and graduate schools
  - 20 bloggers and/or podcasters
» Collect comments, personal anecdotes, and endorsement, from customers and clients.
» E-mail your newsletter.

Your hard work has paid off. By distributing the various materials you have been preparing these past months and booking yourself on media tours, your product or service will have a great advantage over its competition.

Ongoing, Post-Introduction

Continue your publicity campaign. Build even more momentum behind your product or service. Implement the following activities:

- Update your blog and podcasts with post-release news, numbers, and media hits.
- Write updated press releases about your item's success for your Web site and blog, and for the media that will reach your target consumers.
- Publish a monthly e-mail newsletter.
- Place monthly stories in other newsletters including those previously mentioned.
- Collect comments, personal anecdotes, and endorsements from customers/clients. And update and distribute brochures containing excerpts of these to the media, specialty organizations, schools, and libraries.
- Maintain your toll-free telephone number.
- Continually update your Web site.
- Identify and exploit market niches with an eye toward new niches including women, alternative groups, and service businesses.
- Write and distribute articles that link your product or service to news developments and trends.

Publicity is an ongoing process and can only help your product or service. For continued success, continue your publicity campaign after your release.

REMEMBER

Your publicity campaign must be well planned and flawlessly executed. So when surprises occur, as they always do, you will be better equipped to handle them and not incur excessive costs. To make your campaign run seamlessly, examine each tactic you plan to use. Identify how long it will take and what personnel and resources you will need. Then work backwards from the launch date and build in additional time for delays and unanticipated complications.

CHAPTER 14

TRAINING FOR TODAY'S MEDIA

"Training is everything. The peach was once a bitter almond; cauliflower is nothing but cabbage with a college education."

—*Mark Twain*

When the media contacts you, make the most of the opportunity. If you're unprepared or not at your best, you're in big trouble because it may be the only chance you get. The media has many other options, so if you don't perform well your contact will move on to its next story and never give you a second thought. The word will spread and other media outlets will ignore you.

However, if you're a compelling, entertaining, and attractive subject, the media will feature you again and other outlets will contact you. So making a great first impression is imperative—train yourself to be mediagenic.

ON THE OUTSIDE LOOKING IN

When dealing with the media, you're entering a world where the main focus is attracting its audience's attention and delivering the most gripping and entertaining stories available. Media people know the rules. They know how to please their audiences. You, on the other hand, are an outsider.

The media people are in charge of this situation—they ask the questions, direct the action, and determine how your story is told. You do not decide what makes a good story. They do. You may know your business inside and out, but entertainingly explaining it to mass audiences is not your forte.

Many people mistakenly think that they can simply go before the media, tell their story, and look great. They do not factor in that they will be appearing before an audience and answering hard, rapid-fire questions. They think their natural charm, good looks, and intelligence will pull them through—but that's seldom the case. Most people don't know how to *really* handle difficult questions, tough interviewers, hecklers, and even unresponsive or hostile audiences. That's why most companies hire professional spokespersons with acting experience. But if you want to do it the guerrilla way and represent yourself—be prepared, learn the ropes, *invest in a media coach*!

GUERRILLA INTELLIGENCE

To promote your goods or services through the media, you need media training—even if you're represented by a publicist. In the digital age, it's imperative to always make a great impression because every interview and appearance, regardless of how brief or obscure, can quickly be flashed through cyberspace. In literally minutes, people all over the world can view your performance. If you don't look or sound your best, you can find yourself the subject of ridicule and long-lasting scorn.

TRAIN FOR SUCCESS

Media training is essential in helping you to get bookings. Before producers put guests on broadcast programs, they conduct preinterviews to get a sense of whether an individual would make a good guest. "Preinterviews are part audition and part pitch and essential in being booked, but most people don't know what to do," explains Jess Todtfeld, the president of Media Training Worldwide. Media training can teach you how to talk to producers, understand what they want, why they make key decisions, and how you should act.

By going through the training you will learn how to attract the media's interest and know what to do when it bites. A good training program will show you how to make a great impression with producers and convince them to cover your story and put you on their shows. It will also help you after you are actually booked. Media training prepares you to make the best of your opportunity, be a great subject, and get invited back.

THE TRAINING PROCESS

All media trainers operate differently so the precise training you receive will depend on the trainer. Most trainers offer several types of training options. Your best bet would probably be an individual session. This way you will get plenty of one-on-one attention. You can also sign up for special consultations as well as brush-ups or refreshers—in case you need one before an important appearance. Some trainers also conduct group sessions or company-wide presentations. Since the size of group sessions can vary, be sure to check in with the trainer before you sign on.

Media training is predicated on the fact that interviews and media appearances are not normal conversations that everyone can easily handle. "Interviews and appearances are special situations that require special skills," Jess Todtfeld explains. "People have to learn those skills just like actors have to learn how to act."

Trainers teach students the ground rules for interviews and appearances. For example, interviewers or hosts are always in control because they are the ones asking the questions. They also teach their students how to use these rules to their advantage. "Media training teaches people how to take control of their appearances, how to weave predetermined answers into interviews without hijacking them," Todtfeld notes. " It shows them how to get a clear sense of what they want get from the interview, to know the points they want to make and how to make them. It gives them a game plan or a road map to follow."

Today, the primary tool for most trainers is to place you in front of a camera, tape a practice interview, and let you observe yourself.

This helps you to understand what you need to change. After the taping session, your trainer will critique your tape and talk to you about your performance. This way you can make adjustments, get taped again, and be re-critiqued. Once your instructor shows you how to properly handle yourself in front of the camera, he will then focus on what you're actually saying.

HOOKS VS. MESSAGES

An important training tool is distinguishing your "hook" from your message. As Joel Roberts of Joel Roberts and Associates explains: "The message is the information you want to share with humanity, while your hook is what gets you on the air."

What Makes a Hook?

» **Making news.** First and foremost, a media outlet is interested in giving its audiences breaking news. People in the media love to break news stories. If your story is newsworthy, the media will want the scoop.

» **Linking your story to current news.** Connect your story to what's happening in the world today, to items that the media is presently covering because stories that are not topical—even those that are fascinating and highly entertaining—can be replaced by items that the media finds more current and newsworthy.

» **Relating your story to money, sex, and health.** As previously mentioned, the media believes that the public is obsessed with money, sex, and health, and so it is more likely to run stories involving one of those subjects. If you connect your story to two or all three of those subjects, your chances of getting wide media coverage will soar.

» **Debunking myths.** After getting scoops and reporting breaking news, the media love nothing more than to burst bubbles. Media people delight in taking accepted ideas and disproving them. Debunking serves their audiences by continuing the journalistic tradition of muckraking—and it's entertaining.

GUERRILLA INTELLIGENCE

Media trainers also teach you how to broaden your audience and improve your performance. For example, if your product is traditionally aimed at women, they can show you how to pitch it to men or kids. Trainers will teach you how to answer the tough questions as well as the easy ones, how to keep yourself from being diverted and stay on point, and how to slide into your most important points effortlessly. You will learn how to how to sit, stand, gesture, speak, buy time, look at the audience, and remain composed. Trainers can quickly spot your weaknesses and will tell you exactly how to improve them. They also point out your strengths and how to build on them. Many people don't recognize their strengths or know how to build upon them.

- **Creating new angles and approaches.** The media also likes innovation. Media people enjoy explaining to an audience new processes and ways of looking at or dealing with old or existing problems. They like to teach.
- **Reporting on existing problems and explaining how to solve them.** The media wants to serve its audiences. So if you convince media people that you can solve a significant problem, they will give you a platform. The media likes to give audiences "take away" items that they can use in their own lives.
- **Offering tangible benefits to audiences.** If you can offer free, low-cost, or discounted items, the media will pass it on to its audiences.
- **Coming up with catchy words or phrases.** Since people in the media are communicators, many are fascinated with language, especially new and unusual usages. They know that witty and clever language will grab their audiences' attention so they will seize upon the opportunity to include them in their features.

» **Celebrity connection.** The media knows that the public is fascinated by celebrities. If you can connect your story to someone who is widely known, the media will frequently be interested.

What's in a Message?

Media trainers can teach you how to perfect your outer and inner messages. Your *outer message* is how you present yourself—how you dress, how you walk, how you hold yourself, etc. It involves everything but what you say. That is your *inner message*.

For your outer message, your trainer will show you how to dress, stand, sit, gesture, and appear relaxed. He or she will instruct you on how not to slump down, lean back, grimace, or constantly make wild gestures. The job of your trainer as it relates to your outer message is to refine how you package yourself. The more naturally you come off mediagenic, the more media you will attract.

GUERRILLA TACTICS

Don't wear white when you appear on television. White is the most dominant color viewers can see so when guests wear white, viewers don't always concentrate on their faces. This will detract from the impact of your presentation. It causes a major problem because your facial expressions provide insight into your honesty, sincerity, passion, and confidence. This should be one of the first things your media trainer advises you on about on-air dress codes.

Your trainer will also help you develop and present your inner message. "The hardest thing for most people is figuring out their message," Todtfeld says. "It's difficult because they aren't used to boiling their message down into one sentence." People frequently have multiple points they want to make, so trainers help them to focus on the three or four that are most important.

Your trainer will teach you how to crystallize your thinking. You will learn how to add stories and examples to the points you make so that your appearances are more memorable and entertaining. Your trainer will also instruct you how to refine your sound bite, give a proper self-introduction, and gracefully circle irrelevant questions back to the point you want to make.

Visit *www.speakingchannel.tv* to find a qualified trainer and receive even more tips on how to handle the media.

TIPS FROM RICK

At Planned TV Arts, Rick and his staff do not allow their clients to deal with the media unless they have had media training. Rick often conducts media training and he has worked with the best trainers. Here are his tips:

Know your subject thoroughly. If you know your material, you have nothing to fear. You may encounter some initial nervousness, which is natural, but when you know your stuff, you can answer any question.

Write down your five most important points. These should be the five things you want to relate during every media appearance. Write them on index cards so that they are succinct. Carry them with you and frequently review them.

Your first point should explain who you are. People will not listen to you unless you establish your credibility. Let them know why you're qualified and why they should be listening to you.

Answer all questions in three steps:

1. Identify the problem.
2. Give an example that the audience can relate to.
3. Offer a solution.

For example:

1. *The Problem*: You need to lose weight.
2. *The Example*: You're going to a wedding next month and you want to look good.
3. *The Solution*: My new diet drink will guarantee that you lose at least five pounds a week.

Take sixty to ninety seconds to give your first answer and then pause. If the interviewer doesn't ask another question, continue your answer until you have covered all five of your most important points (see above).

Make it your interview. Don't wait for the interviewer to ask the right questions. Work the important points you want to make into your answers. However, don't steal the hosts' or interviewers' limelight. Remember that it's their show, so try to make them look good because if you do, they will usually reciprocate.

Be prepared for irrelevant questions and know how to bring it back to point. Say, "That's a good question. So many people have asked me that." Then segue to where you want to go. We call that "bridging." Study politicians—they're the best bridgers. Note how they don't answer certain questions, but subtly change the subject in order to get to their agenda and put their points across. When you bridge, try to find graceful transitions so the change doesn't seem so obvious or abrupt.

Media people are not your friends. Nothing is off the record. Don't say anything that you wouldn't be willing to see on the front page of the *New York Times*. "A closed mouth gathers no foot" is Rick's golden rule. When in doubt, shut up!

Inform—don't sell. Teach your audiences. If you're an author, don't say, "In my book . . ." Avoid constantly mentioning the name of your company, product, or service (let the host or interviewer do that). If you constantly bring it up, people will think that you're just a huckster. Teach your audiences, gain their trust and respect to build relationships with them.

GUERRILLA TACTICS

An alternative to media training is to join public speaking groups like Toastmasters International (*www.toastmasters.org*) or to take acting classes. At Toastmasters, located in most major cities, you can get experience speaking before groups of people and receive solid evaluations. Toastmasters is also a great place to network and develop contacts.

Also consider taking acting classes. Most community colleges and adult education programs offer acting and drama courses. These can help you overcome the fear of appearing before an audience. Some even focus on improvisation, which can help you to think on your feet.

Although speaking groups and acting classes can help, they are not focused on the media and it usually takes longer for their benefits to sink in.

SPECIAL FAVORITES

Two of our favorite media training programs are run by Bill and Steve Harrison, the publishers of Radio-TV Interview Reports (*www.rtir.com*). They are:

National Publicity Summit: This twice-yearly conference is limited to 100 attendees who get to meet seventy to eighty top journalists from top media outlets. Before they attend, enrollees are taught how to explain in thirty seconds or less why the media should be interested in them. Then they come to New York City and make direct, one-on-one pitches to members of the media. As a result of the National Publicity Summit, enrollees have appeared on *The View*, the *Today* show, *Good Morning America*, and in the most popular print publications. For more information, visit *www.NationalPublicitySummit.com*.

Quantum Leap Marketing Coaching Program: A year-long media-training plus course in which Bill, Steve, and their team teach enrollees how to promote themselves and deal with the media. Enrollees are also trained how to get speaking engagements, develop their own coaching programs, and become consultants. Find out more about this program at *www.yourquantumleap.com*.

REMEMBER

You are probably not used to dealing with the media, so before you begin your publicity campaign, you should get some media training. Media training will teach you how to attract the media's attention, hold a great interview, and get invited back.

CHAPTER 15

ALWAYS BE TOO PREPARED FOR AN INTERVIEW

"Luck is the residue of preparation."
—*Anonymous*

If you are an entertaining interview subject, the media will stampede to cover you and your story. Outlets will run with it. They will promote your products and services and make you a star. You'll become a media darling. That is, of course, if you actually have something to say.

Give a performance. Get on stage and shine. Delight your audience. To consistently get great publicity, learn to become a fabulous interview subject, a media darling.

GUERRILLA INTELLIGENCE

Problems usually occur during interviews because interviewees don't adequately know their subject. This is unacceptable. Interviews are your opportunity to display your mastery of your subject and shine. Not knowing the answers to questions makes you look foolish, unprofessional, and incompetent. Before you're interviewed, you need to prepare and know exactly what you want to say.

GUERRILLA TACTICS

Take these steps to prepare for an interview:

1. Outline your five main points as well as fifteen to twenty subpoints, three to four under each of your main points. As you never know how long an interview will run, you must be able to reel off all points at all times.

2. Strengthen your five main points by preparing anecdotes, stories, examples, jokes, and statistics that will make you more entertaining, interesting, and memorable.

3. Anticipate possible questions that might be asked about you and your product or service. Prepare in advance for questions that may be asked so you will not be caught off-guard.

PRACTICE, PRACTICE, PRACTICE

Rehearse your key points, subpoints, anecdotes, jokes, and answers to predicted questions. The more you rehearse, the more your responses seem unrehearsed. Reword canned replies so they don't sound automatic or robotic. Give them new life.

When preparing your points and stories, be down to earth, avoid going into "esotericland" with big words, complex theories, and wordy answers. This may seem impressive, but it puts most people to sleep.

GUERRILLA TALE: When Rick Frishman appeared on *The Oprah Winfrey Show* about short men, he knew the subject thoroughly because he had lived it all his life. Despite that fact, Rick repeatedly practiced eighteen points about being a short man before he went on camera. Alone in his hotel room standing before the mirror, Rick rehearsed witty stories about the effect of his height on his childhood, dating, marriage, business, and athletics until he could deliver rapid-fire, spontaneous sounding answers. As a result, Rick delighted Oprah and the audience with his amusing stories when answering their questions.

Know your audience. Unless you are addressing select groups, try to connect with average people because they usually constitute the bulk of your audience. Don't act too smart or too dumb—find a happy medium. Remember the purpose of your appearance is to communicate your message and to build public interest. So speak a language that your audience will easily understand, want to hear, and respond to.

TAKE CONTROL

In interviews, seize command. Tell yourself it's *your* interview, *your* performance, and *your* only opportunity to sell yourself. Don't wait for the perfect question, it may never come. Be ready to smoothly transition an answer to an off-topic question into one of your main points.

However, you should always answer the interviewer's question. Even if it doesn't involve one of your main points, you should touch on it before shifting focus onto your main points. This is where having prepared anecdotes comes in handy. One of the easiest ways of bridging the question to a main point is by telling a story. Move into your main points by saying, "That reminds me of a time when I . . ." Having these types of anecdotes prepared will make the transition seem effortless and make sense.

Never alienate an interviewer. Good communicators act as if every question is brilliant, even when they're changing the subject to stress their main points. The more effortless your bridging seems, the better the interviewer's questions appear to be. Interviewers will give you plenty of slack when you make them look good. But you don't want to let interviewers feel that they've lost control. Be respectful and deferential. Never show them up!

BE NATURAL

When writing up your main points and anecdotes, avoid language and expressions you don't ordinarily use in regular conversation. You want to sound like an authority, but you do not want to lose your audience in verbose speeches. All the material you prepare should be written with these rules in mind:

- Keep responses simple and light.
- Avoid long, complex explanations.
- Never lecture or preach.
- Use your thesaurus—but don't include synonyms you have to look up.
- Be humble.

One of the reasons to prepare for an interview is so it will not come off as forced. If what you prepare doesn't sound natural, your interview will still sound forced. The best way to appear relaxed onstage it to be thoroughly prepared.

GUERRILLA INTELLIGENCE

Don't drink coffee before an interview, it will dry you out. Drink water instead. If your mouth gets dry during the interview, drink water—even if the camera is on you. If you're not dry, it's still wise to drink water during interviews to prevent dryness. Sipping some water can also give you time to pause and think before answering tough questions.

THE COMPONENTS OF AN INTERVIEW

To understand how to prepare for an interview, you need to understand the structure of an interview. Interviews can be broken down into three components: the questions, the answers, and the solutions. It is important to know what is expected out of you, the interviewee, for each component.

The questions: Although you have little control over the questions, you can anticipate them. Study other interviews that the host conducted. They generally follow a similar pattern that will disclose the type of questioning you can expect. Then practice slipping your main points into answers to those types of questions.

The answers: When you reply, try to give examples to which the average person at home can relate. Create bonds by asking audiences "How many of you have ever had this happen?" or "Do you know anybody who needs this?" Audiences will remember similar incidents, relate your product or service to their lives, and identify with what you're saying. And most importantly, they'll keep listening to you.

The solutions: When people identify, you've got them. At that point, they want solutions. They want you to tell them exactly what they should have done and to teach them how to act if they face the same dilemma. When they want answers, they'll more than listen, they'll hang on your every word.

GUERRILLA TACTICS Never tease. When you have them hooked—give them enough hard, solid, concrete information to change their lives. Bowl them over! You want them to say "Wow, she wasn't just trying to sell her product, she was trying to help me." Avoid hype and don't self promote. Instead, show, teach, inform, be a resource.

PREPARE FOR THE UNEXPECTED

Interviewers frequently meander from where you would like to go. They will find out your deepest secrets: that you were once charged with insider trading, have been married and divorced seven times, or blew it big time on *Deal or No Deal*. Whatever it is, no matter how personal or trivial, they will find it.

Obviously, you can't ignore these subjects—so prepare for them. Confront all the skeletons in your closet and practice brief responsive answers that sound honest and sincere.

Since the purpose of the interview is to sell your product or service, respond directly to the uncovered secret and gracefully work your answer into one of your main points. If that is impossible, don't force the issue. Answer with your brief, preplanned response and hope that subsequent questions will provide you with openings to make your points.

POSTMORTEMS—PREPARE FOR THE NEXT ONE

After the interview, thank your interviewer. However, your job is not over. You should take this opportunity to prepare for future interviews by stating to your interviewer that you're new to interviews and would like any tips he could offer. Many interviewers are seasoned professionals who can be enormously helpful. Take critiques in stride and work on the things that may need adjusting.

Besides asking your interviewer for his or her input, you can conduct your own postmortem. Take the following steps to evaluate your latest interview and prepare for the next:

- Go over each question asked in the interview and grade your answer to it.
- Ask yourself if you covered all your main points. Did you communicate them effectively? How can you improve your delivery?
- Identify the main points you missed or didn't answer well enough and prepare better responses for future interviews.
- Ask friends and colleagues to objectively critique your performance. Compile their responses and work on what they point out.

Practice *does* make perfect and being able to critique your performance during a real interview is a great tool. Understand what you could have done better and prepare to accomplish it next time.

REMEMBER

Before any interview, plan exactly what you want to say. Outline your five main points with fifteen to twenty additional subpoints. Have anecdotes, jokes, and examples to support your points as well as act as bridges back to your main points from off-topic questions. Listen to the interviewer's question carefully and take control of the interview. Anticipate the questions your interviewer may ask and always be prepared for the unexpected!

CHAPTER 16

PREPARE FOR THE UNPLEASANT

"The expected rarely occurs and never
in the expected manner."

—Former General Vernon A. Walters

Always expect the unexpected. When preparing for interviews, prepare for:

» Hard questions
» Questions that make no sense
» Questions that are totally off the wall or just plain stupid
» Hostile questions

Your job is to be prepared! Usually, interviewers are not out to get you. Most are content with a good, straightforward story, but interviewers know that confrontational clashes can generate interest. As a result, some interviewers prey on their subjects, try to rattle them, and make them react. They thrive on conflict, try to catch their subjects off guard, and agitate them. These mavericks have no scruples and will go to great lengths to make themselves look good at your expense.

PREPARE, PREPARE, PREPARE

As we've stated, the major reason why people perform poorly in interviews is that they're unsure of their subject matter. Simply put, there's no substitute for knowing your stuff. *Do not* seek media coverage until you know your subject thoroughly!

GUERRILLA INTELLIGENCE

To protect yourself, always remember that *nothing* is off the record—even when the media promises it is! Never say or write anything that you're not prepared to see on YouTube. When in doubt, hold your tongue. Silence is often preferable to saying what you might later regret. Think how damaging a brief but thoughtless comment was to Don Imus. Imus's words got his radio shows pulled from the airways after a thirty-year career. Granted he did eventually return to the air, but his verbal blunder will forever tarnish his legacy.

Regardless of the interviewer's reputation, prepare to be attacked. Confrontational interviewers probe for weaknesses and when they find a soft spot, they move in for the kill. Even the most gentle, genial host may ask you a barbed question that you have to answer. Your best defense is to know your material, to firm up those soft spots, and let your knowledge see you through.

The fact that celebrities shine in interviews isn't an accident. It's a product of training, coaching, and practice. Before Jill or Rick let their clients have any contact with the media, they coach them and put them through a series of mock interviews. Mock interviews test clients' knowledge, pinpoint their weaknesses, and identify where they need work. Clients are grilled during mock friendly interviews, hostile interviews, and dumb interviews alike. After the training, they can waltz through the most hostile inquisitions with grace and poise.

ON THE ATTACK

It's hard to stay composed when interviewers are out to upset, confuse, and discredit you. When you're attacked, your adrenaline flows, your heart pumps quickly and you mobilize to protect yourself. Instinctively, you want to lash out, to counter attack. Calmness under pressure isn't easy; it takes practice. It also takes focus and intense concentration to ignore assaults and remain calm.

GUERRILLA INTELLIGENCE

When under attack, always take the high road. Never stoop to your assailant's level by being combative, defensive, or nasty. Stay focused, remain dignified, and stand tall. If you leave with nothing else, leave with your dignity.

Remind yourself before each interview to stay cool and collected no matter what the provocation. Remaining under control lets you think more clearly and shows interviewers that you're impervious to hostile attacks. Most interviewers retreat when their strikes are thwarted and the public admires, and responds to, those who remain poised under fire.

Wait for a count of three before answering all questions or take a sip of water. Pause, gather your thoughts, and formulate a reasoned response. Make it your practice to pause before you answer questions so it becomes routine. Then, when you need to buy time to answer tough questions or to compose yourself, your pause will seem perfectly natural.

Admit when you don't know an answer. Never fake it or bluff! Instead, say, "That's a good question and I honestly don't know the answer, but I'll find out." Audiences respect honesty. Conversely, they detest bluffers and usually can sense them.

When an interview takes a hostile turn, you can save the interview. Remain focused and remember the following words of advice:

- ❑ **Don't be defensive!** Audiences are adept at reading body language; they focus on how you respond. Stay cool—your reactions speak louder than your words.
- ❑ **Don't be argumentative or get into a hostile encounter.** If you disagree with your interviewer,

disagree respectfully and courteously. Remain composed, dignified, and polite. Don't show annoyance, irritation, or anger. Remember, the purpose of your appearances is for you to get publicity, not to get into a fight.

- ❑ **Never repeat a negative question.** Even if you're trying to buy time, don't do it—because repetition reinforces negativity. Take the hit, address it, and quickly move on, but don't reinforce negative comments or implications.
- ❑ **Make positive assertions.** Look directly at the audience and the interviewer and immediately assert, "Everyone who tested our product absolutely loved it! Let me show you how great it works." "This process was originally developed by X Corp., but we overhauled it so it now works with all computer systems." or "No, that allegation is completely false!"
- ❑ **Don't blame others or make excuses.** This will turn people off. Know what allegations could be made regardless of how untrue they may be and prepare responses that directly refute them.
- ❑ **Avoid getting into the gory details.** Make a firm, declarative statement and don't go into detailed explanations. If the interviewer persists, continue to be firm, polite, and brief; sooner or later he or she will back off.

HOW TO HANDLE IRRELEVANT QUESTIONS

Questions that are totally off track may indicate that the interviewer doesn't understand your subject, is not prepared, has lost focus, or has his or her own agenda.

Unless you have reason to think otherwise, assume the interviewer is innocent of devious motives. As a media resource, your job is to protect the interviewer and make him or her look good. Give the interviewer the benefit of the doubt. Answer irrelevant questions with short, pleasant replies and try to steer them to your advantage. Subsequent questions will usually reveal whether the question was an anomaly or if the interviewer was unprepared, confused, or had his or her own agenda.

GUERRILLA INTELLIGENCE

If the interviewer doesn't seem to understand your subject, it could indicate a bigger problem. You may not be communicating clearly. If the interviewer doesn't understand, others could be in the same boat, which is the last thing you want because your job is to clearly communicate the main points of your topic.

Respond by giving more precise answers and avoiding all assumptions and technical terms. Explain everything in clear, simple terms. Study the interviewer and audience for indications of whether they understand.

If the interviewer is unprepared, bail him or her out. Act as if the interviewer asked the world's most intelligent question and try to respond with an answer related to his or her question. Never hint that the interviewer is unprepared. Push your agenda when answering subsequent questions and if the interviewer catches on, great, but if he or she doesn't, keep pretending that you're both on the same track.

With interviewers who are completely off-track, try to spot where they went wrong. Don't articulate or discuss the error with them, correct them or say that they're wrong or confused. Instead, steer the interview back on course by providing brief background information that will resolve the misunderstanding, but don't lecture or go into great detail. Then respond to the question within the proper context. Never embarrass the interviewer, or the interview could dissolve into a disaster.

When interviewers insist on advancing their agendas, you're stuck! You have no choice but to go along. Follow their lead and give them what they want, as long as it doesn't hurt you. And, be gracious—while the process may be painful, don't let it show on your face. Interviewers often switch gears and, with luck, satisfied interviewers will move on and help you deliver your message. As previously discussed, try to bridge what they're asking to the message you want to deliver, "That reminds me of a story," or "It's like . . ." and then make *your* points.

REMEMBER

Expect the worst and you won't be surprised. Nothing is off the record even when the media promises it is! Be well prepared because the major reason why people perform poorly on interviews is that they're unsure of their subject matter. Know your material expertly. Remain composed if interviewers ask hard or unfair questions or questions that seem to push their own agenda.

CHAPTER 17

KEEP UP TO DATE!

"Our Age of Anxiety is, in great part, the result of trying to do today's jobs with yesterday's tools."

—Marshall McLuhan, communications theorist and educator

As we've stated, in media relations, credibility and authenticity are essential. Media relationships are built on trust and the media must be confident that it can rely on information you provide. If you send out-of-date items in your press release, media kit or blog, or your Web site isn't current, the press will cross you off their lists. They can't risk running inaccurate information.

So, if you plan to deal with the media, keep up to date! Update everything regularly including your:

» Press release
» Media kit
» Web site
» Blog
» Voice mail message

Continually read, watch, listen, and browse. Become a media junky and constantly study the media. Categorize the hot stories reported, the outlets covering them, and how they go about approaching them. Are they conservative, liberal, business oriented, New Age, aggressive, passive, or opinionated? Examine the repercussions of their coverage and how long various stories run.

Learn the players. When you contact media people, be in a position to say, "I loved those pieces you did on ________." Talk about their work and then pitch them similar or related items. Go back and read bloggers' blogs and listen to podcasters' podcasts.

Jump on developments that might relate to your business. Copy articles about innovations and trends and add them to your media kit to illustrate the potential of your business. Rewrite press releases and articles to stress how those changes will boost your sales. Spot trends and position yourself to capitalize on those trends. Link your business with items in the news.

ALWAYS INCLUDE DATES

Date every page of all print materials you distribute and prominently post the current date on your Web site. Displaying the current date on Web sites each day can keep your site at the top of some search lists. These search engines sort by the most recent update dates, so daily updates will maintain your priority position. The top-listed sites get the most hits, which means more people and more publicity.

When you make a point of keeping current, it will be noticed and become an asset to you and your publicity campaign. The media will want to deal with you because they know your information is current.

GUERRILLA TALE: Although Planned Television Arts, Rick Frishman's agency, has a central switchboard with a full-time operator, it's company policy that everyone in the agency who works with clients records daily voice mail messages, Rick's message states: "Hi this is Rick. It's Wednesday, November 14th. Hit 1 to skip this message and go straight to the beep. I'm here today until six. Leave a message and I'll get back to you. If you need to speak to someone, hit 0 and the operator will help you."

Rick and his associates give clients their direct phone numbers so calls come straight to their extension. They record a daily message and use the agency operator only as a backup. When clients call, they know whether or not Rick or others at PTA are in the office that day, that their message will be heard, and that their call will be returned. In our voice mail world, knowing that your message will be heard is at least half the battle.

Daily messages tell clients or customers that instead of hiding behind electronic fences, you're innovatively using existing technology to get and respond to your messages. Daily messages give callers a feeling of well-being because they know that they're not in voice mail hell. Clients or customers are impressed by businesses that understand their concerns.

WARNING: If your voice mail message says that you will call back, be sure to do so. Not having calls returned can be infuriating and may cost you clients, customers, or goodwill. Better yet, follow Rick's example and call back as soon as you can. Even if it's just to say, "Sorry, I'm completely jammed up, but I'll get back to you the first time that I get a break."

ACKNOWLEDGE ALL OF YOUR E-MAILS

Acknowledge that you've received and read e-mail messages. Even a few brief words—"Thanks a lot," "OK," "Sounds good," "I'll get right on it"—can make an enormous impact. Senders appreciate knowing that you read their messages. Although most e-mail programs have a return receipt feature, it acknowledges that e-mail was received, not that it was read.

Responding is easy. All you have to do is hit "Reply" and type in a few words and send. Brevity and uncapitalized responses are perfectly acceptable, and if you can respond quickly, even better!

REMEMBER

Media relations is all about credibility, so keep up to date. Read, watch, listen, and browse the media's current offerings. Stay on the cutting edge. It is vitally important to know what's happening in your industry and for people to know what's happening in your business. You should record a daily telephone message and respond to all e-mail so customers, clients, and media contacts are up to date on your status.

CHAPTER 18

THINK "HEADLINES"

"What is written without effort is in general read without pleasure."

—Samuel Johnson, English critic, essayist, and poet

We live in a world of headlines. Headlines are the labels that tell us what articles are about and help us decide what to read. Like their cousin the sound bite, headlines are informative shortcuts for people who don't have time to read, or even scan, the whole story. In one quick line, headlines are supposed to succinctly inform readers what the story is about.

GUERRILLA TACTICS Learn to write great headlines. Besides being a valuable publicity tool, learning to write terrific headlines will force you to sharpen your focus, clarify your objectives, and deliver messages with the greatest clarity and impact. Before you write a headline, answer these questions:

- ❑ What is the story about?
- ❑ Why are you telling it?
- ❑ Who are you communicating to?
- ❑ How do you want them to react?

CHARACTERISTICS OF GREAT HEADLINES

Clarity. If your headline doesn't clearly describe what your story is about, it won't attract its target readers, which means it's failed. Readers must be able to get the message on the first pass—it has to jump right out and grab them. Few readers will spend time figuring out unclear headlines; they'll turn their attention to other items. When readers read headlines they want clear information, not puzzles.

Conciseness. This is essential because most people won't even read long headlines. As it is, most readers simply scan pages for key words that alert them to matters that interest them. When a headline grabs them, they think about it or read further. If a headline is long, most people won't read it all; they will move to another item. Long headlines are counterproductive because readers might as well read the opening sentence or paragraph, which most won't. To write concise headlines:

1. Summarize your material in one sentence. This sentence can be as long as you wish.
2. Scrutinize each word in the sentence.
3. Underline each word that's essential in getting the message across.
4. Circle each word that isn't essential in getting the message across.
5. Rewrite the sentence without the circled words.
6. Examine each remaining word to determine if it can be improved.
7. Put the headline aside at least overnight and then reexamine it with fresh eyes.

Cleverness. Clever, witty headlines attract attention. But, watch out! Drafting clever, catchy headlines can divert writers from the main objective of the story. They can be seduced by their wit and forget the headline's purpose. In their desire to create amusing headlines, writers can fail to clearly convey their message. They also may fall victim to the sins of being too cute and cloying. *Never sacrifice clarity in order to be clever.*

Cleverness can be elusive. Often, writers draw blanks and can't come up with clever headlines. When that occurs, and it will, simply compose clear and concise headlines. Make your point and move on! With narrow-column newspapers, newsletters, and such, keep headlines to two or three lines.

GUERRILLA INTELLIGENCE

Headlines are intended to attract attention, so bending the rules of grammar, style, or even spelling may help—and is generally acceptable. Not having to always comply with the rules of grammar makes writing headlines a little less confining. It also helps in creating clever headlines. Often, an incorrect usage is just the thing that will catch readers' eyes and interest them in the article.

GUERRILLA TACTICS

A great way to try your hand at writing headlines is by asking friends or family members to cut headlines from a newspaper and place them in an envelope. Have them seal the envelope and give the newspaper and sealed envelope to you. Read the headlineless stories and write your own headlines.

Compare the headlines you composed with those that originally ran with the stories. Decide which you prefer; note the reasons why and the particular techniques that appeal to you. Continue this exercise for at least five days until you feel adept at writing headlines.

ADDITIONAL ADVICE

When it comes to writing headlines, writers take different approaches. Although the following suggestions are time tested and seem to work for most, don't be afraid to strike out on your own and experiment with different methods. However, if you're just getting started, it may be advisable to first follow these suggestions and then branch off:

Write the headline after *you've completed the piece.* Writing stories usually crystallizes your thoughts, resulting in sharper headlines. If you write the headline first, you risk making the story fit the headline, which is opposite to how it should work.

Draft at least four or five headlines for every story and let them sit. After you've taken some time away from the process, the right one should jump out at you. Although sometimes they will all stink and you have to write a second batch.

Ask someone for help. Have a friend, relative, or whoever happens to be around sit with you and brainstorm. Come up with buzzwords and angles to take, bounce your headlines off them, and see what your combined efforts produce. Everyone thinks that they can write great headlines, so give them a chance to help you out.

When you're stuck, change gears. Often your approach to writing a headline doesn't work because the idea is limited or unsound. If you try to force it, you will only get more frustrated. When that occurs, abandon your original approach and try something new. Ultimately, the best method for creating a headline is whatever works best for *you*.

REMEMBER

Headlines are meant to provide order by informing us what the article is about. Readers have become very headline oriented and expect headlines to catch their attention. The best headlines are clear, concise, and clever. Headline writing is a learned skill that requires lots of practice.

CHAPTER 19

PARTICIPATE IN SPECIAL EVENTS

"The creation of a thousand forests is in one acorn."
—Ralph Waldo Emerson

Guerrillas see special events as prime marketing opportunities. At special events, a lot of people with similar interests come together in nurturing atmospheres. Everyone who attends has the same focus—to make contacts, talk shop, and do business—so they're easy to approach. Special events are efficient forums for doing business because you're placed together with droves of potential customers, clients, and contacts in a confined area. Most events also have social components so you can get to meet and spend time with others in a nonbusiness context, building stronger personal relationships.

Special events are also ideal settings to learn how to present yourself to potential customers, referral sources, your industry, and your community. Many of these events are inexpensive and are designed to help you to meet and build relationships with peers, resources, and authorities in your field, who can show you the ropes and fast-track your career.

ATTEND EVENTS TO MEET NEW CONTACTS

Attend events in your area sponsored by local groups. For example, business, professional, or trade associations and civic, religious, fraternal, or social organizations often host gatherings for members and perspective members. Most likely, you have family, friends, or business associates who are already affiliated with such groups and you may belong to one yourself. If so, become more active, change your focus, and turn it into a business activity, rather than a social one. Meet and establish relationships with contacts who might buy, support, or promote your product or service.

Get to know your peers in your community as they can be a great source of referrals. They can send you their overflow—clients or customers that they can't serve—and introduce you to valuable resources that could have taken you years to discover on your own.

A great way to meet peers is by attending events hosted by local trade and professional associations such as the Bar Association, the Art Directors Club, the Building Contractors' League, and the Bat Corkers Alliance. Check the calendar of events in your local paper, grab a stack of your business cards, stuff your briefcase with brochures, practice your message, and get ready to shake lots of hands.

Online communities work on the same dynamic as special events. They bring together groups of like-minded people who can focus on their common interests. Although online communities may not have the same pizzazz and excitement that traveling to conventions, conferences, and trade shows do, community members form close bonds and can be invaluable in promoting each others' interests.

VOLUNTEER AND GAIN EXPOSURE

In one way or another, most organizations are involved in community service. So they're always looking for volunteers for community projects as well as their own programs. Volunteering provides you with a platform to display your knowledge, dedication, and ability to perform. Devoting time and effort to others is rewarding on numerous levels. Besides helping those less fortunate, it gives you visibility as a leader, a community pillar, and a good citizen.

Once your presence is known in your local area, it is time to expand. Take the following steps to broaden your network:

- ❑ Attend regional, state, national, and even international events—especially when they're held in your area. Jill recommends that you attend at least four events each month where you can network. She makes it a point to participate in at least eleven trade shows each quarter.
- ❑ Volunteer to assist when national events are hosted locally.
- ❑ Introduce, escort, assist, and house featured guests and dignitaries.
- ❑ Become a central part of the hosting group's efforts.

GUERRILLA TALE: A part-time film critic for a free, county newspaper volunteered to assist at a local film festival. She was assigned to escort the chief critic from a major city's largest newspaper. They spent lots of time together mostly watching and discussing films. The big-city critic liked her knowledge, instincts, and love of films, so after the festival, he assigned her work as an occasional freelance reviewer and interviewer. A few years later, after they had built a strong working relationship, he decided to retire and convinced his bosses to name her as his successor.

TRADE SHOWS ARE A GREAT RESOURCE

Exhibit at and attend trade shows. Shows and expos run by local trade groups and Chambers of Commerce are bargains. Exhibitors are usually charged modest fees and elaborate booths are not required. Local shows help you build a strong network and customer or client base in your community. Frequently, you must join local Chambers of Commerce to exhibit at their events, but it's usually an excellent investment.

It's more expensive to exhibit at state, regional, national, and international trade shows, but the returns can be gigantic. Fees for the least expensive booths at these larger shows run at least a thousand dollars and you'll pay even more to design, build, and outfit a booth. While these trade shows have more potential customers and clients in attendance, many are held in gigantic halls where you can get lost in the shuffle.

Even if you don't exhibit at them, trade shows are worth attending. When you attend put these tips into action:

- ❑ Work the floor.
- ❑ Circulate, visit, and examine every booth.
- ❑ Take handouts and study what's being offered.
- ❑ Sit in on presentations, seminars, and meetings.
- ❑ Get a feel for the pulse of the industry, find out where it is and where it seems to be heading. Look for trends, developments, and new innovations.
- ❑ Learn what your competitors are doing and how they have planned for the future.
- ❑ Talk with exhibitors, attendees, and the press.
- ❑ Introduce yourself, deliver your message, and build your network.
- ❑ Hand out your business cards to anyone who breathes.
- ❑ Distribute printouts of your newsletter, blog, and information about your podcasts.

Meet the Press

It's easy to identify reporters at these shows because of their badges. They usually say "Press" or are a distinctive color.

When you spot reporters, be bold. Stop them, introduce yourself, ask what they're working on, and give them a *quick* pitch. Be brief. Trade shows are not the time to push it with the press because they're working. Instead, just make contacts. Don't go into long, detailed spiels or hold the press captive or you'll blow potentially important contacts.

Exchange cards, ask if you can send them some material, and say thanks before walking away.

If you respect the demands on their time, people in the media will usually remember. Most reporters like to spice up their stories with comments or quotes from trade show attendees and tend to reward those who treated them considerately. So prepare responses in order to be ready in case you are asked. If your comments are clever, witty, or insightful, reporters may want more of the same. Frequent, witty quotes can launch you as a force in your industry.

HOW TO HANDLE YOURSELF AT A TRADE SHOW

Trade shows are not for shrinking violets. They're opportunities to build, deliver your message, and expand your network and customer or client base. Be direct, assertive, and even bold. Walk up to strangers and introduce yourself, tell them who you are, what you do, and how it can help them. Most people will usually be warm and receptive. Trade shows allow you to perfect the delivery of your message, gain greater visibility, and increase your name recognition.

However, you still need to be prepared for rejection, indifference, and curtness, even rudeness. Not everyone will be interested; these types of shows encompass a broad range of industries. Many people will be curious, though, and the more contacts you make, the better your chances of success. And the best way for you to build a contact list is by distinguishing yourself from your competition. At trade shows, many people will be clamoring for attention so it's important to come up with ways to stand out. Try the following:

- Demonstrate or explain how you solve a problem or fill a need.
- Agree to deliver goods or services faster, cheaper, or with less risk and more value.
- Go against the grain. If you're a man, affiliate with women's groups—learn about and volunteer to support their causes.

- Create specific business cards tied to that particular event, trade show, or expo.
- Hand out useful items like pens, pads, or flashlights with your logo on them.
- Sponsor contests, give awards, and donate prizes.
- Become a featured speaker, panelist, host, or master of ceremonies.
- Find ways to capture the spotlight.

It's up to you to take advantage of these situations. They have been organized for people like you, who want to get as much exposure for the least amount of money. Do not take these events lightly—prepare for them as you would any other networking opportunity.

REMEMBER

Special events present outstanding marketing opportunities because everyone who attends has the same interests. Conferences and conventions are solely about learning, making contacts, and doing business. They give you the opportunity to meet, learn from and spend time with your peers and the top authorities in your field.

CHAPTER 20

GET OTHERS TO SPREAD THE WORD

"I quote others to better express myself."

—Montaigne, French writer and philosopher

A single guerrilla fighting alone can wage a heroic battle but to win wars, guerrillas need alliances. Guerrillas need comrades in arms to share the load and spread the word.

GUERRILLA INTELLIGENCE

Unless you've been living in a cave, you already have some sort of network in place. It consists of friends, family, and people such as your doctor, dentist, accountant, lawyer, insurance agent, travel agent, personal trainer, and coworkers. It may also include your plumber, electrician, gardener, and contractor; your maintenance, collection, billing, and repair services; and anyone and everyone else with whom you do business. All your contacts, everyone you know, are members of your network. They're partners with whom you've enjoyed successful relationships and they're all potential sources of business. You've probably recommended many of them to members of your circle and now it's their turn to reciprocate. At the very least, they can attest to the fact that you're a personable and honest person who appreciates quality service.

Everyone is a potential ally, a possible source of business and referrals. Everyone you know, hear about, meet, and do business with is a prospect for your network. Grow your network into an army, enlist battalions to champion your cause, extol your virtues, and recommend you. The larger and more extensive the army, the more ground it can cover and the more business it can produce. Businesses are built on referrals.

HOW TO BUILD YOUR NETWORK

Building a network isn't difficult. You've been doing it your entire life without even being aware of it. It's simply making connections with people and turning those connections into close, long-term relationships. The major difference between these networking relationships and the kind you've been creating for years is that the focus should be on promoting your business. You want to strengthen your relationship with every member of your network so that they will help you build your business.

As with anything, there are certain ways to approach building your network. You must employ the following:

- ❑ Be direct and bold.
- ❑ Explain what you have to offer, the importance of their help, and stress that you're trying to develop mutually beneficial relationships.
- ❑ Ask how you can repay or help them. Most people understand the reciprocal nature of business and know that business relationships are incentive enough.
- ❑ Ask only for the chance to prove yourself.

One of the major benefits of adding new members to your network is that you are then able to access the network that person has already built. When you approach the members of your network for help in promoting yourself, you can:

- Tell your contacts that you've started your own business, or have expanded your existing business and are seeking referrals.
- Ask everyone for three referrals. At first, they may be hesitant, but put them at ease by showing them examples of your past work.
- Point out that you're soliciting their assistance because you've moved into larger offices, put on additional staff, added new equipment or merchandise, or just wrapped up a major project.
- Ask for specific names of people that you can contact and get permission to use their names when contacting those people.

The stronger and larger your network becomes, the easier it will be for you to promote your newest product or service.

REFERRAL FEES

Clarify with all referral sources up front whether they want a *referral fee*—a monetary incentive for providing business contacts. If they do, agree upon the amount in advance. In some industries, referral fees are unethical. It varies from industry to industry. So check out what's acceptable in your field.

When you secure a client or a job through a business referral, reward the individual who recommended you. If they can't or won't accept a referral fee, give them some type of gift—a gift certificate, tickets to an event, or a charitable contribution—or perform extra work at no cost to show your appreciation. Even the smallest gesture will be appreciated and it's good business.

In Your Field

When looking for referrals within your area of business, approach former bosses, former coworkers, and established company heads. Former employers and coworkers are great referral sources because they know you, the quality of your work, and are usually eager to see you succeed.

Another possibility is to contact larger businesses to see if you can handle their overflow, or assist with projects when they need help. These types of relationships will guarantee that you receive referrals down the road.

Some people in your business field may fear that you might steal their clients or customers. To ease their concerns:

- ❑ Be willing to not disclose to referred customers or clients that you operate a separate business.
- ❑ Offer to act as the referral source's employee while handling their referrals.
- ❑ Work out of the referral source's office or use his or her stationery.
- ❑ If, after a referral is completed, the clients or customer wants to hire you directly, don't accept the business without first obtaining the consent of your referral source and agreeing to pay a referral fee.

GUERRILLA INTELLIGENCE

Don't steal customers or clients. Over the long run, you'll be judged on your reputation for ethics, honesty, and loyalty, which far outweighs whatever you might receive from stealing a referral source's clients or customers

In Complementary Fields

Solicit businesses in different, but complementary fields. Create alliances to mutually refer clients or customers. For example, if you're a florist, approach wedding, party, and event planners; caterers; photographers and videographers; and banquet hall operators. If you operate a payroll preparation service, attend events for business accountants, financial consultants, and small business operators.

While soliciting referrals outside of your industry, distribute samples of your product. Let key people experience how terrific it is. Give out samples that will make them want to work with you. Personalize samples to include something unique for each person or business you pitch.

If you run a service business, print a one-page explanation of why your service is superior. (Follow the press release format that we explained in Chapter 6.) Write a great headline, a compelling lead paragraph, and bullet the benefits your service will provide. Use attractive paper that reflects the level of professionalism, design, and inventiveness you want to convey. Include photographs and illustrations. List fee schedules, guarantees, and attach testimonials from customers declaring the excellence of your work, your professionalism, and how much they enjoyed working with you.

Go to workplaces and try to meet business operators. If that's impossible, leave a hand-written note with your sample or written material. In the note, express regret that you couldn't meet face-to-face and explain that you're seeking referrals and would love to speak with them at their convenience. Follow up the note with subsequent visits, phone calls, or e-mails.

REMEMBER

Businesses are built on referrals and everyone is a potential source of new business. Use your existing network to build your customer base. Ask each contact for three referrals and clarify in advance whether they expect referral fees. And when sources produce referrals—show your appreciation.

CHAPTER 21

UTILIZE ETHNIC, RACE-BASED, AND SPECIALIZED GROUPS

"It is in the shelter of each other that the people live."
—*Irish proverb*

The United States' population is made up of countless ethnic, racial, religious, and other groups. In addition, groups exist within groups. For instance, people who are grouped under the Hispanic umbrella may also be categorized as Mexicans, Puerto Ricans, Argentinians, Chileans, or Nicaraguans. In this chapter, we will refer to these groups as specialized groups or communities.

Specialized groups have become powerful markets. They have spawned a dedicated media and provide internal support systems for their people. Some of the largest and most prominent groups are the Evangelical Christian, Hispanic, and the gay and lesbian markets. However, many other specialized markets exist that are based on racial, ethnic, religious, cultural, and social lines.

"It's essential to understand the cultural landscape you target," Elena Miranda, publisher of *Visión Hispana* newspaper, points out. "Anyone who seeks publicity must know the audience he or she wants to address." Then they must find the best way to reach that audience. For example, if you're selling Peruvian food products, learn what organizations and publications serve that market. Learn about special events or celebrations where you could set up a booth to sell or publicize your products."

Reaching specialized groups is important because they have a number of organizations, networks, and events that are fertile grounds for word-of-mouth publicity. "Word-of-mouth publicity is highly effective," notes Bob Witeck, CEO and founder of Witeck-Combs Communications in Washington, DC. "It is the safest and most effective way for members of specialized communities to give each other news and information." Members are closely connected so they put more stock in recommendations from fellow community members. If you can get your product or service publicized in a specialized publication, you are all but guaranteed to have the news of its release spread through that group.

"When we're overloaded with information, we often go back to who we trust," Witeck observes. "For many, the most trusted channel lies within their own community."

The media that serve specialized groups differ from the mainstream media because their members are usually members of the group and they frequently limit their coverage to pieces that only relate to their group. A story may be newsworthy to the mass media, but certain religious, ethnic, or other specialized media may decide not to cover it if the perception is that it does not promote its values.

GUERRILLA INTELLIGENCE

A great place to start building a support base for your product or service is within your own specialized group—be it ethnic, religious, or other. Capitalize on your connections within the group and market your relatability to its media's demographic. If you are able to create a foundation within your community, it will continue to support you throughout the lifespan of your product or service.

GAIN INTERNAL SUPPORT

When you belong to a specialized group, the members of that group can be your greatest, most ardent supporters. Since you're one of their own, they will take pride in your success and will eagerly help you. The members of your community have a great incentive to see you succeed because when their members do well, it can benefit the community. Therefore, group members will show great devotion and go to unusual lengths to help other members succeed.

Group support can form the loyal base that businesses need to succeed. Members can buy your goods or services and form the customer base on which you build. The work you perform for them can be examples of your excellence that you can showcase to others to land more business. Group members can be your unofficial sales force. They can tell others, in and out of the community, about you, how great your product or service is, and how professional and efficient you were.

UTILIZE CHAMBERS OF COMMERCE

Throughout the country, Chambers of Commerce have been formed to serve specialized groups including those that focus on Hispanic, African-American, and Asian communities. Chambers also exist specifically for women. Most of these specialized Chambers are dynamic organizations that are dedicated to helping their members boost their businesses. They collaborate with the mainstream Chambers in their areas and can be especially helpful because they understand the unique challenges faced by members of their communities and share solutions that work.

Joining specialized Chambers of Commerce will also solidify your local base. As Cecilia Zamora, Executive Director of Latino Council of Marin, California, notes, "Chambers try to build a networking component into most of their events and events like mixers can be great networking opportunities." By taking full advantage of your local Chambers you will be certain to corner the market on specialized groups on the local level. If you can build up local support of specialized groups, you can parlay that momentum into national support from the specific group.

SPECIALIZED MEDIA OUTLETS

Specialized groups are served by all types of media (television, radio, print, Internet sites, blogs, and podcasts). The major difference between specialized media and mass media is that specialized media focuses on specific communities' issues, and the various specialized outlets also have extremely loyal and devoted audiences. This can work to your advantage because audiences are more likely to support items that the specialized media promotes or recommends.

As previously mentioned, the members of the specialized media generally belong to the groups they cover. So when you deal with them, understand their values and remember that their main objective is to promote those values.

The types of media outlets specialized groups control are as varied as those run by the mass media. Some groups operate radio and television networks that address their communities. They provide a range of programming that includes variety shows, talk shows, religious programming, and sitcoms.

There are also newspapers and periodicals run by specialized groups at the national and local levels. These publications can be written in English or the language of specific groups. Local publications, which proliferate, inform group members about developments in the community and provide great opportunities for you to publicize your product or service. They usually publish calendars that list upcoming events such as holidays, celebrations, festivals, and other activities of interest. See if you can get your promotional events listed on one of these calendars. They also have feature stories and advertisements. You can either try to get a feature done on you or what you're promoting, or run an advertisement in the specific publication.

The book market is also specialized. Books of faith are huge sellers. Some have sold tens of millions of copies and have crossed into the mainstream market. Christian bookstores do a thriving business; many of them are located in churches. The market for Hispanic books is rapidly growing. That market is made up of

Hispanic-themed books that are written in English and books on a wide range of topics that are in Spanish.

GUERRILLA INTELLIGENCE

Addressing ethnic and national groups has long been a favorite of politicians. Now, publicists are following suit. They are booking clients who are not members of specialized groups to speak to community-based organizations, appear at their events, and sponsor awards. Speaking at houses of worship (especially at mega churches that are attended by thousands of worshipers) can be extremely productive for authors who wish to promote and sell their books. This type of audience is very receptive and buys a lot of books. To be invited to speak, however, authors and their books must promote values that are consistent with those of the congregation. Some congregations even allow authors to sell their books on the premises or at their bookstores after they speak.

TAKE THE SERVICE APPROACH

Specialized groups usually offer programs for community members that outsiders are not eligible to receive. Many have educational, financial, business, health, welfare, and social programs specially designed for their members.

"We meet with a small business, get into the specifics of their businesses, and discuss their marketing goals." Darren Ballegeer, a marketing consultant with Vision Marketing in Alemeda, California, explains. "Then we give them recommendations on how they can meet those goals. We also give them ideas and strategies on everything they're doing so it ties in and works with the actions they will be taking. Some areas we cover are how to get people to turn out to their grand openings, to show up for a seminar, or how they should approach other media for coverage. We are going to support them in all of their marketing efforts even if they only do a little of it with us."

If you have access to such programs within your specialty group, use them. Organizations such as Vision help you in the following ways:

» Identify what you're selling
» Utilize the specific benefits they provide
» Determine your marketing goals
» Identify the core market they should target
» Develop realistic methods to achieve your goals, which include pointing out the specific messages you can use

Most guerrillas can't afford to hire an ad agency and many are not good marketers—especially outside of their communities. "They may be good restaurant owners, great service providers, or manufacturers," Elena Miranda, publisher of *Visión Hispana* newspaper, observes, "but they don't know how to market, which is why there is so much ineffective publicity. We're giving them a real education and giving suggestions that will help them to grow."

VENTURE OUT

If you're an outsider to a specific specialized group, explore how you could promote your items within that group. It could be a ripe, untapped market to pursue. Be aware that the usual methods and approaches you take may not be suitable for all markets.

Many people in specialized communities isolate themselves and don't try to do business outside their own communities. Usually they don't feel comfortable or confident working outside their own communities. So they don't easily accept outsiders—that's why you *really* need to tap into those specialty groups to which you don't belong. And you better act fast. Specialized groups are becoming the target of more and more outside promoters day after day. Ballegeer points out: "Half of *Visión Hispana*'s advertisers are non-Hispanic-owned businesses and they are extremely aware of the power of the Hispanic market."

GUERRILLA TACTICS When you go as an outsider to the media that serves a specialized community, you have to learn about that community first. Subtle nuances often exist with regard to protocols: how a particular community wants to be approached, the type of overtures it responds to, and what turns it off. Sometimes the only way for outsiders to learn these nuances is by dealing with the media that serves those communities.

"Hispanic-owned businesses should promote themselves in both the Hispanic and non-Hispanic communities because outside businesses are trying to move into Hispanic markets," notes Ballegeer.

TIPS ON HOW TO APPROACH SPECIALIZED GROUPS

Before you try and get publicity in these specialized media outlets, you need to gain a foothold in the market. Review the following tips before you approach specialized community members:

Consider how you speak. Think about your tone, voice, attitude, and approach. Learn how to talk to the audience; find out how they communicate among their families and friends.

Dispel myths. Frequently, one community will have incorrect presumptions about another. For example, a widely held belief is that gay and lesbian couples don't have children. However, Bob Witeck tells us that about a third of the women in same-sex relationships and a quarter of men in same-sex relationships are raising children.

Create liasions with leaders of specialized groups. Endorsements from leaders can give you instant credibility with the rank and file who tend to be wary of outsiders. Endorsements from leaders can help you cut through the red tape and formalities that frequently frustrate outsiders. Leaders can tell you how to best approach and serve their communities. They can fill you in on what their community really needs and wants, which may differ from what you thought. They can tell you who to approach and what you should say and do.

Start locally and then build nationally. When you approach the media that serves specialized groups, smaller media outlets may be more willing to run your stories, which can build your credibility and help you make inroads into the group. After you have established a base, you can approach larger outlets, or they may even approach you.

Be aware of special events. Many groups run annual events for holidays, anniversaries, and other occasions such as Martin Luther King Day, the Day of the Dead, Mardi Gras, and Tet. Specialized media outlets will pay special attention to these celebrations, so you can get great publicity during these times by sponsoring events, giving prizes and awards, and underwriting various activities.

GUERRILLA INTELLIGENCE

"When you work within a specialized community, you are expected to give back to that community," Bob Witeck says. "It's a part of the price of doing business there. When you give back, it shows that you're not just asking for your business, but that you are actually participating in community members' lives." Specialized groups can be sensitive about exploitation because they've had to deal with it so often. Many will force outsiders to jump through hoops to prove that the concern for the community they express is not just to make a buck. Show them that you care and make an investment in their community.

GUERRILLA TALE: Jill Lublin's client, Ryan, an Asian-American industrial designer, was "down-sized" from his corporate job at the worst possible time—his wife was pregnant with their third child. Within twenty-four hours of his discharge, Ryan started his own online business and recruited eight employees in seven counties. He then sent out a press release heralding himself as "The Virtual Office Warrior" who vowed never to work in an office again. Both the general press and the Asian-American press ran articles on Ryan, calls from new clients poured in, and Ryan never looked back. The articles on Ryan mentioned that he was an industrial designer, but they concentrated on him being a part of a specialty group. It provided a new angle on an old story—some guy who had the rug pulled out from under him managed to not only get back on his feet, but to land squarely and pointed in a promising new direction.

REMEMBER

Specialized groups are powerful markets that have a dedicated media and provide internal support systems for their people. The media that serves them differs from the mainstream media because its members usually belong to the group and just cover stories that relate to their group and its members and are consistent with their beliefs and interests. Members of specialized groups should seek publicity in media other than that devoted only to their community.

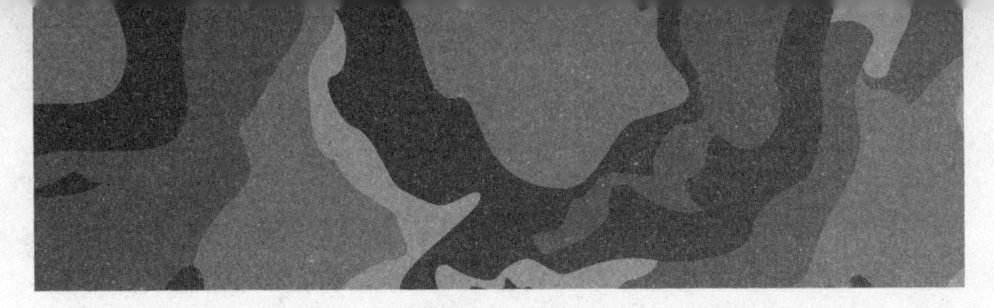

CHAPTER 22

GET PUBLISHED

"Take the top of the mountain."
—David Ogilvy, advertising professional

Publishing a book catapults you to the upper strata of authority figures. It gives you more than credibility; it gives everything you say an increased amount of weight. Authoring a book brings you recognition as an expert, a leader in your business, a star in your field. This helps incredibly when you are trying to launch and publicize a new product or service. Having a book published in your area of expertise opens doors to the media that would not normally be open to you. It puts you on top.

GUERRILLA INTELLIGENCE

Although many people think they've got a book's worth of things to say, *few actually do.* And, even fewer have the ability and the discipline to express their thoughts coherently and get them published. Writing and having your book published is an achievement. It testifies that you're an expert and puts you in an elite group because so few people actually complete all the steps to write and have their book published. Publishing a book demonstrates that you're special and can get things done.

ADVANTAGES OF AUTHORSHIP

A book is a powerful marketing tool. Authorship gets your name out to the public and reinforces that you're an expert. It can take you to the next level by making you a celebrity, and, in our celebrity-crazed world, people are more inclined to purchase a product or service associated with a celebrity.

Authors are respected and sought after. Giving potential customers and clients a copy of your book creates instant goodwill. Writing a personalized message will thaw the most glacial personalities and turn total strangers into grateful, loyal, longstanding devotees. They will treasure their signed volume and continue to support you and your endeavors.

When your book is published, your status as an expert becomes permanent; it can never be taken away. You're listed in the Library of Congress. After you are published, the local media will look to interview you, you'll get cool invitations, and attract a following at conferences and conventions.

Most authors don't make money from selling their books, but their books help propel their careers. If your first is a success, even a moderate one, it will likely open doors for a follow-up. Subsequent books will reinforce your status and help further your career. And, you never know, there's always a chance that one of your books will make the bestseller list, you'll get booked on Oprah or Letterman, and hit the jackpot!

GETTING IT DOWN

Writing a book isn't easy. It takes knowledge, time, and discipline. First, you must have content: information to fill the pages. Clearly articulating your knowledge is time consuming, exacting, and requires deep concentration. It can be hard work.

Ideally, the content you provide should give readers something new or express existing material better—but we all know that doesn't always happen. Like a great storyteller or gifted teacher, you need to make boring old stuff come alive and take on new meaning. You want to capture your unique take on a subject and communicate in an entertaining, intriguing, and understandable manner. Let's face it though, not everyone writes well. You may have a great idea for a book, but you cannot express yourself in written form. That's all right—you can hire a ghostwriter. Working with a ghost is a partnership: you provide the substance; he or she puts it in publishable form. Since it's your book, you have to tell the ghostwriter what to write because he or she probably won't be an expert in your field.

When your ghost has finished writing, though, it's all up to you. You must review every word, every sentence, and every idea because each of them will be attributed to you. As the author, your name and reputation will be on the line.

To test and see if you really have a book in you, draft an outline:

- ❑ Jot down topics; list every possible idea that you might put in your book.
- ❑ Edit the list down to ten to fifteen important topics and organize them in a logical order.
- ❑ Set it up as if you're telling a story or explaining a skill.

This topic list will function as your working outline, or table of contents, which is the structure for your book.

Writing a book is an evolving process. Everything is subject to change. Few authors write straight through; there's always editing, moving, adding, deleting, and rewriting text. Sometimes, it feels like a puzzle. Nevertheless, begin with a structure, even though it will change. Don't wing it. Create a framework and follow it until you're convinced that it needs to be changed. Then make whatever alterations feel right.

Sit at your computer or with your tape recorder and express your thoughts. Forget about grammar, spelling, or logic. Just capture information. Remember, this isn't English class. *Just get the information down!* Spill your guts. Put down everything that comes to mind, whether it makes sense or not. The idea is to get a flow, to build a rhythm and express yourself. Anything that isn't right can always be fixed later.

When it comes to introductions, disagreement exists. Most writers believe that it's usually best to write the intro after the entire text is completed. They begin by writing chapters and if they have thoughts about an intro, they make notes and save them. Others like to write their introductions first. They feel that if they articulate the direction of the book in the introduction it helps them to adhere to it as they write the rest of the book. It really depends on the writer.

When you've completed a first draft of your manuscript, read the entire manuscript and make notes as you read. Then revise the manuscript, editing each chapter in order, until you're satisfied. Recruit a few others to read and comment on what you've composed. Solicit readers, both in and out of your field, and insist that they be honest and severely critical. Thank them in your book's acknowledgments.

Friends and relatives who read your writing usually won't tell you the truth. Most won't read the whole book and those who do will usually go easy on you because they don't want to hurt your feelings. Therefore, take all criticism seriously. If just one person doesn't understand, misconstrues, or dislikes what you have written, others could too. Don't fall in love with your language to the point you are not open to revision. And remember, the purpose of the book is not to establish you as a literary figure, but to enhance your business status.

PUBLISHING HOUSES VS. SELF-PUBLICATION

Entire books and courses are devoted to whether you should self-publish or go with an established publishing house, so we'll cover it only briefly here. You can also pay a "vanity house" to publish your book.

Traditionally, publishers give a book greater prestige. However, that perception is rapidly fading, especially with the advent of e-books and how easy self-publishing has become. If your audience is scholarly or academic, prestige is vital, but with pop culture books, prestige can be a less important factor.

Traditional publishers have in-house sales forces while self-publishers must hire distributors or try to sell their own books. The suggestions of the in-house sales team often contribute to larger sales. However, without a celebrity author or big buy-ins from the large bookstore chains, publishers will usually only print a small first run and seldom push sales.

WARNING: Traditional print publishers' sales forces are often committed to marketing assumptions that may inhibit or not work for innovative and creative projects. Therefore your proposal may be passed on, or radically changed due to their input.

Another in-house feature that self-publishing doesn't provide is a PR staff. Its primary function is to help promote the house's books, but its advertising and publicity efforts for first-time authors are usually small. Authors will often hire an outside PR firm, at their own expense, to work with and supplement a publisher's in-house staff. Outside PR agencies are invariably more accommodating and out-perform publishers' staffs, and would be something a self-publisher should consider hiring anyway.

However, with self-publishers footing the production bill upfront and hiring a distribution service, authors may have limited resources to hire a PR firm. Publishing houses, on the other hand, pay authors in advance against future royalties. Contracts generally stipulate authors will get paid in three installments:

1. On signing of the contract
2. At a middle stage, such as completion and submission of half the chapters
3. On delivery of an acceptable and completed manuscript

Authors may also receive royalties on their books from traditional publishers. Except for celebrities though, first-time authors seldom receive royalty rates of more than 6 to 8 percent of the retail or cover price. They also don't begin to receive additional moneys until after the publisher has recouped all advances through sales of the book. On the other hand, self-publishers get to keep a lion's share of the money a book's sales generate, which can be an enormous amount if the book sells well.

In addition, established publishing houses take a piece of subsidiary rights such as dramatizations, serialization, and merchandising. Whereas self-published authors own 100 percent of these rights, they will probably have to hire an agent or a rep to sell them.

GUERRILLA INTELLIGENCE

Hybrid publishers have emerged that straddle the line between traditional and self-publishing. They offer authors elements of both worlds. For example, some require authors to make up-front payments, but give them larger royalty splits. Since these types of publishing companies offer different deals, look into them and see which could work for you.

THE ADVANTAGES OF HIRING A LITERARY AGENT

Literary agents are the gatekeepers to the publishing world. Some publishers don't accept unsolicited manuscripts (those that come in directly from authors), or even "query letters" that try to get a publisher interested in reviewing a manuscript, while others assign them to over-burdened junior editors, who furiously speed read in order to keep abreast. To get a publisher's attention, hire an agent. Many agents will also not immediately accept an unpublished author. An invaluable reference tool for would-be authors is *The Literary Marketplace* (*LMP*), a massive book in more than one volume, usually available at the Reference desk of your library. Published annually by Bowker Publishing in New York, it contains listings of publishers by different categories and listing of agents, giving their requirements for submission (for example, many agents have a "reading fee" before they will consider your work, or they only want to see a sample).

Besides opening the door with publishing houses, literary agents are also a wealth of knowledge on other aspects of the industry. Agents will advise whether your book is publishable or if you're wasting your time. They'll recommend changes and resources such as ghostwriters, book doctors who can help you shape your book, researchers, and independent editors. Agents know which publishers might be interested in your particular book and how much to ask for it.

Since agents work on a percentage of your book's earnings, usually 15 percent, most are skilled negotiators who try to get the best deal. They become your partner for the life of your book. In addition to negotiating your publishing contract, literary agents relieve you of time-consuming details, oversee the publisher's marketing, expedite promotional tours, monitor distribution, and protect your contractual rights. As book sales take off, agents will push for additional promotion from the publisher and begin talks for a second book.

Good agents earn their keep because they fight for your interests every step of the way. They don't just stop working for you once the book is on the shelves. Agents can be invaluable advisers, comrades-in-arms, and guides who can walk you through the publishing maze and protect your interests.

REMEMBER

Publishing a book establishes you as an authority and gives you a powerful marketing tool. But writing a book isn't easy—nor is getting it published. It takes knowledge, time, and discipline. Authors have many choices: write it themselves or hire a ghostwriter, go with a traditional house or self-publisher, hire an agent or not. You have to make each decision with your best interests in mind.

CHAPTER 23

DESIGN A SEMINAR

"By learning you will teach; by teaching you will learn."
—*Latin Proverb*

People want to do business with the best—the most highly regarded professionals in their field. And they will pay a premium for them. So you want to *be* the best.

Being the best allows you more opportunities within your industry, brings greater recognition to you and your product or service, and translates into big money. One way to get on the fast track to the top is to attend seminars and workshops. Attending them can help you:

» Polish your skills
» Bring you up to speed on industry developments
» Build your network

However, attending seminars is not enough to make you the best. In order to be the best, you need to lead seminars and design your own.

To really cash in on seminars, lead or teach them. Teaching your peers, colleagues, and associates increases your visibility, reputation, and stature in the industry. It establishes you as a respected authority, a leader in your field, and it makes you the subject of media attention, which exposes you to more potential customers or clients. As an acknowledged authority and leader in your field, you can charge more—a whole lot more!

As a seminar leader, you're mentioned in the same breath with the biggest and the best. You can be on center stage demonstrating your expertise to businesspeople who've paid a bundle to hear you and other experts. You can swap ideas and war stories with the finest minds and the most successful practitioners in your industry. They can introduce you to other top people and together you can explore advances and innovations that could further increase your renown and your wealth.

LEAD A SEMINAR

Running your own seminar is hard, demanding work so before trying to start your own, offer your services as a volunteer, lecturer, panelist, or moderator to organizations that sponsor such events. Work your way to the top. Begin by offering your services to local organizations and then, as you gain skill and recognition, graduate to bigger venues.

Service Clubs

A great place to get experience leading seminars is at service clubs. There you can learn the process and make your mistakes. In addition to learning from your mistakes, you can make terrific contacts and, with their help, work your way up. Think of it as the equivalent to an open mike night at a comedy club where comics, both experienced and novice, go to polish their material, try out new routines, and get noticed.

Volunteer to speak at events sponsored by the Elks Club, the Rotary Club, the Veterans of Foreign Wars, the Chamber of Commerce, Women in Business, or organizations for religious, business, or civic groups. Don't ask to be paid, chalk it up to your education. Consider these opportunities to perfect your presentation, build your reputation, and meet potential clients, contacts, and media personnel.

GUERRILLA INTELLIGENCE

Some local organizations appeal mainly to retirees. While events sponsored by these groups may provide opportunities to sharpen your presentation, they're not good opportunities to network and get new business. So when you book engagements, *factor in the audience profile.* To generate business, appear before groups that draw from the active, working community.

Community Colleges

To get experience running larger lectures, teach a workshop or even a course for local educational institutions such as community colleges or adult education programs. Teaching a course can be time-consuming and the networking and business opportunities are not great. However, the experience is wonderful and today's students may be your customers or clients tomorrow.

Internet Conferences

Gain experience and exposure by participating in online conferences. Check search engines, PR services, and your favorite blogs for upcoming conferences on your area of interest. Find out if you qualify to be a panelist or suggest topics that you could participate in or lead.

Promoters

When you're comfortable with your performances at the local level, approach businesses that provide adult education and career-development courses. A wide spectrum of courses are sponsored by state employment agencies and private enterprises such as the Learning Annex, the American Management Association, and other organizations.

These lecturers are paid. They're expected to be highly professional and are graded by audiences. These sessions can be a fertile source of new business opportunities. Lecturing at this level puts an impressive notch on your resume and can qualify you for larger, more lucrative bookings.

See *www.tasl.com*, which offers a comprehensive list of classes and conferences sponsored by universities, industry associations, media, and training companies throughout the country.

Conferences and Conventions

Except for your own infomercial or appearances on major media outlets like *Today* or *Oprah,* conferences and conventions are your best bet to build your profile. Trade and industry gatherings are held locally, regionally, nationally, and internationally. They offer extensive educational programs and are always in the market for dynamic, entertaining instructors and speakers.

Speaking at major conferences means that you are at the pinnacle of your industry. It says you've arrived. Besides interacting with and being treated as an equal by the top people in your field, you're the focus of media attention and potential customers or clients.

Conferences and conventions provide unparalleled opportunities for visibility and advancement in your industry. Since the benefits of leading such seminars are so great, the competition to lead them at the national and international level is fierce. Only the most outstanding are selected, and invited to return.

GUERRILLA TACTICS

As a seminar leader or instructor, your first responsibility is to teach, but in doing so, you must be entertaining. The most popular leaders, instructors, and speakers are accomplished performers. They can rouse audiences, inspire and amuse them, and make them sign up for the next go-around.

Seminars are primarily seen as learning opportunities. In reality, they're equally about networking, socializing, and fellowship. Seminars are not school, they're more like a show or an entertainment event. They often entail travel and are expensive, so audiences—who are used to lively, amusing, and instructive presentations—have lofty expectations. In order to be a successful convention lecturer you need to:

- ❑ Become a performer. Spice up your presentations with humor, anecdotes, and real-life stories.

- ❑ Be newsy. Everyone loves inside scoops about people, companies, and industry gossip.
- ❑ Update attendees on the latest industry developments.
- ❑ Focus on a few hot topics that people in your industry should learn, and cover them expertly.
- ❑ Encourage questions from the audience.
- ❑ Make yourself available after your presentation.
- ❑ Run off copies of news developments, articles, examples, reading lists, and abstracts of presentations so that attendees feel that they're getting value.
- ❑ Provide a list of presenter's names and contact information for everyone who signed up for your sessions.

START YOUR OWN SEMINAR

After working for other people and appearing at conventions and conferences on your own, launch your own seminar. Start small—you can learn on the job and build yourself up. Starting small also establishes your track record and limits your financial risk. When you first start out with your own seminar, follow these steps:

Identify topics that draw on your experience—and can draw a large audience. If you're a financial planner, run a seminar on getting low-interest mortgages; if you're a psychologist, teach stress reduction techniques; if you're a chiropractor, explain how to eliminate neck pain. Give practical, hands-on, how-to instructions so attendees return home with tangible benefits, what we call "take-aways."

Don't charge admission; put on free seminars. Consider them learning experiences, initial steps in your master plan. Either rent a room or convince a local charity, religious, civic, or social group to allow you to use their facility in exchange for a modest contribution and/or publicity.

Hang posters and send out fliers. Place posters in high-traffic areas such as schools, universities, community centers, libraries, and businesses in or related to your field. Send announcements to local radio stations, bloggers, and related Web sites. Get names from your network, media lists, and local organizations. Send them post cards or fliers announcing the event.

Promote your seminar on the Web. Whether you post it on your site or create a separate one specifically for the seminar, get the news out on the Internet. Plug it in your blog and podcast. Create links from your blog to your Web site or the seminar Web site where people can learn more about the course and enroll in it.

The only way for your seminar—and therefore *you*—to be a success is by making sacrifices and doing the legwork yourself. Start small and get the ball rolling. Soon you'll be hosting your own seminars in large lecture halls and charging a hefty admission fee.

GUERRILLA TACTICS

Questions usually enhance presentations because they reflect the audience's concerns, reveal actual problems, and lead to stimulating exchanges. They also provide a rich source of examples that you can incorporate into your future presentations and your work.

Take questions during and after your presentation. Also make yourself available for questioners during breaks and when you're not instructing.

Fielding questions is a skill that often requires delicacy. Every seminar has some bozo who insists on asking an endless string of questions that interests only him or her. Although all attendees should feel free to question, no single person has the right to monopolize a seminar, but some usually try. After a few questions, politely, but firmly, tell incessant questioners, "Let's give other people a chance."

Audience members often think that because they paid for the seminar, they're entitled to professional advice. They won't hesitate to pose questions that don't apply to or interest others. Usually, their questions are long and complex and are followed by a string of additional questions. Answer the initial question briefly and, if the questioner persists, request that he or she see you during the break.

SEMINARS PROVIDE BUILT-IN PROMOTIONS

Although established speakers and authors command handsome fees to lead seminars and address conferences, they routinely make even more money selling a wide assortment of their materials during their appearances. For example, they sell books, audiotapes, videotapes, workbooks, calendars, and novelty items from the back of the room. You can do this as well. If the product or service you're promoting has already been released, sell that. If it still in the development phase, sell previously released materials or novelty items that promote your soon-to-launch product or service.

GUERRILLA INTELLIGENCE

Seminar promoters estimate that 20 to 25 percent of those who attend engagements buy speakers' goods. And the top attractions exceed those amounts. Product prices tend to be high because they're narrowly focused and purchases are deductible. If you make five presentations to audiences of 500 people, you can pull down substantial, additional money.

Veteran speakers frequently offer discounted packages at seminars. They might package three or four items that usually sell for $250 for half that price. To encourage sales, they'll autograph their wares, chat with attendees, or pose for photographs. Audiences, inspired by rousing speakers, gobble up goods that will remind them of, or supplement, the experience—especially when the speaker autographs them.

REMEMBER

Seminars are a fast track to success and leading them can rocket you to the top of your field. Gain experience and visibility by organizing small workshops on specific topics that you've mastered and then work your way up. As a seminar leader, your first responsibility is to teach, but in doing so you must also be entertaining. Take questions from the audience during and after presentations.

CHAPTER 24

TELESEMINARS AND VIRTUAL TOURS

"You don't make money writing books,
you make money explaining books."
—Alex Mandosian, Internet marketing specialist

For many people in this fast-paced world, there is not enough time to travel to various locations to take in the latest seminar or lecture. Luckily for them, they don't have to. Between traditional teleseminars and increasingly popular virtual and blog tours, seminar leaders and goers do not have to leave the comfort of their office. Now, you can use both options to get more publicity.

TELESEMINARS

Instead of going to a store and sitting jam-packed in uncomfortable, folding chairs, people who attend teleseminars don't have to leave home. They can stay in the comfort of their homes or wherever they have access to a telephone and listen to people talk about interesting, informative subjects. They can hear writers read excerpts from their books and discuss and answer questions about their work; or they can listen to businesspeople explain the latest industry innovation, and hear how they came up with the idea and overcame problems. Since teleseminars are primarily informational, listeners can sit back and learn a great deal on a great many subjects.

Hosting a teleseminar is an ideal way to strengthen your reputation, build your contact list, and help promote your product or service. It can expose you to new and fascinating information, involve you in stimulating discussions, and help you form relationships with exceptional people.

To run a teleseminar, get a bridge line that will enable you to host a telephone call with a large group of people. Listeners phone in to hear you conduct interviews with guests. During the interview, the listeners' phones are muted so you're not interrupted. However, as the host, you have the option of opening up the phone lines so listeners can comment and ask questions.

Also, if you're a guest on a teleseminar, you can receive great publicity. You can promote your product or service and drive traffic to your Web site. Your interview may also be logged so listeners can call in and replay it at their leisure. Or replays can be put up on your and the interviewer's Web sites. Teleseminars can also be recorded and put on MP3 players or converted into podcasts. One interview has the ability to take on many different lives.

Two distinctions between teleseminars and virtual tours are:

1. In virtual tours, you ask a question prior to the call so you can create a back-and-forth with listeners. In teleseminars, your audience can ask questions when you no longer mute their phones.
2. Virtual tours ask listeners to do something—usually buy goods or services. Virtual tours try to sell, while teleseminars focus on trying to inform. At the end of a teleseminar, you may make a special offer if you wish, but do it only at the end. "You have to give content," Rick stresses. "You have to teach. Otherwise people think its just one giant sellathon and they won't tune in."

WEBINARS

Webinars or web seminars are essentially teleseminars delivered via the Internet that include a visual component. Visuals can range from simple slide shows to full-scale productions of live video-feeds of the host and his white-board presentation. The audio for webinars can be transmitted by telephone, as it is for teleseminars, or through the Internet.

GUERRILLA TALE: On a warm fall evening in 2002, Alex Mandosian, an Internet marketing specialist, drove to a restaurant for dinner, but he couldn't find a place to park. The large parking lot was completely filled because a nearby bookstore was hosting a book signing by Al and Tipper Gore. After the signing, when the crowd had disbursed, Mandosian stopped by the bookstore and asked how many books they sold. About 450 he learned, which was enormous for that store and vastly more than the amount sold at most book signings.

How pathetic! Mandosian thought. He couldn't believe a former Vice President of the United States had to spend so much time and effort to sell so few books. Suddenly, the idea of producing virtual book tours dawned on him. He could use the telephone and the Internet to conduct virtual tours that would not require authors to travel and they could sell infinitely more books.

Since then, Mandosian has perfected the virtual book tour and has run them for an impressive array of bestselling authors. In addition, he has adopted the concept for many other products and services. "It works for anything that needs an explanation," Mandosian notes. As you read about the virtual tour format later in this chapter, think how you could adapt it to work for you.

Viewers can interact with webinar presentors by sending instant messages to the hosts. During the presentation, webinar systems can provide polls and surveys so the host or presenter can gauge the audience's interests and needs. Webinars also can be recorded and logged for later viewings, accessible through the host's Web site.

VIRTUAL TOURS

Virtual tours are primarily used for authors to promote their books, but they can also help entrepreneurs publicize their products or services. The general idea of a virtual tour is that it is a live question and answer session with the author or entrepreneur, done over the Internet, in front of a "live" audience. A moderator asks the interviewee questions that listeners have submitted and steers the session to generate interest so listeners will buy their books, products, or services. The interviewees provide answers to the questions and explain their thought process during the creation stage.

Typically, producers will stir up interest in a virtual book tour by sending e-mails that offer two free chapters of a book to those who attend the tour. The names and addresses of people to e-mail come from the publisher's list, the author's lists, and from huge lists that tour producers and their strategic partners have compiled. The e-mails contain links that those interested in the tour can click in order to sign up.

When people sign up to attend a virtual tour they are asked to submit questions for an author or entrepreneur to answer. Many people attend these tours because they want to hear answers to their questions and would not normally be able to take part in such events in real life.

On the day prior to the tour date, those who have opted in to the tour receive an e-mail reminding them when the tour will take place and the number to call. These reminders are automatically generated by auto-response software, which is readily available. Reminders can also be e-mailed on the day of the tour.

At the appointed time, listeners call a phone number and listen to what is called the live call or session, even though it is usually prerecorded. Calls usually take an hour or less. Anytime thereafter, a recording of the live session can be accessed from a Web site. Mandosian estimates that 10 percent of all listeners phone into live calls while 90 percent hear replays. Replays can also be downloaded to CDs, iPods, or other media players, which gives listeners the flexibility to listen to the tour when and where they want. "They can have the [person] in the palm of their hand," Mandosian notes.

GUERRILLA TACTICS Repackage the content generated by virtual tours. Virtual tours have a very long tail; many products can be created from them including CDs, podcasts, blogs, and newsletters. Transcribe your recordings and put them on your Web site and use them for your newspaper column, in articles, speeches, or on your radio show. You can also save the names and e-mail addresses you receive to build your list and constituency of readers for your next publicity campaign.

BLOG TOURS

On a blog tour, you appear on a series of blogs to provide information about your industry and promote your product or service. Whether the focus is put on providing information or promoting your material will depend on the nature of the particular blog on which you appear. On business-oriented blogs, you can be overtly promotional, but on others you may have to provide more information and downplay your wares.

During the tour, you appear on a number of blogs instead of traveling to stores or media outlets to promote your items. The blogs should contain links for readers to submit questions and comments, and to your Web site where they can order your items.

To set up a blog tour, first identify blogs with audiences you want to target. Search to find those sites in your area of interest that get heavy traffic. Then contact them and make your pitch. Since most bloggers always need content, many will be happy to feature you. Setting a tour schedule is important to drum up interest and to emphasize that your appearances will be limited.

Since search engines index all blog content, blog tours can have long tails. After the tour, searchers will find you; they find your appearances and can check them out. In addition, outstanding blog posts build a lot of buzz and may be picked up by other bloggers.

"The blog tours of old no longer really work," Internet marketing expert Penny C. Sansevieri, CEO of Author Marketing Experts, Inc. revealed. "The tours in which we would take clients to blogs are not as effective because everybody has moved online and their first target is bloggers. So you end up taking a number and waiting for a blogger to get back to you. We now combine our blog tours with blog comment tours. On comment tours, our clients comment on high-traffic blogs. It's a great way to get your message on high-traffic blogs that you would otherwise have to wait to get on and to do some virtual networking with people in your market."

The Dos and Don'ts of Teleseminars and Virtual Tours:

Do: Create interest in your tour by posing questions. For example, what is the single most important question on how to win the inner game of wealth? Find your target markets' concerns, identify their problems, and figure out what they want. If you're on track, the questions you ask should fit right in with your promise to buyers.

Do: Build your contacts list. Now, more than ever, names and e-mail addresses have enormous value and can be used to promote future products and services. They can be used to create strategic liaisons with other promotions that can greatly benefit you. When you ask questions, they generate content for future goods, services, and promotions.

Do: Promote the recorded, replay version. After they have recorded a tour, many people forget about it, which is a huge mistake. Since replay versions can be accessed for extensive periods of time, they have long tails. That means that they can generate lots of sales, sales that frequently amount to vastly more than the sales made from the initial version. Promoting the replay version also builds your list.

Don't: Rely on straight-through replays of your interviews; repurpose your material. Don't just record your virtual tours, put them, or parts of them, on CDs that you can give away at events or in other promotions. You can also put them online, in podcasts, blogs or transcribe them. Use material from virtual tours in brochures, fliers, newsletters, columns, speeches, and your radio show. When you repurpose, make sure that all the items you produce drive people to your Web site.

Don't: Forget to remind people to attend your tours. E-mail reminders the night before *and* the day of your virtual tour, webinar, or teleseminar. People are busy and tend to forget. So nudge them to increase their chances of listening to your tour.

Do: Address your audiences' concerns. Many people push their agenda by only giving the information they want; they ignore what their listeners need and want to know. Answer your audiences' questions; address their concerns. Your audiences' needs and questions are of the greatest importance; focus on answering them in order to connect and build beneficial relationships.

Don't: Treat your audience members like strangers. If people who submit questions give their names and cities, announce them on the call. Stating this information will personalize the session. When you publicly mention people's names, they will become your loyal supporters and advocates; it will help you forge stronger relationships.

Do: Remember that a virtual tour is always about the promise of your product or service. Build your tour around the promise made by the subtitle. Make sure your audience knows why you're bringing this into the market and how it can help them.

REMEMBER

You can great publicity without leaving your home through a virtual tour, blog tour, or teleseminar. Send e-mails to those on your lists and your strategic partners' lists to create interest in your tours. Treat each audience as if they are seated in front of you, make a personal connection with them, and be sure they are aware of your product or service's promise and how it can help them.

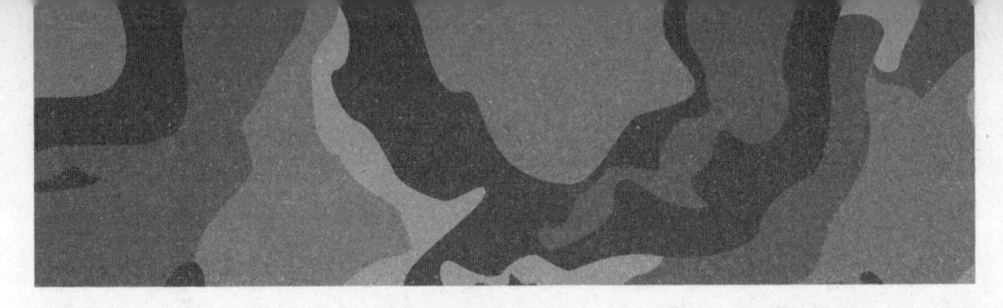

CHAPTER 25

BECOME A PUBLIC SPEAKER

"Public speaking is the art of diluting a
two-minute idea with a two-hour vocabulary."

—John Fitzgerald Kennedy

Public speaking puts you on center stage. It places you on an elevated platform in front of people who are eager to learn. Giving a public speech provides you with visibility, name recognition, and enhanced industry status, which can strengthen your publicity campaign. The fact that you were invited to speak is something in itself—it gives you the host organization's endorsement. The invitation conveys your authority to the organization's members.

Speaking is the most personal, intimate, and powerful form of communication. It's also the most effective and influential. When you speak, all eyes are on you, and you're in command of the room. You're the featured performer; everyone is listening to what you are saying.

When your talk is interesting, informative, and entertaining, an amazing dynamic takes hold. You and the audience come together; you share the same focus and explore similar ideas and beliefs. You feel the same emotions. Your minds meet and you arrive at similar conclusions. They will become supporters who champion your cause.

When you speak to organizations, they promote you. They feature you in their newsletters, Web sites, blogs, and podcasts. You become recognized as an expert, a leader in your field. Other experts and authorities take interest in you, which moves you to a higher echelon where you are grouped with the best. They want your advice and are happy to pay you more for it.

When an organization asks Jill to speak, she requests it to promote her appearance by running an article about her in its newsletter, Web site, blog, or podcast. These articles help Jill draw larger audiences and build her name recognition.

Write an article for the organization to publish before your speaking engagement. Customize the article for that organization's members and their concerns. Then ask the organization to publish your piece. Most will be happy to run your article if you request this. Don't wait for organizations to ask because most won't. Furnishing an article lets you control the information the organization distributes about you and stress the points you wish.

Ask organizations to give you the names and contact information of the attendees at the events where you will be speaking. Many organizations prepare lists and will give you a copy, but again, you must ask. If the organization does not compile a list, pass out sheets for audience members to sign and collect their business cards. When you transfer the information you receive to your records note that these individuals heard you speak at the event so you can personalize future communications to them.

If you have products or consulting services, speaking will help you increase your sales. Speaking can be extremely fulfilling, but speaking alone usually can't pay the rent. The people who get the most monetary return from speaking use it to support and generate sales for their other enterprises.

BUILD YOUR CAREER—ONE SPEECH AT A TIME

Before you launch your speaking career, take some time to prepare. Jennifer Geronimo, who runs Life Enlightenment, a business that manages speakers and authors, says, "Find your niche. Determine why you want to speak, what is unique about you, what you will speak about, where you will fit in and your goals." When you decide on your target market, supplement your publicity campaign by giving speeches. Here are some pointers on how to make an effective speech:

Research your audience. Learn about the types of people that make up the association you'll be speaking to. Find out who has delivered speeches to them in the last five years. See who they liked and who they disliked—and why. Use this to your advantage.

Be clear about what you will cover. Select a topic that you have an expert knowledge of and that people need to learn. Ask yourself what information the audience members need to know and think about what they will want to hear.

Stress three to five main points in your presentation. As discussed in Chapter 15, each point should clarify a fact about something the audience may not be clear on, or provide them with new information. Be sure to limit your speech to five points; more than that can confuse and overwhelm your audience.

GUERRILLA TACTICS

Create a one-sheet that gives your name, your topic, briefly explains your topic, lists the points you will make, and specifies how your talk will benefit the audience. Also consider adding a few testimonials to your one-sheet.

Send your one-sheet to meeting and event planners for organizations you'd like to speak to. Organizations are approached by many speakers so providing your one-sheet will show them how you separate yourself from the rest. If you have a videotape of a prior appearance or appearances, also offer to send it along.

Address your audience's problems. Before you speak, identify the members' concerns. Then in your speech, give them clear, practical, and concrete solutions that they can apply to their lives. Provide examples, step-by-step directions, and personalize your speech so the audience feels that you understand its problems and needs.

Get your message down. The better you know your message, the better you can deliver it. Part of giving a speech is to make it as entertaining as possible. You will only be able to make it entertaining if you have it down pat.

The more speeches you make, the better you will get at delivering them, and the better you get, the more jobs you book. If you can prove yourself as a great speaker, you will become the go-to resource when professional organizations want information on your industry. This platform will benefit you greatly during your publicity campaign.

GUERRILLA INTELLIGENCE

Have products to sell. Most people give speeches in order to promote something else, usually a product or service. Use your speaking career to increase the sales of your consulting services, handbooks, workbooks, or a CD.

PREPARE A SUCCESSFUL PRESENTATION

Before you speak, visit the venue. If possible have someone assist you in evaluating the space. See how the room is laid out, stand on the stage, and test the acoustics. Walk around the hall to see how the sound carries. Familiarize yourself with the sight lines so you know what the audience can and cannot see. Make sure they have supplied all the needed equipment (a stand, pointer, easel, blackboard, chalk, eraser, projector, and screen). Test that everything works flawlessly. You don't want any surprises during your presentation.

Make sure any visual aids—slides, posters, or even very brief films—you plan to employ are ready. The same goes for any handouts, worksheets, handbooks, or lists, you are thinking about using. If they will give your audience a better or fuller understanding of your presentation, use them, but be sure to prepare the materials carefully before your talk. Make certain they are neat and look good, but place more emphasis on content than on looks and design. Don't spend a great deal of time, money, or effort on producing visual extravaganzas because the speech itself is much more important.

Q & A WITH THE AUDIENCE

An important part of your presentation that you cannot fully prepare for is the questions from your audience. While questions create listener involvement and can produce stimulating dialogues, you have to stay on your toes. Try to prepare for a variety of questions before you give the speech. Announce at the beginning of your talk whether you will answer questions during your presentation or if there will be a question period after you finished speaking.

After you speak, make yourself available to answer questions or to speak with members of your audience. If they ask, sign autographs (especially if you're an author). Build relationships with audience members by being accessible, pleasant, and responsive.

At the end of your presentation, show your Web site address. Project it on the screen or display it on a poster. Include your Web site address on all handouts to direct your audience to your site where you can build relationships with them and they can learn about and purchase your goods and services.

GOALS AND GROWTH

Set goals and timetables. Determine how many talks you would like to give within a certain period of time. At the start, Jill recommends trying to give one speech per month, which should be a realistic goal if you focus on local groups to which you, your friends, or family belong. You can also target organizations run by specialized groups that you belong to, or that you may have an affiliation with.

Speaking once a month will give you an idea as to whether or not you like being a speaker, and if it's work you wish to pursue. After you have been speaking for a while, measure your success. Decide what you like about speaking and what you dislike. Then try to develop the areas you enjoy and eliminate those you do not. Somewhere along the line, you will instinctively know that it's time to move to a higher level. This may mean that you must speak more often, target larger audiences, or seek higher-paying engagements.

To move up, contact organizations that sponsor the bigger events. Find out if they will need speakers, when and if you might be able to schedule a time to speak. Have tapes made of your performances for potential bookers that you can send to them or that they can watch on your Web site. Sign up with several bureaus that book speakers and build relationships with them.

WARNING: Speakers bureaus have many clients so don't count on them to be your only marketing arm. Continue trying to get bookings on your own and consider any engagements that bureaus book to be gravy. If bureaus secure speaking engagements for you, understand that they will take a portion of your fee as a commission.

As you move up the line, keep your options open. You may be on an upward ascendancy when you get an offer to speak to a smaller group, one that doesn't pay as well or pay at all. Don't immediately rule it out as being a step back. It may offer other benefits such as great exposure and publicity, or help open the door to bigger, higher-paying engagements.

Jill gives one speech each month for which she does not charge. She selects events where she can address her primary markets or simply give back and help worthy organizations.

JILL'S TIPS FOR LAUNCHING A SPEAKING CAREER

As a popular and frequent public speaker, Jill has the following suggestions for you on how to launch your own speaking career:

1. Continue to train. You can always improve your speaking and presentations. Get media training or take lessons in acting and/or improvisation. Join different groups to learn a variety of techniques. In addition, join organizations such as Toastmasters or Business Networking International where you can perform on a regular basis, receive insightful critiques, and make important business contacts.
2. Constantly study your subject in order to stay at the top of your field. Keep your expert status by attending workshops, seminars, and educational conferences. Read publications on your area of expertise. Round out your knowledge and get different views by subscribing to a wide variety of newspapers, magazines, blogs, and podcasts.
3. Join the National Speakers Association (NSA) to meet and hang out with other professional speakers. Other speakers can give you leads, referrals, tips about speaking, and inside information about organizations that hire speakers and vendors you might use. They can also become good friends. NSA hosts conferences where you will be trained to be a world-class speaker. At NSA events, you can make terrific contacts while you learn. NSA also publishes a newsletter that can keep you informed about news and information related to public speaking.
4. Think of yourself as a speaker. Constantly focus on looking for new material that you could add to improve your presentations. Continually look for new places where you could speak. Tune in to words and phrases, stories, anecdotes, and technology that could make your talks more powerful, informative, and entertaining. Form

liaisons with other speakers, discuss common problems, techniques, developments in the industry, and exchange leads.

HOW TO BOOK SPEAKING ENGAGEMENTS

Select your targets carefully. "You don't want to contact meeting planners and find that they get hundreds of requests each week from speakers on the topic you address," Jennifer Geronimo, who manages speakers, advises. Check out the competition. Go to the National Speaker Association's Web site, *www.nsaspeaker.org*, and in the "Find A Speaker" section search who is speaking on your subject and where they're speaking.

Many directories are published where you can find organizations that employ speakers and information about them. New editions are published annually so most are up to date. They include: Douglas Publications' *Association Meeting & Event Planner's Directory* and *Corporate Meeting & Event Planners* (*www.douglaspublications.com*), and Columbia Books' *National Trade & Professional Associations of the United States* (*www.columbiabooks.com*).

Through directories you can find the names and contact information for national, regional, local trade and industry associations, corporations, professional societies, and labor unions. You can discover which groups use paid speakers, how many events they hold each year, and how many people attend. Directories also provide the names of contact people and information about meetings such as the types of meetings, their location, duration, booking requirements, and more.

When you find the names and contact information for meeting or event planners, go to their Web sites to learn which speakers they hired in the past and the topics they covered. Web sites will also tell you the theme of their next event and who they have scheduled to speak.

Send an introductory e-mail or letter to the planners for the organizations you want to target. Use the information you found on their Web sites to tailor your pitch toward what they seem to be looking for and stress the value that your presentation will provide. For example, you will show them how to save money, improve their health, or take fabulous low-cost vacations.

GUERRILLA INTELLIGENCE

Include your one-sheet with your introductory e-mail or letter. Make sure to give your Web site address, blog and podcast links, articles and any other information you think might help. Then follow up with a phone call—don't just expect the planner to contact you. When you call a planner, it won't be a cold call because he or she will have received your one-sheet. He or she will know why you're calling and may have reviewed the information you sent or visited the speaker's Web site. Keep in mind that planners need speakers and that you are calling them to provide a resource they need.

REMEMBER

Public speaking puts you in front of people who are eager to learn and be informed. It boosts your visibility, name recognition, and status in your industry. Before you launch your speaking career be clear on what you want to say, identify your audience, and get your message down. Continually take training on speaking and study your subject. Join the National Speakers Association to meet and spend time with other professional speakers.

CHAPTER 26

RADIO: HOW TO GET BOOKED, GET ON-AIR, AND START YOUR OWN PROGRAM

"Brains, integrity, and force may be all very well, but what you need today is charm. Go ahead and work on your economic programs if you want to, I'll develop my radio personality."

—Gracie Allen, comedienne

Alex Carroll (*www.radiopublicity.com*) is a self-promotion guru. His specialty is teaching people how to promote themselves on the radio. He has booked himself as a guest on 1,264 radio shows over the past ten years, which adds up to $5 million in free airtime. Although he has never spent a dime on advertising, Alex has sold over a quarter of a million books and made millions of dollars in book sales due to his radio publicity. Some of Alex's secrets are:

1. *Focus on radio.* According to Alex, radio is the easiest to get on—and it also reaches the biggest audience—of all the media. Being a radio guest is fun, gets you cost-free publicity, establishes you as an expert, and builds your reputation and brand. Hosts are happy to let you promote your Web site or whatever else you're selling and you don't have to dress up or travel because most interviews are done by telephone.
2. *Aim for big shows.* Over 10,000 radio stations operate in the United States, but most have only a handful of listeners. The 80/20 rule applies to radio: 20 percent of the stations reach 80 percent of the listeners. So get on the big shows if you want your sales to skyrocket.

3. *Identify the big shows.*
    a. People mistakenly assume that stations with high wattage (50,000–100,000 watts) have lots of listeners. However, many high-wattage stations are in low-population areas so they have fewer listeners.
    b. In contrast, many low-wattage stations are in high-population areas and have millions of listeners. Example: KBOI in Boise has ten times the wattage of KABC in Los Angeles. But KABC has ten times as many listeners.
    c. Many people assume that stations in big markets (cities) have lots of listeners. Again, often wrong. Example: WKXW in Trenton (Market #138) has eight times as many listeners as KKLA in Los Angeles (Market #2).

GUERRILLA INTELLIGENCE

Learn about the radio market from Alex Carroll's database. He has the only database of top radio shows that is based on actual listener numbers. All of the stations in Alex's database have at least 100,000 listeners. To obtain Alex's database, visit *www.radiopublicity.com.*

4. *Get booked.* The best way to get booked on big radio shows is by calling them. Since they're in radio, they want to hear what you sound like. If someone else—such as your employee or your publicist—calls in your place, be sure that they have interview sound clips of you or that sound clips are available through your Web site. Don't send faxes or e-mail blasts to radio shows; they probably won't be read by producers at big stations.
5. *Write a pitch script.* Before you start calling radio producers, be clear on what you're going to say when they answer the phone. Write it down. Practice it out loud. Have others listen to your pitch. It should take no longer

than sixty seconds (preferably thirty). Practice by calling your voice mail and pitching yourself on your recording. Then listen and critique yourself. Keep practicing until you can continually make a perfect pitch.

6. *Pitch drive time shows*. At 7:30 A.M., five times the amount of people listen to radio than at 9 A.M. Why? People are commuting to work. Ask for an interview slot between 7:30–8:30 A.M. For afternoon shows, try for 5:15–6:30 P.M., which is also prime commuting time.
7. *Follow up*. After you speak with a producer at a big radio station, send him or her an e-mail with a link to your Web site's media page, or a media kit that pitches your idea for a show. An e-mail may not be enough, but your media kit will get your idea to the almost daily meetings held between producers and hosts. Your media kit can seal the deal and get you booked.
8. *Pitch a show, not a story.* Most media kits and press releases pitch stories and for radio that's a big mistake. Stories are great for magazines and newspapers because they're in the story business, but radio people are in show business and they want to know how you will entertain and educate their audience. Tell them what you will cover and state specifically what you can share with the audience if you're booked. Give them seven to twelve bullet points. Your entire pitch should fit on one sheet.
9. *Include sample questions*. Radio hosts and producers don't have time to sit around and come up with questions to ask you. They're much too busy. If you give them a script for the interview, your chances of being booked will skyrocket because they won't have to do any work and they can see what the interview will cover. Send only one page with ten to fifteen sample questions. Most (but not all) hosts will follow your questions pretty closely, which will let you direct the course of the interview.
10. *Prepare for your interview*. Listen to the show before your interview to get a feel for the host and the show. Many

stations also broadcast on the Internet so you can listen to them at your convenience. Get the studio hotline phone number in case an emergency arises the day of the interview. Send the producer some freebies that they can give to the audience. They could be samples of your product, books, tickets, or novelty items. Ask the producer to run a promo prior to your appearance; it can attract lots of additional listeners who will make it a point to tune in for your interview.

11. *Send thank-you letters*. After each interview, write a personal thank-you note to the producer. Offer to be an emergency fill-in guest. Ask the producer to post favorable comments about your appearance on bulletin boards such as Bitboard or Radio Online. These member-only boards are read daily by thousands of radio professionals and can generate more interviews.
12. *Get an endorsement*. Ask the producer to send you a letter on the station's letterhead saying how great a guest you were, how much the audience liked you, and how professional and easy to work with you were.

GET YOUR OWN PROGRAM ON INTERNET RADIO

While we're on the subject of radio, how would you like to have your *own* radio program? Dr. Proactive, Randy Gilbert, did, so he created the Internet radio program *Inside Success Radio*. The site now has a strong following and has brought him great publicity. Through this program, he has also strengthened his network and created new, lucrative business ventures including a course—the Secrets of Internet Radio (*www.secretsofinternetradio.com*)—that teaches people how to start, operate, and promote Internet radio programs.

On Gilbert's radio show he interviews authors. His program has allowed him to read many interesting books, talk about them with their authors, and create relationships with many of those authors. It's also boosted his name recognition and helped his other business ventures, which include running e-mail blasts.

Starting an Internet program is easy and inexpensive. Interviews are recorded by telephone without using special, high-priced equipment. Software to record interviews on your computer can be obtained free of charge. Telecasting requires a camera and can be a bit more complex, but it's still relatively easy.

GUERRILLA TALE: "I instantly get past gatekeepers when I tell them I'm the producer of an Internet radio show," Gilbert revealed. "I'm immediately transferred to the person I want and they're happy to talk. It opens doors everywhere, exactly like a press pass. I get in to conventions, meetings, seminars, where I meet really interesting people. When people learn that I have a radio show, they readily share information with me that they haven't previously disclosed. When they know it's for the radio, they want to give something special."

REMEMBER

Radio is the easiest media to get on and reaches the widest audience. Your best bet is to try and get booked on big, drive-time shows by contacting them yourself. Be sure to pitch the show—not the story. Write out your pitch before you call and provide sample questions. If it feels natural enough, think about starting your own Internet radio program.

CHAPTER 27

ONLINE PUBLICITY STRATEGIES

"A fundamental new rule for business is that the Internet changes everything."

—Bill Gates

Before we get into online publicity strategies in depth, we would like to thank and acknowledge Steve Lillo, CEO of PlanetLink (*www.planetlink.com*) for his great help in consulting with us on the chapters. As we all know, the Internet is an expansive place, and if you need help traversing it—get some!

If you aren't familiar with the Internet, it's easy to get intimidated by the massive amount of information out there. It can be frustrating to try and find your online niche where you can publicize your product or service. You have to establish what market you're going to target and set up an online publicity plan.

You also have to be flexible. "If you commit to Internet marketing you must be willing to go through constant change." Penny C. Sansevieri advises. "Things are going to go away, come back, and fluctuate. So you have to be ready for it and your success could depend on how flexible you can be."

In this chapter, you will learn about basic online publicity strategies that you can implement. Following these strategies will help you launch your campaign into cyberspace, where it can expand and grow.

POST PRESS RELEASES

Announce the launch of your product or service on your site and post your press release. Summarize each press release with a brief story on the main page of your site's press release section. Then link the summary to the full text of the release.

Simultaneously send your press release to:

- Those on your media list (See Chapter 7, Media Lists: Play the Numbers Game.)
- Online distribution services
- Everyone in your organization and network

Add links to your press release to connect it with information on your Web site and information on other sites that might interest your visitors. For example, link to financial statements, government statistics, and prior press releases.

WARNING: Since the Internet is constantly evolving, by the time you read this book, the information and sites in this chapter may have changed, or no longer exist. In that event, don't give up. The information you want is somewhere on the Web. You just have to look.

UTILIZE DISTRIBUTION SERVICES

Distribution services circulate press releases to thousands of media outlets. Many of them also offer other services, including providing contact information for journalists, editors, and industry analysts while continually supplying updated news reports and financial information and furnishing links to other information.

GUERRILLA TACTICS Don't send the same press release to more than one distribution service because most of them send items to the same media outlets. Bullet key points in electronically distributed press releases so that they'll pop right off the page.

Key distribution services can be found at:

- Business Wire (*www.businesswire.com*), on- and offline distributions
- InternetNewsBureau (*www.internetnewsbureau.com*), online distributions
- Marketwire (*www.marketwire.com*), online distributions
- PRNewswire (*www.prnewswire.com*), on- and offline distributions
- PRWeb (*www.prweb.com*), e-mail distributions

ONLINE PUBLICATIONS

Submit promotional materials to online publications or create your own Web publication as either part of your site or as its own site. Established blogs address the sharply focused communities that you want to reach, but there is a big advantage to creating your own online publication—you make the rules. Although podcasts are technically not publications, submit your material to them as well because they are also excellent promotional vehicles.

Submitting promotional materials will help you build name recognition and credibility. You can demonstrate that you're an expert and a visionary who is respected, dedicated, principled, articulate, clever, well connected, and well liked.

Meanwhile, if you choose to start your own publications, you can begin to build a following that's all your own. As the publisher of your own media site, you select the content and decide how to present it. You can dedicate your entire publication to unabashedly promoting your own goods or even to knocking your competitors. You're in charge. You're writing it, editing it, and publishing it. Your publication can include text, audio, and/or video.

However, this freedom will also require you to do a tremendous amount of work. You may end up diverting all your time and resources to your online publication rather than focusing on other important aspects of your publicity campaign. To solve this problem you can contract out some of all of the work. You can hire others to do the legwork while you still make all the decisions. But contracting out could be costly.

GUERRILLA INTELLIGENCE

Successful publications reflect their creators. So, develop a newsletter, e-zine, blog, podcast, search engine, or mailing list that is an extension of you. Use it as a platform to express your insight, ideas, knowledge, sense of humor, passion, conviction, and world view. Remember, as we stated way back in Chapter 1: *You are the product*! But you also have to remember that it's not *all* about you. Even though you are the product, the items you offer must appeal to your audience. Your publication must be filled with information that will benefit your audience so that they'll depend on it and look forward to reading it.

ONLINE NEWSLETTERS

Newsletters usually are industry, product, or interest specific. They're information intensive, but can carry some advertising space. Most newsletters are all business with little fluff. It's assumed that readers want and need their information so they get straight to the point.

Newsletters come in all sizes, shapes, and approaches, and thrive on alerting visitors to developments in their fields. Visitors read them to stay up to speed. Some newsletters go into exhausting detail while others are brief reports on developments that subscribers can explore in greater depth elsewhere.

Generally, online newsletters occupy a separate section of a Web site and, in some cases, are password protected. Most of the time, access is free, but they can also be fee-based.

Subscribers like newsletters because they're so specifically focused and can be quickly read and easily printed, circulated, transported, and stored. Most newsletters are published in-house and intentionally avoid the formalities of traditional magazines and newspapers.

Publish new newsletter editions on a regular basis—at least quarterly. Marketing experts suggest following the rule of 75/25: provide information of worth and value in 75 percent of the newsletter and sell stuff with the remaining 25 percent. Find a mix that fits your needs and those of your readers.

Don't charge for access to your newsletters, unless you're prepared for a big drop off in your readership. However, if your information is essential and not otherwise available, your readership may hold, or even grow, when you charge for it. It depends on what you're offering the reader and how others in your industry function.

Before starting a newsletter, become familiar with other newsletters in your industry. Focus on newsletters in your field, as well as a few in other fields. This way you have a good idea of what's going on in your sphere, and also what else is available and working in the wider world. Examine all of them closely. Note features you like, dislike, or wish were included and develop a template of your own. If your newsletter appeals to a large number of readers, you may attract advertisers.

E-ZINES

E-zines (or zines) are electronic newsletters delivered via e-mail. They're similar to online newsletters, except they aren't posted on a site, but sent to your inbox. Usually, they're free of charge and published by companies to support their business. However, some are like magazines, supported by advertising. Most e-zines are sent to subscribers on a regular schedule, but many others are published sporadically.

The content of e-zines runs the gamut of human imagination from the highly specialized to the diverse and eclectic. E-zines often contain articles submitted by authors in exchange for publicity. If you don't feel that launching your own is worthwhile, piggyback off someone else's e-zine.

However, if you *do* launch your own e-zine:

- » Solicit subscribers from your Web site, by e-mail or postal mail, through seminars, conferences, and speaking engagements.
- » Ask your customers, suppliers, colleagues, friends, and family to subscribe.
- » Don't twist arms, or force subscriptions down anyone's throat.
- » Don't send your e-zine to those who didn't request it. Send it only to those who actually want to receive it.
- » Build a loyal following rather than inflated circulation figures.
- » Don't sell the names on your subscriber list. If, for any reason, you decide to sell their names, tell them beforehand. If you don't inform your subscribers that you intend to give their names and e-mail addresses to third parties, your subscribers will consider the third-party e-mail to be spam.
- » Don't inundate subscribers with additional mailings.

If you charge for access to e-zines, expect to lose subscribers. However, as with online newsletters, your readership might hold or even grow if your information is essential and not otherwise available. Again, you'll have to feel it out for your specific industry. Mention your friends and colleagues in your e-zine and ask them to include items about you in their e-zines. Mentioning each other is a great guerrilla way of building name recognition and increasing everyone's subscriber base. Check out Jill's e-zine (*www.jilllublin.com*) and Rick's (*www.rickfrishman.com*).

Directories listing e-zines can be found at:

- » eZineSearch (*www.ezinesearch.com*)
- » Ezine Universe.com (*www.bestezines.com*)
- » Tile.Net/Lists (*www.tile.net/lists*)

Look around at other people's e-zines and see what they have to offer. If it's something that you think you could handle, include its launch and mailings in your campaign timeline.

FORUMS

Millions of people find and discuss information within their areas of interest on online forums. Forums are interactive discussion groups and they exist on virtually every imaginable subject.

People from all over the world participate in these forums and businesspeople join to monitor discussions and get feedback on their goods and services. Participants send messages about their interests that are circulated to other participants who can comment on messages and generate dialogues. Some forums moderate or screen messages while others allow all posts.

> **WARNING: Some groups prohibit commercial messages and advertising. Check the particular forum's rule on advertising before you join.**

You can get publicity by joining existing forums or starting your own. Since forums are communities, they are great places to virally market, promote, and network. In fact, they can operate like free focus groups. You can receive insightful comments and critiques from people with extensive interest and experience in your field. Their input can enhance your product or service and provide ideas on how you can promote it. And if participants like your wares, they will often work hard to promote them.

REMEMBER

If you don't know how to use it or have a plan, the Internet can be overwhelming. Set up a specific Internet publicity strategy. Whether it includes posting your press releases to your Web site, using an online distribution service, starting your own online publication, commenting on forums, or all of the above, your plan should be specific to your product or service.

CHAPTER 28

GROW YOUR BUSINESS WITH A WEB SITE

"When I took office, only high energy physicists had ever heard of what is called the World Wide Web. . . . Now even my cat has its own page."

—President Bill Clinton

For guerrillas, the Internet continues to be a bonanza because it has exponentially expanded their media opportunities and their reach, and brings potential consumers to them. A Web site makes it possible for a guerrilla to address wider target audiences more effectively and efficiently. Instead of having to beat the bushes to generate interest in their goods and services, guerrillas can use the Internet to bring people to them.

The Internet gives the public direct access to Web sites so anyone can get your information, not just the media. The content you provide isn't filtered through the media, who usually decide what's news, what gets printed, aired, and publicized. Before the Internet, publicists focused their time and energy courting the media. If they were lucky, the media told their story to the public, but the media usually added their own spin, which the publicists hoped was the spin they wanted.

The Internet lets you tell your story directly to your target audience and in the manner *you* want to tell it.

Many visitors to your site are looking for more information than they get from the media. They come to you. They visit your site because they're interested in viewing your information or forming a relationship with your company. Before they do business with or invest in your company, they want to see all your press releases and financial information. They don't want information that's been interpreted by others; they want to see original documents so they can draw their own conclusions.

GLOBAL REACH

In the past, when guerrillas began to publicize their businesses, they were forced to conduct local or regional campaigns. Usually, the cost of national campaigns was prohibitive, so guerrillas concentrated on promotions close to home. High costs limited their entry into larger markets and slowed their growth. That's the past. Today, the Internet recognizes no such boundaries; the Internet erases boundaries.

The Web blankets the globe. When you visit a site, you don't know whether it originated next door or in Timbuktu. Once your site is up, you can attract customers from all over the world. From the outset, the Internet gives you access to it all: local, regional, national, and international markets.

Global reach increases the possibilities exponentially. Before the Internet, guerrillas with narrowly focused specialties slaved for years to expand their customer base. Today, simply by launching a Web site, those guerrillas can leapfrog regional borders and immediately offer their wares to a vastly larger clientele. Technical advances have also provided the ability to have the Web change a site's default language so it can reach international markets.

UNEQUALED VALUE

As a promotional tool, a Web site is an unequaled value. A Web site can reach an international audience for less than the cost of advertising in most local media. It's global reach and ability to target potential customers can lift a guerrilla from obscurity to riches faster and more economically than any other marketing method. Through the Web and the new media, obscure individuals can reach colossal target audiences and receive worlds of publicity. As these new approaches take hold today, they and refinements of them will become even more important in the future.

GUERRILLA TALE: Marie Digby never dreamed that the music videos that she recorded in her living room would make her a YouTube sensation, bring her huge publicity, and skyrocket her career. Digby's simple, acoustic covers of popular songs have been viewed on YouTube over 2.3 million times and led to numerous radio and TV appearances plus performance dates. The strategy to make these videos and use YouTube to promote her was hatched by Digby and her record company, Hollywood Records. This shows how traditional businesses are turning to the Internet to promote their wares. Digby, who was a musical unknown, recorded popular songs, rather than her original material, in order to get the spill-over from searchers who were looking for the well-known songs she covered—and it *really* worked.

SPECIALIZATION

Web sites also speed guerrillas' ability to shape the direction of their careers. It lets them focus their marketing efforts on more sharply defined areas. In the past, it took years to establish your niche, but now guerrillas can, from the outset, use the Web to proclaim that they're specialists.

GUERRILLA TALE: In law school, Mark showed an aptitude for copyright law, a field dominated by powerful law firms and corporations. Upon graduation, he took a job as a licensing attorney with a major publishing company. He worked hard, got great experience, and after a year, opened his own, one-man office. Although he only had a handful of clients, Mark had a friend who was a Web site designer. Mark put up a Web site that promoted him as a copyright specialist for authors and from there clients poured in. Mark's site quickly established him as a specialist.

The Internet also enables people to specialize more narrowly. In the past, specializing in narrow segments of a market was frequently not commercially viable because the specialists could not reach enough potential clients or customers. However, since the Internet reaches so many people, specialists can now draw from a vastly larger group of prospects.

BECOME A TWENTY-FIRST CENTURY PLAYER

A Web site also places you in the twenty-first century. It testifies that you understand the new economy, that you're using the latest tools and providing the most easily accessible information.

Your Web site is the first thing prudent potential customers or clients and peers examine. It speaks directly to the businesses you want to attract: innovative businesses that are blazing trails into the new millennium. It shows that you're a kindred spirit, a player in the twenty-first-century economy. It also tells them who you are, what you're doing, and where you're headed. Remember, most people prefer doing business with those who are on the same wavelength . . . don't you?

MAKE FRIENDS WITH THE INTERNET

For those of you who aren't familiar with the Internet, stop here and get to know it. In fact, get to know it well. Visit a wide variety of sites. Experiment, play, try it out. Examine content, design, speed, and ease of use. Don't be afraid to make mistakes, they're part of the process. Then decide what would work best for you.

WARNING: A bad Web site can be worse than no Web site at all. Visitors won't waste time with sites that are weak in content, poorly designed or slow, or difficult or unreliable to navigate. A bad Web site will be a blot on your reputation and will cost you business. So, don't jump rashly into the Web site waters. If you plan to promote your business with a Web site, do it right!

GUERRILLA TACTICS

Before designing a Web site, ask the following questions:

- ❑ Who is my target audience?
- ❑ How do I best reach them?
- ❑ What information do they need to know?
- ❑ What is the intended result?
- ❑ What is the best way to achieve that result?

After you've answered the above questions, build your Web site from three perspectives:

1. Marketing
2. Technology
3. Design

All of these overlap and influence each other. Answer the following questions from all three perspectives:

- ❑ Who is the site being created for?
- ❑ What are their needs?
- ❑ Should the site have audio or video?
- ❑ What information do visitors want and expect?
- ❑ How do I want to communicate with them?
- ❑ How should I lay out the site so it's easy and intuitive to navigate?
- ❑ How should I organize the site?

Have your Web site listed by search engines. To decide which search engines would be best for your site conduct some research. Start by typing a phrase such as "major search engines" into the search engine you use most often. Review the information you find and select the appropriate search engines. One of the most productive ways to increase your search engine ranking is to have sites link back to your site as often as possible.

To get publicity for your new site:

» Notify the media when it launches.
» Notify the media when you update it with new content.
» Notify the media about new awards and distinctions.

Sites for notifying the press include:

» PR Newswire (*www.prnewswire.com*)
» Business Wire (*www.businesswire.com*)

The more often members of the media visit your site, the more likely they are to find something they are interested in. Keep them coming back and you are likely to get some publicity hits.

TURN YOUR SITE INTO A MEDIA CENTER

Encourage other sites to reprint your articles with a link at the bottom, or to just link directly to your articles. Let those other sites use yours as an industry resource. If they begin looking to your site for news, you're building your name recognition and authority. You are the place to come for information on the industry.

Make your Web site function as a press center or a press room. Provide content for the media and make it easy for them to use. Prominently display the link or button "Media Room," "News Room," or "Press Room" on your site's navigation area and link them to a series of pages or subsections with:

» A listing of all your press releases by their headlines. Place the headlines in reverse chronological order and link each headline to the full-text press release, which visitors can view, print, and download.
» Format your Web pages so that visitors can print them in easily readable, printer-friendly versions.
» Provide supportive documents including: spreadsheets, fact sheets, multimedia, photographs of products and manage-

ment, company and management bios, logo, articles, client list, testimonials, awards and recognition, events and programs, links to other sites, and other information that visitors can download. List date-sensitive material in reverse chronological order and group documents according to categories. Consider creating a separate page for each category. Also consider including audio and video from your previous media exposures.

» Give contact information on every page. It's amazing how many Web sites don't provide the phone number, fax number, or e-mail address for the site. Don't force visitors to search madly when they want to contact you.

WARNING: Don't post financial or any other type of sensitive information on your Web site if you're concerned about your competitors getting access to it. However, if you wish to provide limited access, your site can be constructed to let you designate who has access to sensitive information.

» Make it easy for the media to use information from your site.

» Include information about your product or service on your Web site's "About Us" section or in separate product/services sections.

» Include a request form on your site that visitors can complete and submit in order to ask questions or get information.

By creating a media-friendly area of your site, you can get more traffic and increase your exposure. If lots of people read the articles you post, it will showcase your expertise.

Another way to get your information circulating through cyberspace is by enlisting a distribution service. Internet distribution services send out press releases to thousands of reporters and media outlets.

You can send your releases to:

PR Newswire (*www.prnewswire.com*)
Business Wire (*www.businesswire.com*)
Marketwire (*www.marketwire.com*)
Internet News Bureau (*www.internetnewsbureau.com*)
eReleases (*www.ereleases.com*)

WARNING: Only send your press releases to one distribution service because they all reach virtually the same audiences and charge similar fees. The media doesn't want or need to receive the same releases from multiple services.

KEEP TRACK OF YOUR VISITORS

Create a registration system on your press center through which the press can tell you who they are and what material they wish to receive. Get registrants' names, e-mail addresses, and topic areas like general news, financial reports, new product news, etc. Categorize the data according to the media they represent (radio, TV, press, and Web) and the interests indicated. Build in the capability for visitors to subscribe to your e-mail list(s). Systems can be added to your Web site that will automatically send messages to list members.

WARNING: Registration systems that require detailed information can be barriers because many visitors will leave the site rather than complete them. Only ask the fewest questions possible, clearly state the value that the visitor will receive and post your privacy policy.

It's important to create a loyalty among your site viewers. You should ask visitors to:

» Bookmark your site
» Join your mailing list
» Subscribe to your newsletter, blog, and/or podcast
» Purchase your other goods and services

Collecting information about visitors to your site is essential. Not only does this add members to your contact list, but it also starts a personal relationship with them. Visitors will be more likely to offer you constructive feedback on your site.

MAKE YOUR SITE EFFECTIVE

Visitors to Web sites are demanding and they have plenty of options. If your site has problems, they won't waste their time with it and probably won't return. They might even turn to your competitors' sites. So don't put up your site until it's well tested and easy to navigate, and you're convinced that it's effective.

Before launching your site:

- Test it on friends or family members who have little computer/ Internet experience and note the problems they encounter.
- Don't accept excuses or explanations from Web designers. Care only that your site is easily navigable by everyone from novices to experts. The bottom line is that the site be easy to use.
- Be certain that it works smoothly with all operating systems and browsers.
- Fix all problems.

Once your site is fixed and up and running, make sure that it is always:

Easy to use. Make your Web site as easy and intuitive to use as possible. If it isn't, visitors won't return. Visitors are fickle. They have loads of other options and if they have to jump through hoops to use your site, they won't waste their time. Waiting for your site to appear will frustrate and anger visitors. It will undermine your hopes of turning them into satisfied customers or clients. So, make your site simple to use!

Informative. Your Web site should be *the* repository of vital information about your industry. Design may attract visitors and ease of operation will keep them happy, but content will bring them back. Ultimately, visitors want content. They want to see who you are, what information you provide, and how it can benefit them. Web sites can describe:

- Your business
- Its history
- Specific projects
- Financial information
- Your portfolio
- Staff biographies
- Staff photographs
- Customer or client lists
- Testimonials
- News
- Newsletters
- Games
- Contests
- Privacy and security policies
- Links to other sites
- Product descriptions
- Product specifications
- Price lists
- Photographs
- Illustrations
- Audio
- Video
- Ordering information
- Shipping instructions
- Direct e-mail links for questions, comments, or for ordering goods or services

Has a great look and feel. The first thing visitors notice is a site's look; it's the first impression that it will make. Site design reflects how you would like to be perceived: classical or modern, traditional or progressive, avant garde or straightforward, etc. A bold design that features unusual colors combinations and typefaces can signify a dynamic, aggressive, and vigorous approach. However, it can also come off as distracting, visual noise. Web site design is akin to dressing appropriately for a job interview; it may not get you the job, but without it you decrease your chances of making it to the second round. What constitutes appropriateness depends on the audience you hope to reach. Also, Web design isn't just about looks. It also controls many other features including the site's structure, organization, and ease of navigation, which are essential if a site is to succeed.

Reflective of your mission. Remember, the purpose of your Web site, the reason for its existence, is to support your mission. It's easy to be seduced by the glitter of new, exciting technology, brilliant writing, startling color combinations, and groundbreaking design. But what value do they provide if they divert visitors from your site's main purpose: to support your mission? Identify your site's mission. Be specific. Your site should reflect and support the mission of your business. For example, if the mission of your business is to sell tools, create a Web site that allows you to sell tools. On your site, give visitors information about your tools and make it easy for them to buy your tools online. Also make it clear to them why it's to their benefit to buy your tools.

Quick to download. As previously stated, visitors to Web sites hate to waste their time. "The site took too long to download," is a constant complaint that Web designer Steve Lillo of Planetnet hears. According to Steve, slowness is a major turnoff.

To be successful, Web sites must download fast! If visitors have to wait long, most won't stick around, especially if they have other options. They'll be off and running to other sites, including your competition. The most terrific, prize-winning site won't attract many visitors if it takes forever to view. Slow downloading can be expensive; it can cost you customers and clients.

In the past, a site could either be downloaded quickly or be graphically exciting, not both—you had to make a choice. Fortunately, that's no longer true. Today, Web designers can give you the best of both worlds: sites that download fast and look great.

Web designers know how to best use color, optimize and compress images, and judiciously incorporate graphics to make your site "lean and mean" and visually appealing. They can write code that tells your browser how the Web page looks while taking minimal space and using downloadable audio, video animation, and additional programming sparingly.

Steve Lillo shared his secrets on how to assure that visitors come back to your site. They are:

- ❑ Always tell the truth. State the facts clearly and avoid hype, buzz words, and jargon.
- ❑ If you're stating your opinion, make it very clear that you're merely giving your opinion, not quoting facts.
- ❑ Employ appropriate technology to ensure that every element of your site is easy to use. Keep in mind that use of the latest technology doesn't always produce the most effective Web site. Ease of use is especially important with large, complex sites. Make sure all links connect properly.
- ❑ Make your site lively and entertaining. Create great content that visitors will look forward to reading. Give advice, the latest news, and plenty of "how-to" explanations. Include anecdotes, jokes, industry gossip, tips, contests, surveys, and discussion groups. Award prizes and give discounts on merchandise.
- ❑ Keep content updated so that the information you provide is always correct.
- ❑ Remember your Web site is a research tool. Visitors will depend on you for reliable information and won't

use your site if your information isn't current. Provide information that's updated regularly such as daily tips or monthly articles.

- ❑ Notify people via e-mail about significant news developments, updates to your site, and other information that may be of benefit or interest to them. Create a link in your e-mail messages to your site so those interested can easily access your site.
- ❑ Deliver what you promise—if you can't deliver it, don't promise. As previously stressed, results are ultimately what count, and once you get past the glitter, results are what visitors to your site want. If you don't provide as advertised, you'll lose credibility and most likely your business.
- ❑ Update the look of your Web site so it's consistent with your other marketing materials. Periodically freshen it by adding content—press releases, articles, blog posts, event listings, and more. Consider adding some interactive components to your site to allow registered visitors to also contribute content.
- ❑ Never litter the Internet with spam. Don't host or use services that specialize in circulating spam. The wide distribution they offer is more than offset by the resentment they arouse. Sending spam can also cause you to lose your account, which can result in lost business.
- ❑ Provide added value. What information or services can you provide that will cause visitors to return to your site? Fill your site with newsletters, industry analysis, calendars of events, industry directories and other interactive services. Create a Web site that visitors will want to return to and recommend.

REMEMBER

The Internet is a bonanza for guerrillas because it has exponentially expanded their media opportunities. Before designing a Web site, identify your target audience and their needs. Register your site with search engines, create a media center, and make it easy for the press to use information from your site. Test it thoroughly to make sure that it's easy to use, informative, attractive, reflective of your mission, and quick to download. Make sure you stay true to your mission—and don't lose your visitors to the competition!

CHAPTER 29

WELCOME TO THE BLOGOSPHERE

"Blogs are the new black, the new Web site."

—Michelle Price, CEO of A Third Mind

When we wrote the first edition of this book, blogs were in their infancy. In fact, when we drafted material on blogs, we had to define the term and explain what it meant. Before we went to press, we decided not to include the text we had written about blogs because they were still so rare.

Well, things have changed!

GUERRILLA INTELLIGENCE

The search engine Technorati (*www.technorati.com*) reports that 103 million blogs now exist and 175,000 more are created each day. According to a Pew Internet study, 50 million people read blogs in 2005. Blog readers are exceptionally loyal; 85 percent read at least one blog per day.

In case you still don't know, a *blog*, or Weblog, is a journal that is posted on the Internet. Blogs cover every conceivable subject, whatever their authors wish. They tend to be opinionated, highly niche-oriented, and encourage dialogue with their readers. They do not have to be fair, objective, or balanced. Authors publish blogs to establish themselves as experts; they build loyal readership by displaying their knowledge, insights, observations, personalities, and writing skill.

Bloggers are at the forefront of the new media. The new media distinguishes itself from the traditional media because of its willingness to freely provide content to its audience. The new media operates according to the belief that when it gives its content, it builds communities and corps of loyal customers and consumers.

Writing and maintaining a blog is inexpensive and can reach large, devoted audiences. Blogs have taken off because their authors can express who they are and the benefits they can provide. Since blogs are updated frequently, their authors build close relationships with their readers and hold their attention. Unlike traditional Web sites, which are slow to change or static, blogs continually issue new posts and they promote conversations with and among their readers. So bloggers can air their ideas and get prompt feedback. Feedback from readers helps them customize their messages for their audiences.

Successful blogs can be more powerful than other Web sites because they forge close relationships with their readers. In addition, search engines treat every blog post as an individual Web page so blogs can receive preferential listings and generate more traffic. Nevertheless, both are important because blogs and traditional Web sites complement each other and work best when they coexist.

GUERRILLA INTELLIGENCE

Steve Lillo, CEO of the Web site design firm PlanetLink, says, "When we set up a blog for a client we generally integrate it with their Web site. The design will look like the rest of their Web site, with their unique branding. The navigation elements for the rest of their Web site are also included in the blog. We want visitors to come to the blog, and more importantly, we also want visitors to come to their Web site. By integrating the blog within the main Web site, we increase the odds that visitors coming to the blog will also go to the other areas of our client's Web site."

Blogs are ideal vehicles for getting publicity in two ways:

1. Your story can be discussed in other people's blogs.
2. You can discuss your story in your own blog.

Since search engines index every word in every post, blogs give you a strong Web presence and make it easy for people to find you.

USE OTHER PEOPLE'S BLOGS

"To get publicity through blogs, start by reading a bunch of blogs," Web presence developer Jeff Nordstedt, CEO of City Desk Design, recommends. "Understand the community, and get a feel for them, their style. Find out how different blogs work, their passions, their pet peeves, their format, and preferences."

Your information can be included in other people's blogs if you establish relationships with the bloggers or if you pay them. If you have relationships with bloggers, ask if they will run your items. Or you can sign up with organizations that will place your information in blogs for a fee. These organizations include Federated Media Publishing (*www.federatedmedia.net*), Pajamas Media (*www.pajamasmedia.com*), and BlogHer (*www.blogher.org*).

"Getting published on other people's blogs is the essence of new media," Tia Graham, The Blogsultant (*www.bloggingwithflair.com*), explains. "A beginning blogger may not understand the traditional methods for getting publicity such as press releases, media kits, and the like, but blogs leapfrog all that because they're instantly publishable. If you know people who publish blogs, contact them to see if they will publicize you."

Leaving comments on other people's blogs can build your following. Many bloggers read other blogs and they may pick up your comments or contact you.

Conduct keyword research. Go to Wordtracker (*www.wordtracker.com*) and similar sites and search keywords and phrases that relate to what you're promoting. Choose words that will tell where to reach people who are having problems that your product solves. For example, when Jeff Nordstedt promoted the *Serotonin Power Diet*, a book aimed at readers who gained weight from taking antidepressants, he searched "fighting antidepressant weight gain." His search directed him to sites that were concerned with the problem. Nordstedt also searched "diets or weight loss for people taking antidepressants."

Search key terms that identify both the problem and the result. See how many times people have searched for the key terms within a certain period of time and how many results were provided. Ideally you want your words to have been searched often, but not to produce thousands of results. Then create traffic by implanting your key words in everything you put on the Internet—your Web site, articles, and blogs—and by linking them to other sites and blogs. To be placed high on search result lists, optimize your Web presence. For example, if you're selling electric drills, frequently include the term "electric drills" wherever you sell them; on your Web site and your blog.

GUERRILLA TACTICS "The real key isn't necessarily how many blogs you hit," Penny C. Sanservieri adds, "but how much traffic you drive to your site. Every link from a high-traffic blog, e-zine, or Web site won't necessarily generate traffic. The key is to conduct research to find high-traffic, high-impact programs that really send highly qualified buyers to your Web site."

Go to directories and search engines to find blogs that might be interested in covering your story. Leading search engines include Technorati (*www.technorati.com*), IceRocket (*www.icerocket.com*), Sphere (*www.sphere.com*), GoogleBlog Search (*http://blogsearch.google.com*), and Yahoo! Search Blog (*www.ysearchblog.com*).

Search to find other blogs in your niche. Find out who they are, what they cover, their perspective, and how you can connect with them. Although they may be your competitors, the blogosphere is about connections, even with your competitors. If you try to go it alone, your blog will be cut off like an island; you'll be alone and won't have the connections you need to succeed. With your competitors' help, your blog can be a part of a community from which you can become a center of influence.

BUILD STRENGTH BY BUILDING LINKS

It's hard to link with other blogs if you don't have a blog. Without a blog, you're left to try traditional methods like sending press releases, product samples, and offering discounts. If you don't have a blog, you can write articles and submit comments that you send to bloggers who cover your areas of interest.

If you approach bloggers, understand that they are a part of the new media so you should also be a part of the new media. Bloggers will be more receptive to those who they consider members of their community, who have blogs, and who share their values and beliefs.

Blogging differs from traditional media because most bloggers feel that blogging is the process of developing communities, not just a method of marketing. Most top bloggers really enjoy blogging, and don't consider it their "job." They enjoy dealing with people who are part of their community as opposed to the traditional media. The best way to approach a blogger is by becoming part of his or her community.

"Most blogs are personal. They state their authors' opinions, insights, and feelings," Tia Graham believes. "Building personal relationships works better than paying for postings because blogs tend to be about the blogger. So bloggers can be protective of what they post. If you have a good relationship with them, it can help."

If your blog contains great content, the word will usually get out. Other bloggers will learn about it, enjoy it, respect it, and support it. They may comment on your blog, plug it, link to it, and include material from it on their blogs.

Jeff Nordstedt encourages his clients to start blogs so they can participate in the community. Then he helps them reach out to other blogs that address the same market or customers. On your blog, place links to your competitors and list them as resources. Link and post comments to your competitors blogs because they may link back to you, talk about you, review your blog, or make you a part of their community, which is called "link love."

Contact your competitors:

» Send them an e-mail asking them to look at your new blog.
» Briefly tell them about yourself.
» Briefly explain why you're qualified to write your blog or have an interesting perspective on your subject.
» State that you think their blog is great so you put up a link to it on your blog.
» Say that you would appreciate it if they would link back to you.

Be straightforward and honest. Don't try to link with blogs you truly don't like. The more you read other blogs, the better you will be at approaching their authors about their content and setting up link exchanges. Linkage is what establishes a community.

The more links you post, the more traffic you can receive. The idea is to build an extensive network. If you use this approach to promote your blog, understand that it may take time. However, try to make connections, promote others, and hope they respond.

SETTING UP YOUR BLOG

Before you create your blog:

» Identify why you want to create a blog and how you think it will help you. Write down your reasons. If your main reason is to make lots of money, expect to be disappointed.
» Determine how you want your blog to look and read. Study other blogs, note what you like, don't like, and what has been successful. Then incorporate the features that seem right for you. When you have identified what you want and like, it will

help you communicate with blog consultants, designers, and other bloggers.

- Decide if you want to write the blog yourself. You should give writing your blog a chance—even if you don't like writing. Some people who initially don't wish to write a blog really get into it once they get rolling. If you don't want to write a blog, hire others to write if for you.

If you're not expert and want your blog to promote your goods, services, or business, get expert help. Once you have an idea of how you want it to look and function, you can employ help for both the design and content if you don't think you're up to the challenge, or have the time. Think of hiring help as a business investment, equivalent to hiring a CPA, a computer technician, or a sales associate.

If you create a blog, it will give you these advantages:

You will have 100 percent control of the content. People can hear your voice, get a sense of who you are, and learn about your unique ideas and approaches.

You can build relationships. After you attract their attention, you can build relationships with fellow bloggers and consumers, which is the essence of the new media. The new media is more relationship and connectivity minded; those involved are looking to forge close connections.

It will show that you care what your customers and clients think. Value their insights and opinions, and invite their responses and input. Allow them to enter into conversations with you.

It will establish you as a player in the new media. In today's world, this is the way of doing business. You need a strong Internet presence to make an impact on your market. Hosting a blog will show that you are up to date, innovative, and forward thinking.

GUERRILLA INTELLIGENCE

"A ton of blog clutter is out there," Tia Graham notes. "So if you want to promote your goods and services on a professional level, you want to stand out from the noise. Your blog must be well written, fresh, and of interest to your core readers. They must believe that they can rely on the information you provide."

BLOG FATIGUE

Continually writing and publishing blogs can be exhausting. Constantly keeping your readers and yourself excited is hard. It's not easy to always come up with new information, slants, and approaches that will keep your audience and you engaged. Most new blogs fizzle out after six to eight weeks because bloggers lose their inspiration and run out of steam. You can avoid blog fatigue by:

Reaching out. Invite guest bloggers from your field and related fields to share their ideas. This will provide new content and generate stimulating conversations. Invite people whom you respect, admire, or would like to get to know, or those who have different opinions than you. Guest contributors can underscore your message, create controversy, as well as alter the tone and direction of your blog to keep it fresh and unpredictable.

Prewriting posts. Write a number of blog posts at one time and program them to publish on specific dates. For example, take one day to write all the blogs you will post the following week. Ironically, when people prewrite their blogs and are relieved of the burden of constantly having to compose and post them, it often spurs their creativity and they come up with terrific content. During those periods when they don't have to post their blogs, they find information and think, "Hey this idea could make a good blog." Then they can sit down and write it.

Getting help. Producing a blog by yourself is a lot of work and finding someone to share the load can help. A blog consultant or designer can teach you shortcuts that will simplify or reduce your work. Consultants can also monitor how often you're posting, what you're posting, and how relevant it is. They can give you advice and recommend strategies to strengthen your blog and keep you motivated and on track.

HIRING A BLOG CONSULTANT

The work involved in creating, writing, and marketing a blog is substantial. Although excellent online services can get you up and running, it may be advisable to hire a blog consultant or designer to help you get started, create your first blog, and assist you with tasks you don't do well or don't like.

A blog consultant or designer can teach you and save you time by doing much of the work. They can help you build a solid foundation for your blog that you can easily follow and expand upon. Once you form a relationship with a consultant or designer, he or she can serve as a coach or adviser who can guide you when difficulties arise (as they will).

Consultants can also help you plan and execute your online strategy. They understand how to optimize your Web presence, know great shortcuts, are up on the new innovations and have fabulous contacts. "We have relationships with many high-profile bloggers," Penny Sansevieri explains. "So many of them let us post items such as excerpts of articles and books on their Web sites."

Deciding who to hire can be tricky because blogs differ from other types of Web sites and not all Web designers are experts on blogs. Many people can do both, but not many specialize in both.

The best way to find a blog consultant or designer is through recommendations. Contact people who publish your favorite successful blogs and ask who they use. Question them as to whether they are satisfied with the service they received and ask what problems arose.

When you contact consultants or designers, talk with them to get a sense of who they are, how they work, and what you can expect. Trust your instincts. "Blog design is very intuitive," Tia Graham observes. "Pay attention to the undercurrents and how you feel because with blog design, you're trying to attract a loyal audience that just doesn't come and get your information, but stays. Blog readers care about the content, quality of the writing, the layout, and ease of use. So a blog doesn't have to be flashy or expensive to be effective," she stresses. "Flash may initially attract readers, but it's the content and constantly providing high-quality access that keeps them coming back."

Question consultants and designers out about their experience. Learn what blogs they worked on, what their involvement was, and read those blogs. Ask for references. Get their clients' names, contact them, and question them.

BEWARE OF BLOGGING FAILURE

Besides the necessary commitment and constant work, blogs fail for a number of reasons. They can become predictable, repetitive, pedantic, preachy, diaryish, journalish, sloppy and stale. Some give too much information, or are too technical or verbose. Authors often stray because they don't keep their mission and brand in mind. The social networking aspect of the blogosphere can be seductive and divert you. "The blogosphere can be a black hole that sucks you into areas that throw you completely off course," Tia Graham notes.

If you lose your direction, you may be penalized by search engines. If they feel that your blog is filled with content and links that are irrelevant to your stated objectives, search engines may lower your ranking. So don't fall into the trap of letting your posts stray. Stay on message; focus on your core audience, and be vigilant.

As soon as you place anything online, it leaves your control and you can't take it back. Even if you delete your blog, your site or the specific content, it can come back to haunt you because someone may have copied it before it was removed. So be cautious. From the start, form the habit of examining every word and every thought in every posting because they're permanent. Getting it right from the beginning is crucial because false starts can be fatal and impossible to overcome.

Occasionally, bloggers must stop and take a break, which can cost them readership. If you plan to temporarily discontinue writing your blog, inform your readers before you stop. Tell them when you will be stopping and when you will be coming back. Better yet, bring in guest bloggers to fill in during your absence to hold your readers' interest. If readers go to a site plastered with your name and picture, but find no new content, they may not return.

If you create your own blog, you will also have to market it. Marketing can require you to network in the blogosphere, which may not be your interest or forte. Either way, it can require you to do a lot of additional work.

REMEMBER

Blogs are usually opinionated, highly niche-oriented, and encourage dialogue with their readers. You can create publicity by having items about you or your product or service published in other people's blogs. You can also start your own blog to drum up publicity. Most new blogs only run for six to eight weeks before the bloggers throw in the towel. Keep yourself and your audience motivated and excited about your blog by working with blog consultants or designers and inviting guest bloggers and readers to contribute to your blog.

CHAPTER 30

PODCASTS: SEND OUT YOUR MESSAGE AND REEL IN PUBLICITY

"Good communication is as stimulating as
black coffee and just as hard to sleep after."

—*Anne Morrow Lindbergh, author of* A Gift from the Sea

A producer for a popular television talk show is interested in booking you for an appearance on her show but needs more information. So she visits your Web site and goes to your media page, where she finds a podcast along with your press release, bio, photo, and the details of your media experience. Like most producers, she's pressed for time so she downloads your podcast and saves it to listen to at a more convenient time.

Just discovering that you have a podcast tells the producer that you're a media-savvy professional who's up to date with current trends. It immediately gives her a favorable impression of you. So she has a good feeling before she listens to your podcast. And when she finishes and likes your podcast—it seals the deal.

WHAT IS PODCASTING?

Podcasting is a method of distributing content through the Internet to portable media players, personal computers, cell phones, and other devices. "Podcasting is a tool to syndicate content," according to Jody Colvard, founder of the Women in Podcasting Directory and the FMG Network. "It gives us the ability to put our content in one location and springboard it off to different places in one shot."

Podcasts can contain text, audio, video, or a combination of all or any of them. This versatility enables you to expand your audience because you can give your subscribers more than just text. It also helps you form emotional bonds, which is the highest form of connection.

A podcast can be a single segment or a series of segments or episodes like a radio or TV show. When people subscribe to a series, which most do, they automatically receive new segments when they are released. A podcaster's objective is to turn subscribers into devoted listeners of every episode. Like others in the new media, podcasters want to build large groups of loyal subscribers, communities that they influence.

GUERRILLA INTELLIGENCE

Podcasting is a pillar of Web 2.0. It faces you in the direction where business is heading and it puts you with people who are forging forward, pushing the boundaries, and looking for new and better ways of doing things. Launching your own podcast positions you to be noticed by your industry's innovators. "Podcasting is very popular with social networkers," Denise Bach, CEO of Yaktivate, reveals, "It's powerful because it's easy to use and it's very viral. People love to send interesting content to one another. So if they like your podcast, they will recommend it and send others links to it. It's a big social activity."

Podcasters submit their podcasts to searchable directories that are the equivalent of the telephone Yellow Pages. They include iTunes, Podcast Alley, Yahoo!, and Odeo. If you want wide distribution, list your podcast in a number of directories so searchers are more likely to find them. For lists of directories see *www.podcastingnews.com*, *www.podcastdirectory.com*, and *http://audio.search.yahoo.com/audio*.

Since podcasts are frequently played on portable devices, their content is more mobile than content distributed in other formats. When a podcast episode or series is stored on a portable media player, that player can be slipped in a pocket or purse and taken anywhere. This gives listeners the option to hear and see podcasts when and where they want, not just at certain times and places. Listeners can hear podcasts while they walk, jog, commute, or just hang out.

PODCAST YOURSELF SOME PUBLICITY

As YouTube has shown, visuals are remarkable communication tools. People watch them, play them over and over, remember them, and tell their friends about them. And they have extended lives. Podcasts can do the same because every day, millions of people download and listen to podcasts on every conceivable subject and they can keep what they download for ages.

You and your product or service can be publicized on other people's podcasts or you can create and distribute your own podcast. Either way, your goal should be to get listeners' attention, build relationships with them, and route them to your Web site where you can introduce them to or remind them about goods and services that they can obtain from you. As with blogs, the best way to get mentioned on other people's podcasts is to build relationships with them. If they like what you're doing, they may speak favorably about you.

As mentioned at the beginning of this chapter, the media now routinely checks podcasts and blogs looking for new stories. When they find those that they consider special, they approach the individuals who created them. So enhance your written material with audio and video, and really get noticed. When the media can see and hear your message, it becomes more powerful than just text.

The publishing industry has led the way in using podcasts to publicize their books. Publishing companies have created podcasts that they post on their Web sites and their authors' sites. Their podcasts contain information about their authors, their authors' books, discussions, interviews, excerpts, and reviews of their books. When publishers consider whether to publish proposed books, most now factor in whether the authors have podcasts and blogs.

GUERRILLA INTELLIGENCE

The impact of podcasting is clear from the fact that over 70 percent of the automobiles manufactured in 2007 included technology for devices that play podcasts. And podcasting is expected to have an even greater impact in the future.

Companies like Colvard's FMG Network work with clients to produce and distribute publicity-oriented podcasts. "Our focus," Colvard stated, "is to help find out:

» What their message is.
» How to deliver it.
» Where they want to put it.
» How to market it to create an emotional bond.
» How to get the media's attention."

If you create your own podcast, it must be well planned and structured like a radio or television program. You must know exactly what each podcast will be, what material will be covered, in what way, and by whom.

When you schedule your content to post, it will be fed all over the Internet. If you're conducting a campaign, you can time it so that updates are sent out at the same time other campaign initiatives begin.

GUERRILLA TACTICS

"When people create podcasts, they often give everything away right at the beginning," Colvard observes. "Don't give it all away; take snippets; think in terms of movie trailers. Pull out the meat and put it in 30-second to 3-minute podcasts. Then get them to the media. If they're too long, the media

> won't download or watch. At the end, include a call to action that brings them back to your Web site where they can make the next move such as opting into your e-mail list, contacting you, or buying a product."

HOW TO CREATE A PODCAST

Explaining how to create and publish podcasts makes it sound much harder than it actually is. Excellent, easy-to-use, free software is readily available and the Internet is brimming with instructions and tutorials on how to proceed. Or if you prefer, you can hire consultants to do all or parts of your setup. Consultants can produce, index, and distribute your podcasts. They can complete all the technical work so you can concentrate on the content.

You can record your own content on your computer or a recording device. In fact, at one sitting, you can record all or a number of segments. You can also record telephone calls, including conference calls, and edit them. Then you route your recordings in files to a platform, such as iTunes, where other people can download and play them.

Without getting too technical, the following are the essential steps involved in creating a podcast:

1. Come up with your idea and develop the content. If you plan to do a series, be sure that you have enough interesting content for each segment.
2. Record your content.
3. Save the recording to a file.
4. Upload your file to a Web hosting service to put it online.
5. Create a feed (a text file with a .rss extension) that lets people find your podcast and receive it. When they subscribe to the entire series, they will automatically receive new segments and updates that contain new content. Most software will do this for you.
6. List your podcast on directories so people can find it. Directories include Podcast Alley, iTunes, Yahoo!

Podcasts, and Odeo. At Author Marketing Experts, Inc. (*www.amarketingexpert.com*), Penny C. Sansevieri publicizes podcasts in two ways:

- By syndicating the podcasts to directories such as iTunes and Podcast Alley
- By having it transcribed and syndicating it just as you would with an article that has a link to the subscribed feed for the podcast

Focus on how to circulate your podcast because creating one isn't worth anything if it doesn't reach the largest audience possible. When you list with directories, searchers can find your files. They can search by categories to find podcasts on topics that interest them. Then, when they do, they can download and listen to those files.

Services such as Denise Bach's Yaktivate use podcasting, social networking, and user-generated content to create Web presence for their clients. Yaktivate teaches clients how to podcast and gives them an online studio for their audio podcasting. For music podcasts, they teach their clients how to edit and how to create musical podcasts. Yaktivate's channel masters are assigned to podcasters to help them leverage their podcasts in the most efficient way.

GUERRILLA INTELLIGENCE

Podcast subscribers get information on a regular basis without having to go to a Web site. Whenever new content is added to your podcast, it is automatically sent to subscribers. Podcasts also have no viruses or spam, and subscribers have complete control. When they no longer want to receive a podcast, they can easily unsubscribe.

Yaktivate also conducts market research and helps its clients position themselves in their markets. From its research, it tells its clients the types of podcasts to create to build relationships with listeners. They create the show and support it. For example, each time a new show is posted, Yaktivate puts out a press release to spread the word.

They also work with all of the social networking sites and they have tours that try to transfer traffic from social networking sites to their clients' sites by targeting the appropriate social networking sites for their clients.

BUILD INTEREST IN YOUR PODCAST

First, provide outstanding content. The podcast community has endless options and won't put up with poor-quality podcasts for long. Great content will help you build a large and loyal following. If subscribers really like your podcasts, they will tell others, more people will listen to your podcasts, and your audience will soar. Your listeners will get involved in discussions, providing their insights and opinions, making your podcasts more dynamic, interesting, and alive.

Build your audience by telling everyone about your podcasts. Forward your podcasts to them, ask them to listen, and to forward them to others. Tell your listeners to give you feedback. Stress that it's important in order for you to improve your podcast, make it more interesting, or move it in new directions.

You can also participate in discussions generated by other podcasts. Create links on their Web sites and blogs to your podcasts. Or find discussion groups or forums that target your audience and make a post that informs them about your podcasts.

Keys to a Popular Podcast:

» Well-planned segments that flow smoothly and professionally
» Fresh content for each new segment
» Featured guests and experts who have interesting, unusual, or controversial opinions
» Mixed formats—interview shows, educational shows, and tip shows

» Regular features that listeners seem to like such as product reviews, new product information, profiles, listeners' comments, photos and other graphics, contests, and games
» Acknowledging listeners' comments and interchanges

Provide excellent, high-value material that people will read, watch, and listen to. If you can tell a publisher that you have an audience of X number of people who read your newsletter, visit your Web sites, and listen to your podcasts, it shows that you have a loyal following who will be more likely to buy your book. People in your community will want to support your endeavors, so continually give them lots of added value.

Your main goal as a podcaster is to keep listeners interested and engaged, but your main goal as a guerrilla publicist is to sell yourself and your product or service. You can accomplish both. Just remember:

» Work your product or service into your podcast, but don't make it a sales pitch. Think of yourself as a reporter, journalist, or newscaster and inform rather than sell. Try to entertain, but make sure your message gets across. Build your credentials and trust. If you try to sell and promote, you can lose your credibility and your listeners.
» Customize your delivery for your audience. For example, if your podcast is targeted at the media, make it brief, snappy, and direct because the media is busy and won't waste its time. If you're clear about who your audience is you will be able to work your message in more effortlessly.
» Be brief. Forget about the old sales tactic of repeating your message to drum it in prospects' heads. No one has the time or patience for that any more. In most cases, podcasts should not exceed fifteen minutes or you'll lose your audience.
» Don't make the podcast all about you. In your first segment, briefly introduce yourself and give your credentials, but after that focus on giving information that will help your listeners.

Build a community that shares common interests—not a cult that centers around you.

- At the beginning of your podcast, while you are introducing yourself and establishing your credentials, briefly mention your goods or services and their benefits. Then leave it alone until the end. At the end, tell them to visit your Web site for information on your goods and services. Then give your Web site address.
- If you have a number of products or services, promote a different one in each segment.

Steve Lillo suggests, "When you include a link in your podcast, create a specific page for it in your Web site. Make a separate page for each podcast, so you can include links on the page for products that are specific to that podcast. Also include a form that visitors can complete to receive a free item, but first require them to answer a simple question related to your podcast. Track the hits your Web site pages receive so you can determine which podcasts are providing the most traffic to your site. When a topic or area of interest is extremely popular, consider adding an entry form for a contest that offers a great prize. If you do, you can also publicize the contest and increase subscriptions to your podcast and your newsletter."

Use all the traditional and Internet-based promotional methods to generate interest in your podcast. Send press releases, write newsletters and blogs, and don't forget the social networking sites. You can also take unorthodox approaches to building publicity by doing something like holding a contest. You could deliver a series of clues in your podcast that tie in to a larger promotional campaign. Have weekly winners who become eligible for a mega prize.

REMEMBER

Podcasts are a pillar of the new media and are extremely popular with social networkers, so they can bring you tons of great publicity. They can be made on every conceivable subject and people love them because they can listen when and where they want. When listeners like podcasts, they play them repeatedly, remember them, and tell their friends about them.

CHAPTER 31

E-MAIL BLASTS AND OTHER ONLINE OPTIONS

"Publicity is easy to get. Make yourself so successful you don't need it and then you'll get it."
—*Anonymous*

The Internet is a laboratory filled with scientists who are constantly inventing new ways in which it can be used to help all facets of society. One of the areas in which this online lab has made major advancements is marketing. Whether you are the one lighting the fire, or opt to have your target audience carry the flame, the Internet is *the* place for guerrillas to create some hot publicity.

One of the ways to get your product or service out there is by launching an "e-mail blast." This is something that you as the publicist have to create and circulate. On the other hand, you can use the millions of people out there in cyberspace to circulate your message through viral marketing, which spreads product awareness through pre-existing social networks. Both types of online marketing are beneficial and should be utilized in your campaign.

SEND OUT AN E-MAIL BLAST

E-mail blasts, or e-mail campaigns, are promotions that can generate a great amount of quick sales and build interest in your product or service. The objective is to conduct a low-cost saturation campaign aimed at potential buyers with whom you and your strategic partners have established relationships. These highly effective promotions are inexpensive to run, but some work may be required for their initial set-up. However, after you run your first blast, others are usually much easier to produce.

First, you enlist strategic partners, who are also called joint venture partners. The people you approach should have large e-mail lists, or have lists focused in the particular area that you would like to penetrate.

Also, try to solicit partners who will give bonus items to those who purchase the items offered in your blast. Your objective is to enlist a lot of partners who will offer lots of bonus gifts. Try contacting those who run Web sites, newsletters, and blogs that generate heavy traffic; they tend to have large lists. Ask your friends and business associates to recommend potential partners. The more partners and e-mail addresses you obtain—and the more your target audience matches, the better.

Finding partners can be an involved process that requires approaching people, being stalled, rejected, asking for leads and referrals, and then repeating the process again and again. Increase your odds of finding partners by being well organized and prepared. Before you contact potential partners, make a list of the benefits that their working with you will provide. It takes a lot of confidence and preparation, but the benefit of having a sizable e-mail list is well worth it.

Then you and your strategic partners e-mail those on your respective lists a special offer if they buy your goods or services. Design your e-mail offers so it's easy for recipients to place orders. In your e-mail, clearly explain the benefits and value you offer. If you can quantify the benefits in dollar amounts or time savings, do. Stress that this is a special, one-time offer that only you can give and that they must act quickly to get. Create links that potential buyers just click to place orders.

Before you send your e-mail offer, test all instructions to be certain that they work. Send them to your employees and friends to try them out. Double-check all sites and e-mail addresses you may include and triple-check all numbers, dates, and, especially, amounts of money.

Since spam filters can send communiqués to e-mail oblivion, always send e-mail using the name and e-mail address that you normally use to communicate with those on your list. Also write a subject line that will motivate them to open your offer. Often the best approach is to simply identify what you're offering. For example, enter "Special Offer on *Guerrilla Publicity, Second Edition*" in the subject line. When you make it clear what you're offering, those who are interested will be more likely to open your e-mail, which is what you want.

WARNING: Don't burn out your list subscribers by inundating them with offers. They signed up for your list because they want your expertise and to be in contact with you, not to be bombarded with offers. Being sensitive to your subscribers will bring you greater rewards. If you have a newsletter, consider including offers with your newsletter rather than sending multiple e-mails.

In exchange for your strategic partners' help, agree to reciprocate and e-mail those on your list when your partners have items they want to sell or promote. If you enlist a number of strategic partners who have good-sized e-mail lists, and if all contribute bonus items, your promotion will reach a substantial number of people.

GUERRILLA TACTICS

Don't structure your e-mail offers to look like traditional sales pitches. Recipients don't want to read e-mail that is obviously intended to sell them; most will quickly delete them. Also avoid offers that run on for pages, constantly repeat themselves, and sell, sell, sell. If you're offering a quality item or a good value, come straight to the point, be brief, clear, and direct. Don't take up more than two computer screens; better yet, confine it to one. Don't badger recipients and let your offer stand on its own merits; trust its value and worth.

GUERRILLA INTELLIGENCE

The beauty of e-mail blasts is that they can be run for large-scale promotions or for smaller, more precisely targeted groups. For example, you can focus on specific demographic groups according to factors such as age, sex, family status, careers, locale, buying habits, and much more. You can affiliate with bloggers and those in the new media who address communities that share common interests.

SOCIAL NETWORKING

Social networking sites are those where users create a profile and build personal networks or communities that connect them to other users. Social networks can be based on the members' common values, interests, activities, friendships, and ideas. They can socialize, explore their interests, discuss problems, and give their views and opinions. Popular social networking sites include MySpace, Facebook, and LinkedIn, which is a business-oriented networking site.

In social networking, you can become a center of influence in your community. You create personalized profiles, post information about yourself, and stress areas you wish to pursue. In your profile, you can provide information about your interests, your career, your background, experiences, and a wide range of other subjects.

If you have a product or service, you can include it in your profile. People who are interested in items you mention can search, find you, and add you to their communities. If you're a cabinetmaker who specializes in making Shaker-style dressers, someone can search and find you. They can communicate with you and learn more about you and your work. If they hire you and like your work, they can endorse and recommend you to others. Your fame can spread and help build your business. Of course, they can also rip you to shreds if they feel your work fell short.

Although social networks were originally purely social, they have now expanded to business, education, health, religious and other applications. Social networks sites such as LinkedIn (*www.linkedin.com*), ryze (*www.ryze.com*), and XING (*www.xing.com*) focus on business and others, including Facebook (*www.facebook.com*), offer business networking.

Penny C. Sansevieri creates tours for her clients that move traffic from social networking sites to her clients' Web sites. She looks for appropriate social networking sites for her clients. "Every social networking site is not appropriate for every client and some like MySpace don't like commercial posts." Sansevieri says. "First, you have to find the appropriate site and then populate it, whether by keywords, content, or giving freebies. It's not enough to put up a page on Facebook and hope people show up. You have to figure out what are they are searching for and what will drive them to your site. Then you take that information and populate the site with things that are unique, interesting, and valuable to the people who go to that site."

LENSING

A "lens" is a blog or a Web page that conveys peoples' expertise or opinions on their interests. Lenses are created by lensmasters. A lensmaster can create a lens on any subject and post it on a single page on Squidoo, *www.squidoo.com*, a Web site that is a network of user-generated lenses. A lens is primarily a guide that refers people to content; it is a place to start.

People can find lenses through search engines and rate them. If your lens is rated highly, you can be acknowledged as an expert on that topic. Lensing is free and you can create as many lenses as you want.

For example, if you're into portrait photography, you can create a portrait photography lens on Squidoo. You could also put up portrait images, links to affiliates that sell portrait products, or information about your own products. Visitors can also leave comments on Squidoo and interact with your lens.

If visitors to Squidoo click on advertisements or buy items from companies that are linked to it, Squidoo receives a commission. Squidoo then gives half its commission to the lensmaster who generated the sale and a piece to charity.

VIRAL VIDEOS

The use of online video is moving in many directions. You can create your own video content and distribute it for free on video-sharing sites such as YouTube (*www.youtube.com*), where it could become a big hit. You can also include video in your blog or podcast. Sites like Mogulus (*www.mogulus.com*) enable you to develop and broadcast your own Internet video channel from your computer.

Internet videos can be made on any subject, at any length, and in virtually any format. They can follow the lines of newsletters, talk or variety shows, or infomercials. You could create a show about marketing, offer a daily inspiration, provide cooking tips, or host an entertainment show—it's totally up to you.

To get more publicity, you can syndicate your videos by allowing other people to imbed them in their sites, blogs, or podcasts.

WIKI AND OTHER NEW DEVELOPMENTS

Wiki are Web sites that anyone can add or edit. The best known is Wikipedia (*www.wikipedia.org*), an online encyclopedia filled with entries or articles written by contributors. After articles are posted to Wikipedia, anyone can edit or add to them. If you want to promote your product or service, you can write your own description and submit it to be posted on Wikipedia.

Alacra Wiki (*www.alacrawiki.com*) is a guide to business information companies, publishers, and databases, and anyone can update these. Alacra also posts marketing materials, product reviews, product announcements, and executive biographies.

Newsvine (*www.newsvine.com*), reddit (*www.reddit.com*), and Digg (*www.digg.com*) are Web sites that provide community-submitted news stories and opinions. Slashdot (*www.slashdot.com*) is a news site oriented toward science, science fiction, and technology. Users can submit articles, provide links to other sites, vote, comment, and chat.

Other emerging technology allows you to create your own search engine comprised of sites you like and provide it as a service to others. On your search engine, you decide which sites you want. They could be sites you like to visit and want to recommend or are your favorite resources. Naturally, your own site would be included. Creating your own search engine can bring you great publicity and help you establish you as an expert.

REMEMBER

E-mail blasts and viral marketing can generate a lot of quick sales for you. Using the Internet to spread the word about your product or service, as well as build up your network, will help you reach much larger audiences and markets. Inexpensive to run and easy to navigate, all these options are perfect for guerrillas looking to promote themselves on a budget.

CHAPTER 32

GROWING PAINS—HOW TO HIRE THE RIGHT PR PEOPLE

"Winning isn't everything, but wanting to win is."
—*Arnold Palmer*

Now that you've put the principles of this book in practice and they're working beautifully, your publicity campaign is generating tons of business—in fact, it's producing more work than you can handle.

Something's got to give. Obviously, you can't process all the new work, run your PR campaign, and have a life outside the office. You also can't afford to turn down new business; it's senseless to stop a campaign that's paying big dividends. What do you do?

Clearly, you need to hire help. You can hire additional staff, but finding and training good workers takes time. Instead of hiring additional workers for your business, it may be smarter to seek help from publicity professionals. Hiring professionals can allow you to concentrate on your business, which after all should be your main focus. And since you've now learned so much about publicity, you can monitor their work without surrendering all control.

For help with publicity, you have three basic options.

PR Agencies: We know that hiring large PR firms can be expensive. Most large agencies are geared to corporations, not guerrillas. However, a large agency may offer you a good deal because it sees the potential in you and your business or wants to get into your particular niche. They may also agree to handle parts of your campaign, such as your radio or Internet efforts.

Smaller agencies may be more reasonably priced, can provide more personal service and may better serve your needs. Plus, you're less likely to get lost than you might be with a bigger firm.

PR firms are usually well staffed. They can handle every aspect of your campaign in-house and don't have to contract out. Firms usually work on monthly retainers, but many will take you on a project basis and charge an agreed-upon, set fee.

WARNING: Be wary of agencies that claim to do more than just PR, like PR and advertising or PR and branding. They seldom do each well. PR is a unique discipline. It takes special talents, so if you want PR, go to a firm that specializes in PR only, not also in advertising and/or branding.

Consultants: Freelance PR professionals usually operate one-person operations without staffs. Generally, consultants worked for large PR agencies or corporations and then went out on their own. Since they seldom have staffs, you'll probable incur additional expenses for services they aren't equipped to perform. Consultants are usually less expensive than agencies because they have less and lower overhead. Some will work out of your office or place of business. More on consultants is included at the end of this chapter.

In-house Publicists: You can hire experienced PR specialists to become employees on your staff. Generally, guerrillas can't afford in-house publicists and their resources are better spent concentrating on their core business. However, they could work for you on a part-time basis, for a percentage of job fees, or you could barter for their services.

GUERRILLA RESOURCES

If you choose to go with a PR firm, do your homework. Check *O'Dwyer's Directory of Public Relations Firms.* It lists 1,900 of the largest firms worldwide cross-indexed with 8,500 of their clients so you can look up a company and learn which PR firm represents it.

Identify firms and/or consultants that specialize in your product or service and in the type of promotions you envision. Although firms may claim to do everything, few do everything well. The key is to match the type of services firms provide and the clients they represent with your objectives. Check out their Web sites.

After you've had a chance to explore your options, complete the following steps to find the firm that's best for you:

1. Select four or five firms and/or consultants to interview.
2. Before you contact any firms or consultants, define your needs and objectives.
3. Set a figure of how much you're willing to spend.
4. Then meet and interview each firm and consultant.
5. Get a gut feeling for the firm or consultant; see how they work and the results they claim.
6. Ask for client names and contact them.

DEALING WITH EXPERIENCE

After you've signed on with a PR agency, you may discover that the impressive gentleman you first met, who always had the right answers, isn't working on your account. Instead, a kid six months out of school is handling it.

Experience is important, but it isn't everything. It can also pose problems. Publicists, like anyone else, get into ruts. They tend to stick with what traditionally worked in the past and can be reluctant to change. Publicists can be committed to assumptions that no longer apply or lack the boldness to distinguish you and make your campaign fly.

GUERRILLA INTELLIGENCE

Before you hire an agency, learn who will actually work on your campaign and his or her experience. If it's a newer employee, ask who'll be supervising your account and to what extent they'll be monitoring it.

Turning to an experienced PR professional who comes from outside your targeted field is often effective. New faces can bring fresh ideas, new approaches, excitement, and flair. They can see what others may have been too close to notice. For example, a publicist who worked only with automotive clients might be just the right person to create a breakthrough campaign for a non-profit hospital.

THE HIRING PROCESS

Obtain the names of recent and current clients. Specifically request the names of those that worked with personnel who'll be handling your account. Call those clients. Learn how they liked working with the agency, or individual publicist, and if they were pleased with the results. Ask them to list the agency's strengths, weaknesses, and what they would change. Find out how promptly agency personnel return calls.

Ask the agency what it will bring to your account. Is it creativity, large agency backing, entrepreneurial background, media placement, booking speaking engagements? Find out what you can expect.

Once you are close to making a decision on hiring an outside firm or individual, conduct an interview. The questions that you should ask prospective publicity professionals will vary project to project. However, the following basic questions should be asked in most cases.

Interview Checklist

1. Who will lead my account?
   a. What is his or her experience?
   b. How much time will he or she spend on my account?
2. Who will work on my account?
   a. What is his or her experience?
   b. How much time will he or she devote to my account?
3. Who will supervise the work on my account?
   a. What is his or her experience?
   b. How much time will he or she put in on my account?
4. What is the plan for my campaign?
5. How long will my campaign run?
6. How much access will I have to strategists who design my campaign?
7. How much input will I have in my campaign?
8. Will I receive weekly communications about my account?
9. How often will I get updates on my account?
10. How many calls will be made on my account?
    a. Each week?
    b. Each month?
11. What specific results will I receive?
    a. After one month?
    b. After three months?
    c. Upon completion of the project?
12. How do I measure results?
13 What can I do if I don't receive the results promised?
    a. Can I terminate our agreement?
    b. Will you refund fee payments?
    c. If so, how much?
    d. Will I receive extra work at no charge?
14. What specific results have you created for past, similar clients?
15. What are your strong points, your advantages over other agencies?

BE PROACTIVE

You are always the expert. No one knows or cares as much about your business as you do. You must be involved in your campaign and make or approve all major decisions.

Insist on this right for all final decisions that will cost more than a stated monetary amount.

You should also insist on weekly updates. Updates will inform you whether your campaign is proceeding on schedule and what problems occurred. Updates will also help you make quick adjustments to address problems. However, in your involvement, avoid interfering and preventing, or complicating the publicity professionals' work. Such involvement will be counterproductive, breed resentment, and your campaign will suffer.

Leave the details to the professionals. Assume the role of a consultant, an adviser, a resource who has inside knowledge that can enhance the experts' performance.

GUERRILLA TACTICS

Hire the top consultants. Identify the experts in your industry. Go to bookstores, libraries, and the Web to find out who wrote the best books in your field. Find out who ran a PR campaign that impressed you. Check out the most effective instructors on the seminar circuit and at schools and universities. Ask your friends and peers.

Obtain and study publications written by these experts before you approach them. Contact information is usually given at their speaking engagements or can be found on their publications or Web sites.

When you make contact with one of these professionals, be willing to pay. Don't try to merely pick their brains, but tell them, "I want to buy some of your time. I've read your books and I want to hire you as a consultant to walk me through this project. I want you to tell me exactly what to do." This will show them that you're a professional and that you understand that their time is valuable. They'll also treat you as a professional.

If consultants refuse to charge you, send them a gift equal to or of greater value than the fee they normally charge. This small gesture will buy goodwill and ensure that you have access to the experts in the future.

Although hiring the top authorities as consultants may not come cheap, it's usually a great investment. Most experts are familiar with most problems, they know:

- The industry
- The short cuts
- The players
- Who to approach
- How to get the best results
- How to prepare you for unforeseen changes

REMEMBER

When you hire publicity professionals, you can concentrate on your business while the pros run your campaign. You can hire, work with, and supervise PR agencies, consultants, or in-house publicists. Identify those that specialize in your products or services and in the type of promotions you envision and interview them. In hiring and working with professionals, keep in mind that you're the expert—no one knows or cares as much about your business as you.

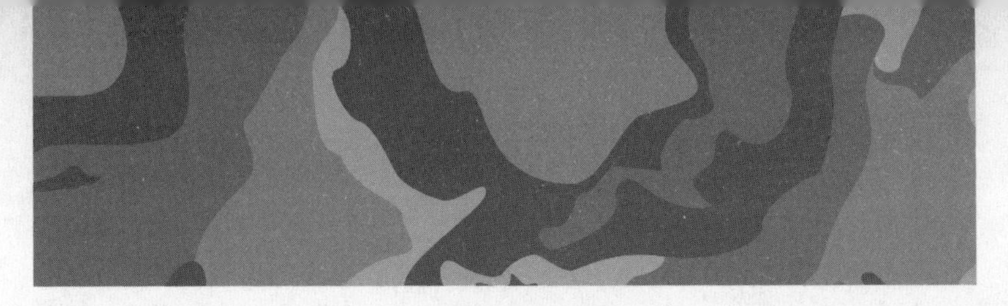

CHAPTER 33

CRISES CONTROL—CONFRONT DISASTERS AND TURN THEM AROUND

"Crises and deadlocks when they occur have at least this advantage, they force us to think."

—Jawaharlal Nehru, former Indian Prime Minister

Your brand, your business or product name, is your most important asset and once you've established it, it must be protected at all costs. Otherwise it can destroy your business.

Every book seems to include a warning about Murphy's Law—and our book is no exception. When you're working to publicize your product or service, whatever can go wrong will go wrong. Mistakes will be made; accidents and screw-ups will occur. If you're not prepared to deal with them, they can take you down. When something bad does occur, you need to act immediately. Fix the problem and face the public or else you'll lose the trust and confidence of both consumers and the financial community—and you might never get them back.

WHAT TO DO

In business, it's all about trust. Trust takes years to create, but can be destroyed in an instant. Your customers or clients want products and services that work, that won't fall apart, and that will do their job. (It's what they're paying for.) Furthermore, they want you to stand firmly behind your goods, without excuses or blame. When disasters occur, your first concern should be to do everything in your power to restore your customers' confidence because if you don't, you're gambling with your business' future.

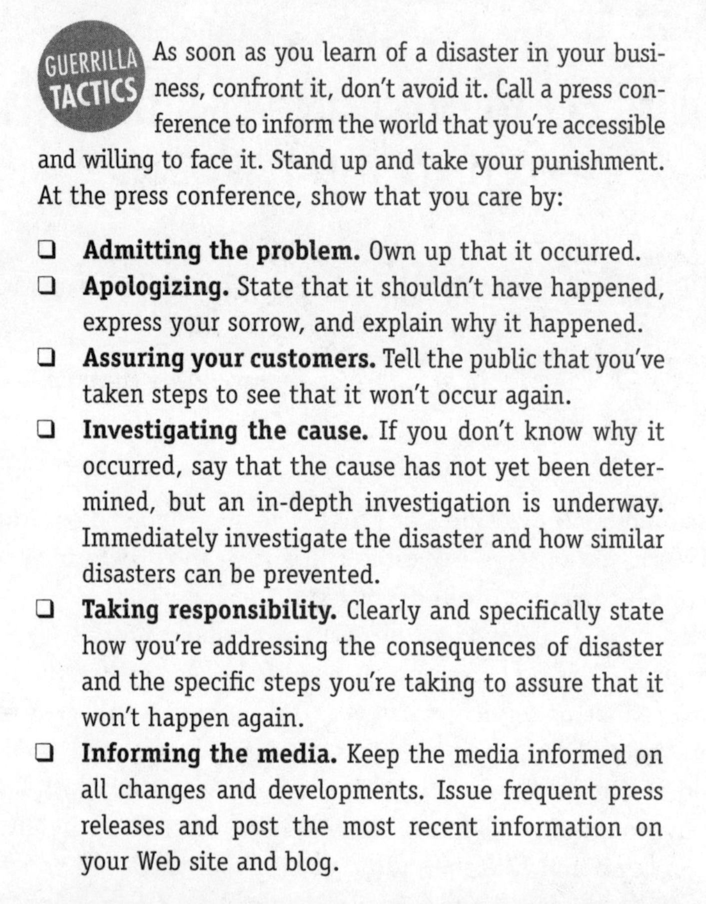

As soon as you learn of a disaster in your business, confront it, don't avoid it. Call a press conference to inform the world that you're accessible and willing to face it. Stand up and take your punishment. At the press conference, show that you care by:

- ❑ **Admitting the problem.** Own up that it occurred.
- ❑ **Apologizing.** State that it shouldn't have happened, express your sorrow, and explain why it happened.
- ❑ **Assuring your customers.** Tell the public that you've taken steps to see that it won't occur again.
- ❑ **Investigating the cause.** If you don't know why it occurred, say that the cause has not yet been determined, but an in-depth investigation is underway. Immediately investigate the disaster and how similar disasters can be prevented.
- ❑ **Taking responsibility.** Clearly and specifically state how you're addressing the consequences of disaster and the specific steps you're taking to assure that it won't happen again.
- ❑ **Informing the media.** Keep the media informed on all changes and developments. Issue frequent press releases and post the most recent information on your Web site and blog.

GUERRILLA TALE: When Odwalla's juices were pulled from the market because consumers got sick after drinking them, the company acted promptly and decisively to protect its good name. It held press conferences and issued press releases to inform the public of its test results and steps it was taking to address problems. By acting quickly and being honest, Odwalla was viewed as a concerned and responsible company and was able to minimize the damage that could have ruined its brand.

PEOPLE UNDERSTAND

If you move swiftly and take responsibility, the public will understand and it may forgive you. The public knows that people aren't perfect, that they make mistakes, and that accidents occur. While it may forgive errors in judgment, it will not excuse mistakes in motive or attempts to hide or cover up.

If you admit to what happened, sincerely apologize, and move quickly to fix the problem and prevent future disasters, your customers or clients will stand by you. The public will not forgive you if you hide, avoid responsibility, and cover up. You will win the public's trust and confidence by being forthright, up front, and apologetic, and by taking prompt remedial action.

GUERRILLA TALE: When bottles of Tylenol were tampered with, the company immediately yanked every bottle off the shelves. As soon as the news broke, Tylenol called a press conference. It announced that although only a few actual tampering cases had been detected, it was pulling every bottle in distribution in order to protect the public. Tylenol's prompt action is a textbook example of how to respond to a PR disaster because it turned Tylenol into the most trusted name in America. Consumers knew that they could depend on Tylenol because the company cared, was unwilling to compromise the public's safety, and would do, absorb, and spend, what was required to resolve the problem. Ever since, Tylenol has enjoyed unprecedented public support and respect.

In contrast, revered stalwarts of American business, Firestone Tires and Ford Motors, steadfastly refused to accept responsibility for defects in tires that had been supplied as original equipment on some Ford vehicles. In reaction, consumers lost trust in both Firestone and Ford and withdrew support of their products. Sales dipped and consumers went so far as to return Firestone products that were never suspected of being defective because they lost trust in the Firestone brand. While Ford continues to stagger, Firestone has been absorbed by a foreign tire maker.

REMEMBER

Disasters will occur. When they do, protect your brand and reputation by immediately addressing the problem. Call a press conference, admit that a problem occurred, apologize for it, assure the public that you've taken steps to prevent it from happening again. If you take responsibility, the public will understand.

CHAPTER 34

CONCLUSION

"An idea can turn to dust or magic, depending on the talent that rubs against it."

—*William Bernbach, advertising legend*

Thank you for reading this book! Now that you've read and digested all of this information, it's time to act. You've learned about the publicity tools that are available and what you should do. Now it's time to apply what you've read and put it to use.

As you do, add a few extra ingredients—your creativity, inventiveness, and daring. Be bold, take chances, blaze new frontiers. Distinguish yourself from the rest of the pack.

When you analyze problems and evaluate possible solutions, ask yourself how you could:

- » Do it differently?
- » Do it better?
- » Break new ground?
- » Make a bigger splash?
- » Enjoy it more?

Take the rules and techniques you've learned and *break them*. Explore how you could do things differently, what changes you could make, and what variations you could add. Figure out what you could do that has not been done to make everyone take notice and create a more successful campaign.

Build on your uniqueness; add your personal stamp. Push the limits, rethink the process, and question all accepted rules. Analyze everything from new and different angles. Stand it on its head.

Think big. Give your campaign gusto and vibrant colors. Overscale. Put on a spectacular show. Make a big and lasting impression and continually challenge yourself. Make your life and your work stimulating, exciting, and constantly fresh and new.

Let your mind loose, unleash it, and let it soar. Don't worry about financial realities, making sense, or being practical. Ignore all boundaries—mine ideas—and remember that you can always pull back. When you return to reality, some remnants of your venture into creativity may remain. They may take root in the back of your mind and they, or parts, aspects, or variations of them may just become viable somewhere down the road.

POINTS TO REMEMBER

Before we finish, we would like to emphasize some final points that we consider worth repeating. Although we've covered these points, keep them in mind because they pervade virtually every aspect of publicity. If you understand them, you'll have a better perspective as to how to apply the information you've learned and deal with the situations that you're going to face.

> *Think publicity*. Publicity must become a mindset, a constant and instinctive focus in your life. Always look for opportunities to publicize your products and services. Not just when you're in your office, but when you're home, out with the family, or at a social event. Continually ask, "How can I publicize my restaurant, my book, or my dog-walking service?" "How about this newspaper, magazine, station, Web site, or event?" "How should I approach them?" "Who do I know who can help me?" and "What is the best strategy?" When you come across other promotions, always ask, "How could it work for me?"

Credibility is everything. You are the product, so never claim to be what you're not or promise what you can't deliver. Integrity is crucial because consumers ultimately want results. They want, and are entitled to, products that work and services that deliver as promised. When people don't believe, or even doubt you, they won't support your efforts. Your failure to deliver will alienate customers and clients and quickly destroy a lifetime of credibility, reputation and goodwill. To compound the problem, it's infinitely harder to regain lost credibility and goodwill than it is to first establish them.

Build for the long run. Choose your battles wisely. Don't wage a life-or-death fight on every issue or you may not get the chance to do battle tomorrow. That doesn't mean that you should always give in easily or not make repeated efforts. It means that you shouldn't press an issue with a media contact to the point where you could destroy the relationship. Take the long-term view. Remember that you may need that contact down the road. Think in terms of campaigns, rather than ads; in careers, instead of jobs; and in decades, rather than years.

Media relationships are not equal. In your relationships with the media, the media holds the upper hand because they can deliver publicity. Don't take it personally when media doesn't respond. The fact is they're usually busy. The media has a short attention span and once they have your story and you're not on their schedule, you're no longer in their minds. Don't fall apart when they pull away. Instead, maintain the relationship by becoming a media resource. Since the media is a voracious machine that must be fed, feed them. Serve them up heaping portions of your stories, information, and contacts, even after they keep chewing them up and spitting them out.

Build relationships and communities and work within them. Join or start groups that share your interests and values. Support their efforts. Solicit their opinions and advice and be open to their comments and suggestions. Concentrate on a few groups and don't spread yourself too thin.

Follow up on everything. Persistence is the key to publicity; without persistence your story probably won't be told. Following up can be the difference between languishing in the crowd and emerging into the spotlight where you can shine. Remember the Rule of Seven: it takes seven calls to get a Yes. When following up, don't be a pest and never be rude!

Never give interviews unless you're totally prepared. The major reason people mess up interviews is that they lack command of their subject. First, learn your subject expertly. Prepare five main points to cover in every interview and another fifteen to twenty subpoints, three to four under each main point. Strengthen and spice up those points by using anecdotes, stories, jokes, and statistics. Practice, practice, practice—in front of the mirror and in front of your friends and family. Have people grill and pepper you with questions. Consider hiring a media coach or taking media training.

Become an authority. Learn your discipline expertly and then increase your visibility by teaching, speaking, and/or writing about it. Design, organize, lead, teach, and participate in seminars or workshops. Publish materials on narrow subjects that you've mastered and clearly explain your knowledge to others. As a recognized authority, you'll meet and spend time with other experts and your peers. You'll expand your knowledge, your contacts, your network, and your business.

Master the Internet and new technologies. Explore both the Internet's research and marketing capabilities. Visit many different Web sites, read lots of blogs, and download many podcasts. Visit different social networking sites to learn what they're all about. Then draw on all of these tools and utilize those that will best support your business objectives. Keep on the cutting edge by continually reading and discovering what is new and on the drawing board.

Maintain contact with the publicity community. Attend trade shows, conventions, and conferences. Contact the authors of this book. Send us your comments on this book and information that we might include in future versions. Tell us about your own experiences, insights, and stories.

Contact us as a team at:

www.guerrillapublicity.com

Contact us individually at:

Jay Conrad Levinson:
www.gmarketing.com or *www.guerrillamarketingassociation.com*

Rick Frishman:
www.plannedtvarts.com

Jill Lublin:
www.jilllublin.com

BACK MATTER

APPENDIX A

NEWSLETTERS

Guerrilla Publicity
www.guerrillapublicity.com

Guerrilla Marketing
www.jayconradlevinson.com

Jill Lublin
www.jilllublin.com

ClickZ
www.clickz.com

InternetPRGuide
www.internetnews.com/bus-news

Ragan Communications
www.ragan.com

Radio-TV Interview Report
www.freepublicity.com

APPENDIX B

THE GUERRILLA MARKETING HALL OF FAME

Besides being innovative, dedicated guerrillas, the following individuals have been a constant sources of information and inspiration to other guerrillas. After blazing new trails, these pioneers have authored books that explain how other guerrillas can follow their lead. Their books stand as landmarks, testimonials to the principles of guerrilla marketing, its ease of implementation and the results that guerrillas can achieve.

We salute and thank these guerrillas for their daring, their insights, wisdom, and most importantly, for their generosity in graciously sharing their experiences, understanding, and knowledge with us. And, we hereby recognize them as outstanding examples of the best of guerrilla marketing:

Jay Abraham, author of *Getting Everything You Can Out of All You've Got.*

Jack Canfield and Mark Victor Hansen, coauthors of the *Chicken Soup* series.

Greg Godek, author of *Intimate Questions, Love: The Course They Forgot to Teach You in School*, *The LoveQuotes Coupon Book*, *Romantic Essentials: Hundreds of Ways to Show Your Love*, and *Enchanted Evenings.*

Seth Godin of Yahoo!, author of *Permission Marketing, Unleashing the Idea Virus, If You're Clueless about Starting Your Own Business and Want to Know More (If You're Clueless)* and coauthor of *The Guerrilla Marketing Handbook.*

Daniel S. Janal, author of *Dan Janal's Guide to Marketing on the Internet, The Online Marketing Handbook,* and *101 Businesses You Can Start on the Internet.*

Jerrold Jenkins of the Jenkins Group, publisher of *Independent Publisher* and coauthor of *Publish to Win* and *Inside the Bestsellers.*

John Kremer of Open Horizons, coauthor of *High-Impact Marketing on a Low-Impact Budget,* author of *1001 Ways to Market Your Books* and editor of *Book Marketing Update.*

Harvey Mackay, CEO of Mackay Envelope, syndicated columnist and author of *Swim with the Sharks Without Being Eaten Alive, Pushing the Envelope All the Way to the Top,* and *Beware the Naked Man Who Offers You His Shirt.*

Jan and Terry Nathan, executive and assistant directors of Publishers Marketing Association, sponsor of PMA's Publishing University.

Dan Poynter of Para Publishing, author of the *Self-Publishing Manual.*

Tom and Marilyn Ross, cofounders of the Small Publishers Association and coauthors of the *Complete Guide to Self-Publishing* and *Jump Start Your Book Sales.*

Dottie Walters (deceased), popular speaker and coauthor of *Speak and Grow Rich, The Mighty Power of Your Beliefs,* and *101 Simple Things to Grow Your Business.*

APPENDIX C

REFERENCE MATERIALS

PRESS RELEASE

For Immediate Release

National Association of Women Real Estate Investors
Contact: Lisa
(555) 555-5555

Women Invest "Not To Lose"
and Lose 73 percent of Income upon Loss of Spouse

(Denver, CO)...Women lose 73 percent of their income when they lose their spouse through death, divorce, or desertion. Yet, our culture continues to teach us to rely on our spouse to bring home the bacon. Wealth-building expert C. L. Osborn, founder of the National Association of Women Real Estate Investors, creates simple solutions for women to become millionaires in 3 to 5 years. Osborn says "I tell women: 'Ladies—a man is not a plan, no more than buying a lottery ticket is a retirement plan.'" The divorce rate is over 51 percent and women outlive men, so why do so many women leave the control of their financial destiny up to others? "Lack of education," says Osborn. According to Osborn, there are three investor types in the world:

- People who do not invest at all, expecting someone else to take care of them.
- People who invest not to lose, investing in CDs, mutual funds, stocks, etc.
- People who invest to win and take responsibility for their financial freedom.

For women investors who want to win, Osborn says the best plan is learning to invest in real estate with people who do most of the work for you and help you with the money and credit issues. Then, she advises, develop a long-term strategy to make your money make you money.

-continued-

A big believer in real estate, Osborn says "You can get started with what I call Monkey Dust; which is little or no money or credit." Real estate offers women three substantial leveraging opportunities that other investment options do not:

- Invest in real estate without spending cash. In other words, investors can expect a return without putting money in. That's leverage.
- Refinance and use the proceeds used to reinvest in more real estate. That's called compounding.
- Grow your wealth with real estate appreciation while you live your life. That's called passive income, the key to becoming a mutimillionaire.

C. L. Osborn

From an uneducated single mother to multimillionaire real estate investor, C. L. Osborn simply conveys that the journey to financial freedom starts the minute you decide that you were destined for prosperity, not scarcity—for abundance, not lack; the freedom of being your own boss—without the limits of a job. Ms. Osborn is the author of the upcoming book *Wealth Formula One™*, *Wise Women Invest in Real Estate and Tell Their Secrets*, based on her groundbreaking training formula. Ms. Osborn, CEO and founder of the National Association of Women Real Estate Investors, is also on the faculty of IBI Global, an international executive education organization.

Founder of Autism Today Is Changing the Face of the Special Needs Community

An amazing story of how one woman raises six children—two with special needs—survives a near-death experience while giving birth, creates the world's largest online resource for those with autism, and writes several books—without accepting a dime from the government, special interest groups, or corporations! Every cent received from product sales has been reinvested into the organization.

> "Karen wanted her son to understand his autism, so she ended up teaching the whole community a lesson."
> —*Woman's World*

Karen Simmons is the face of the newly evolving special needs community, shining light on the special needs of others.

America has 6.2 million people with special needs, of which one-fourth have autism. Karen has two special needs children—one with ADHD and the other with autism, as well as four other healthy children. Rather than see herself as a victim of circumstances, she was empowered to help the millions of others who are forced to confront the challenges posed by their "invisible disability." She launched, just four years ago, what has now become the world's largest online resource for those with—or who care for those with—autism spectrum disorders.

www.AutismToday.com, which receives over two million hits every month from 55,000 unique visitors, is a vast resource of information, experts, resources, research, books, early intervention tools, conferences, workshops, and educational services for those diagnosed with autism spectrum disorders—including Aspergers syndrome—as well as for their caretakers, parents, doctors, therapists, and educators.

-continued-

Membership is free and all of the net proceeds from the sale of online courses, books, or other services and materials have been poured back into the Web site.

The site's concept and direction germinated through one parent's extremely frustrating process associated with finding the best quality treatments and resources for her son with special needs. Karen's young son, Jonathan, was diagnosed in the early 90s at age two and a half. It overwhelmed her.

She sifted through an overwhelming amount of material, much of which was contradictory, depending on which faction within the medical or holistic fields was dishing info out. "I knew how important early intervention would be to the long-term prospects for my children," says Karen. "I needed to find ways to tend to the needs of all my children without completely depleting our family's physical, emotional, and financial resources. Doing nothing was not an option, yet there were times when I was paralyzed by indecision. I needed to choose a course of action now, but I was exhausting myself trying to locate and evaluate pertinent information. While I was going through this maze, I realized I was also doing so on the behalf of other parents and children with autism."

Karen also founded the KEEN Education Foundation in 1996, which seeks to help special needs children attain their fullest possible individual development and to secure social inclusion within the community. As a speaker and organizer of conferences that are each attended by up to 750 people, coupled with her four books, a CD, and her interactions online, she has influenced hundreds of thousands of people, who in turn impact many more.

-continued-

Karen is available to the news media to discuss how:

- She launched Autism Today and offers help to the special needs community
- Parents, siblings, and professionals can help those with autism
- Families can cope with the devastating impact autism has on their children
- Early diagnosis and intervention is crucial for those with autism
- The autism epidemic needs the attention of the federal government
- Popular myths surrounding autism must be discarded

Autism is a biological disorder of the brain, though the exact cause has not been determined. Three main areas of development are impaired: communication, social development, and the acquisition and use of language. There is no cure available at this time. But Karen believes a lot can be done to help those diagnosed with autism and to help decrease the severity of the disorder.

She will also speak about how:

- Kids with autism can really thrive
- To be an advocate for your child and seek the best treatment for them
- The social stigma associated with autism needs to be changed

"I want to educate the public on possible causes, warning signs, potential treatments and therapies," says Simmons. "There is an enormous impact this 'invisible disability' has on families. If we can spare others of this—or lighten the burden of those living with it—we should do all that we can in this area."

-continued-

Autism has transformed from a barely diagnosed disorder to one that impacts 1 in 68 families. An estimated one in every 166 children is affected by autism, cases of which are being diagnosed 60 times more often now than two decades ago.

"We envision a positive future for the many significant children and adults with autism in our lives, all beings of light and love regardless of where they sit on the spectrum," says Karen. "Each individual is here to teach us to open our own heart and to be more understanding of others. That's what my intention is . . . to bring out the stars in everyone—and to shine light on special needs."

Contact: Planned Television Arts
Brian Feinblum, 212-583-2718, *feinblumb@plannedtvarts.com*

Offshore

"Don Corace's corporate thriller is the breakout book of the year! *Offshore* is a page-turner that entertains and educates."
—Talk show co-host Sean Hannity, *Hannity & Colmes*, FOX-TV

"I was hooked from the first page. *Offshore* is a roller-coaster ride with unexpected twists and turns. Buy it!"
—Nationally syndicated talk-show host Neal boortz

"*Offshore* can do for Houston what the TV series *Dallas* did for that city."
—Sam Fletcher of *Oil and Gas Journal*

In the background of raging oil prices, a new energy policy being debated in Congress, and the recent government approval for drilling in Alaska's Arctic National Wildlife Refuge, Don Corace, a Florida land developer and former Texas oil roughneck and oil-lease speculator, delivers an explosive debut novel with the page-turning corporate thriller, ***Offshore***.

In ***Offshore***, Corace has taken the complex and controversial subject of drilling for oil offshore—the first widely distributed thriller revolving around the offshore business—and created a host of colorful characters to engulf us with a fascinating look behind the scenes and in the boardroom of what it might be like for the nation's most powerful oil barons.

He takes us into the high-tech world of deepwater exploration and skillfully weaves a tapestry of corporate greed, romance, and murder with unexpected outcomes. His book's timely launch coincides with a hotly debated topic—the potential of expanding offshore drilling to address our energy needs.

-continued-

Corace sheds insight on the following:

- How deepwater technology and offshore drilling hold the future for new oil.
- Why gas prices are skyrocketing and could hit $5/gallon this summer.
- The pros and cons of drilling in the waters of Florida or the Gulf of Mexico.
- How oil companies explore, drill, refine, and deliver gas to consumers.
- How oil companies invest in crude oil futures and how this impacts us.
- The critical issues facing the offshore drilling business and the oil industry.
- Informs and educates on our nation's dependence on foreign oil.

"Deepwater drilling is not outer space, but the deep water is a hostile and unforgiving environment, where leading-edge technology meets complex geophysical conditions from extreme temperatures and water pressure to strong ocean currents and underwater landslides," says Corace.

For his book's research, he spent several days on a large deepwater drill ship, as well as interviewed several executives in the offshore oil industry.

Offshore pays tribute to the early pioneers of the offshore oil industry and today's men and women who continue to push themselves and deepwater technology to new frontiers. "The public takes the oil industry for granted and it's misinformed about all that goes into the process of delivering oil to our cars and homes," says Corace.

-continued-

"This is a story about an industry that had to be told. I wanted to pay respect to the industry and the people in it, especially the diehard Texans, like my fictional D.L. Drummond, who not only demonstrates a can-do entrepreneurial spirit in spite of his flaws, but also represents American enterprise at its finest."

Sixty percent of the world's offshore acreage is unexplored. Ninety-five percent of that lies in water that is at least 3,000 feet deep. Corace believes, as his novel demonstrates, the only way for the United States to sustain its insatiable appetite for oil (we consume twenty-five percent of the daily oil used in the world) is to pursue drilling offshore.

"There are no easy answers when you look at our energy policy," says Corace. "It is unrealistic to assume that the U.S. can become energy independent. We must continue to drill in the deep waters of the Gulf of Mexico. We must open up the Arctic National Wildlife Refuge for development. At the same time we must be environmentally responsible, promote conservation, and research economically viable alternative energy sources."

Deepwater exploration in the Gulf of Mexico, which his book ***Offshore*** revolves around, could yield as much as 25 billion barrels of oil—as much as Alaska's Prudhoe Bay and the Arctic National Wildlife Refuge combined.

Corace, aware the public has concerns over oil drilling, relates to the topic of environmental concerns as a real estate developer. In fact, his Naples, Florida, condo building project has been delayed by 3.5 years of permitting issues and a million-dollar public battle with environmentalists over a single bald eagle's nest within a project.

-continued-

Corace is participating in the Offshore Technology Conference, the world's largest conference on oil with over 50,000 attendees and 2,500 exhibitors. He provides a unique perspective on offshore drilling—the physical challenges, the political obstacles, the cost-effectiveness, the environmental issues, and the role it plays in our energy policy.

Offshore is sure to strike oil with those seeking a fast-paced corporate thriller.

Publication Data: ***Offshore*** by Don Corace; Emerald Ink Publishing; May 2, 2005; 312 pages; Cloth; $21.95; ISBN: 0-9760426-0-6; *www.Doncorace.com*

Contact Information: Planned Television Arts
Brian Feinblum, 212-583-2718, *feinblumb@plannedtvarts.com*

About Autism Today

www.AutismToday.com launched on May 1, 1998, was created to provide easy access to information about autism for parents and professionals. This site now enjoys two million monthly hits from 55,000 unique visitors. The site also brings participants together to conduct useful studies on the needs of the autistic community. Founder and CEO Karen Simmons, the mother of an autistic boy, has poured back every cent she receives in proceeds into the Web site.

Autism Today, a free-membership site, offers the following:

- Up-to-date medical information about autism and Aspergers syndrome
- A public discussion forum where people can share stories, tips, and ideas
- A library of articles containing thousands of pages on autism
- Poems, art, and stories by—and for—members of the autism community
- A store containing hundreds of books and other materials
- A listing of conferences and events for the autism community
- The latest information on treatments and alternative therapies
- A database to locate physicians, psychologists, speech therapists, occupational and behavior therapists, schools, camps, programs, employment organizations, and recreation facilities that service the autistic community
- A free newsletter with a summary of the latest news media articles on autism
- Opportunity for participants to submit their books for publication

-continued-

Autism Education Online

Is a program that brings world-renowned authorities into your home or office through your computer or Internet connection. Using the speakers' PowerPoint presentations and their professionally recorded audio, we have developed a system for you to watch their presentation online at any time, anywhere. A sample of the topics covered include: managing feelings, making friends, language development, communication skills enhancement, advocacy for those with autism, bridging to adulthood, and many others.

Nearly 50 world-class experts are available on site, including:

- **Dr. Tony Attwood**, a world-renowned clinical psychologist, best-selling author, and expert on Aspergers syndrome.
- **Dr. Temple Grandin**, who also suffers from autism, is a world-leading speaker on autism spectrum disorders.
- **Dr. Lisa Lewis, Ph.D.**, provides research that supports the use of dietary interventions for individuals with autism
- **Raun K. Kauffman**, diagnosed as severely and incurably autistic at age 18 months; he overcame his disorder and now has no signs of the disease.
- **Andrew S. Bondy, Ph.D.**, has worked with children and adults with autism for 30 years and is the director of the Delaware Autistic Program.
- **Arnold Miller, Ph.D.**, a language and cognitive development specialist.
- **Jackie Marquette,** a transition specialist and a family coach.
- **Bart Stevens, ChLAP**, a chartered lifetime assistance planner.
- **Dr. Darold Treffert**, a psychiatrist and savant syndrome expert.

After You Say 'I Do'

7 Tips to a Happy, Lasting Relationship

Dozens of interesting and atypical tips for keeping your relationship alive are offered in a witty new book, ***What Happy Couples Do: The Loving Little Rituals of Romance*** (Fairview, February 2008). Below are seven proven ways happy couples can bond:

1. Come up with colorful and meaningful nicknames. Here are some affectionate monikers (repeated lovingly): Snugglebutt, Stinker, Cuddle Bumps, Love-Cheese, Lassie, Queen Diamond, and Colonel Sanders.

2. Find a private, personal way to say "I Love You" to one another. Sample phrases and gestures used by couples to express their love include three hand squeezes, curling the pointer finger, a scratch above the ear, or saying "Noodle," "I.U.," "Me More," and making the "cluck, cluck" sound.

3. Do something to switch your regular routines into more joy-filled rituals. Do something that will shift a mindless event into a mind-exhilarating one (or at least one that you don't mind as much).

4. Gestures in long-lasting marriages need not be extravagant. Something simple—every day—can keep a marriage healthy. Many couples make an effort to simply call or e-mail each other at least once during the day. Sometimes it's just a quick hello. Sometimes it's a more lengthy conversation. But a call can say "I care" or "I want to be in touch" or "I like that you're in my life."

-continued-

5. Do make sure you're not missing those moments by thinking only about what could be. Should be. Ought to be. Once was. Recognize that this is it. These moments are your marriage. That doesn't mean you can't do them better, differently, or more thoughtfully. What it does mean is that your invisible bond is being tightened or undone through and by those conversations. Those events. Those gestures. Little by little—forever.

6. Do get more actively engaged in your marriage by finding even one activity you both enjoy—bargain hunting, cooking, cleaning out the basement, playing cards, running like track stars—and commit to doing that activity again as if it's the first time you've ever done it. You'll soon see how beautiful this thing called marriage was meant to be—and can be again with a little bit of time, a little bit of effort, and (why not?) a little bit of healthy competition!

7. Do lower your expectations a little so that your happiness can be a little greater. And expect the weeds. For if you do, they won't be such a disappointment when they do pop up (because, without a doubt, they will).

Oil Industry Facts & Stats

- The U.S. is the world's largest oil consumer—using up to over 7 billion barrels of oil per year.
- The U.S. consumes a quarter of the world's daily usage, 20 million barrels a day—yet we represent only 5 percent of the world population.
- U.S. demand is estimated to increase 50 percent by 2025.
- The peak in oil productivity in the world is predicted to come within the next 5 to 34 years. The peak in the U.S. (continental 48 states) occurred in 1970.
- Nearly 55 percent of the oil consumed in the U.S. is imported.
- The world consumes 84 million barrels a day (42 gallons per barrel).
- The average American consumes three gallons of oil daily.
- The world's top drill ships, each the size of aircraft carriers, are able to operate in 12,000 feet of water and can drill over 5½ miles beneath the ocean floor.
- Raising a single steer, weighing 1,250 pounds, uses up 283 gallons of oil.
- It's estimated that to produce a pound of beef it takes three-quarters of a gallon of oil—for fertilizers used on cornfields and diesel fuel to run farm equipment and trucking.

-continued-

- Ounce for ounce, gasoline is cheaper than any liquid in the grocery store—water, milk, orange juice, detergent, shampoo, ketchup, etc.

- The tar-sand deposits in Canada—primarily in Alberta—hold the equivalent of more than 1.6 trillion barrels of oil—an amount that may exceed the world's remaining reserves of ordinary crude. But most of it lies too deep or in deposits too sparse to be exploited. Still, about 174 billion barrels of oil could be tapped economically, placing it second to Saudi Arabia as the most oil-rich nation.

- Oil experts estimate that the deep waters of the Gulf of Mexico will yield more than 25 billion barrels of oil. That's twice as much as Alaska's giant Prudhoe Bay Field, and far more than in any untapped U.S. prospect, including the controversial Arctic National Wildlife Refuge.

- In the lower 48 states, we produce less than half of what we did at the production peak in 1970.

- Deepwater well production could increase U.S. supplies by 33 to 40 percent in the next few years.

- Offshore drilling operations cost $450,000 to $500,000 per day.

- Sixty percent of the world's offshore acreage is unexplored. Ninety-five percent of that lies in waters deeper than 3000 feet.

- There are thousands of oil-based polymers and plastics we use in everyday life: medical implants, fertilizers, computers, sneakers, soccer balls, bike helmets, toys, plastic bottles and containers, clothes, etc.

-continued-

- It takes seven gallons of oil to produce a single tire.
- Two-thirds of U.S. consumption of oil goes toward fuel for cars, trucks, planes, military, buses, motorcycles, etc. One-third of our consumption goes toward producing synthetic fabrics and plastics.
- Around 25 percent of the price of a gallon of gas is in taxes.
- The Energy Information Administration projects in 20 years the Persian Gulf will supply 50 to 75 percent of all oil in the world—the same percentage before the 1973 Arab oil embargo.
- The U.S. Geological Survey predicts total U.S. production will peak in 20 years.
- Russia recently bypassed Saudi Arabia as the largest oil-producer in the world. It exports two-thirds of its daily production of 9 million barrels. Production could crest in 10 to 15 years.
- Saudi Arabia's proven oil reserves are estimated to be 260 billion barrels compared to Russia's 100 billion barrels.
- The U.S. imports 13 percent of its oil from Venezuela.
- The Gulf of Guinea could hold as much as 30 to 50 billion barrels of oil.
- Chad, Nigeria, and Angola account for 15 percent of U.S. imports and is expected to rise.

-continued-

- China, the world's most populous nation (1.3 billion), has become the second-largest oil consumer in the world, surpassing Japan.

- China's economic growth rate is surging. The new rich professionals have snapped up two million cars in 2003—up 70 percent over 2002. By 2025, China could be using 10 million barrels of oil per day, most of it imports.

- The world has burned through over a third of a trillion barrels of irreplaceable oil.

Karen Simmons

Founder of Autism Today

Biography

As the mother of six children—two with special needs, one of whom has autism—Karen Simmons is the founder of Autism Today, the nation's leading clearinghouse of information, resources, tools, and experts designed for parents, educators, doctors, therapists, and those who service the community of those afflicted with autism or Aspergers syndrome. She has also published four books on the subject (her fifth is due out this fall). Karen is also an active presenter at autism conferences and workshops that she has constructed, bringing in the nation's top experts and speakers for events that attract 500 to 700 new and repeat attendees each time.

An unexpected diagnosis of autism in her two-year-old son threw Karen into an unknown world without a clue, in search of information and support to deal with the special needs of a child with autism. The journey was far from easy.

Determined to find solutions to further her son's development she delved relentlessly into the mysterious terrain of autism, accumulating knowledge, insight, and information about the unusual world of people with autism.

Her experience as a mother of a child with autism inspired Karen to found the Keen Education Foundation in 1996. Their mission is to build a life for children with exceptional needs and to ensure that support, equipment, services, and education are available. They seek to help special needs children achieve their fullest possible individual development and find social inclusion.

-continued-

After years of personal research, trial and error, and discussions with other people creating pathways through the winding maze, Karen recognized a need for an "exceptional resource" to assist those individuals and families struggling in a world where easy answers were not readily available. The company is dedicated to making autism-related books, videos, tapes, and educational resource materials easily available to parents and professionals.

In May of 1998, Karen launched Autism Today's Web site, *www.AutismToday.com*, an interactive online newsmagazine and community for people whose lives have been touched by autism. It receives over two million hits monthly from 55,000 unique visitors. Karen speaks regularly at conferences throughout North America. Her monthly newsletter has a subscriber base of 22,000.

She has been featured in international publications such as *Woman's World.* A former jeweler in Seattle and Edmonton, a distant relation to Woodrow Wilson, and a former member of the U.S. Air Force, she resides with her husband and family in Alberta, Canada.

Don Corace
Biography

Don Corace applies real-life lessons and wisdom from his 25 years of experience in numerous entrepreneurial ventures in his corporate thriller set around an oil company fighting bankruptcy and a hostile takeover while drilling for offshore oil. *Offshore* was inspired by his days as on oil field roughneck and an oil and gas lease speculator throughout Texas, New Mexico, and Oklahoma. He also incorporates his experiences as a land investor, a bank director, an influential lobbyist, an owner of an environmental contracting company, and a real estate developer.

Prior to his life of oil, real estate, and business, he had a vision of being a professional baseball player.

A back injury suffered during his senior year in high school sidelined him from continuing on a baseball All-Star team sponsored by the Los Angeles Dodgers. His ninety-mile-per-hour fastball and 16-4 record as a pitcher made a fond memory. His dream of playing professional sports was replaced with the intent to study law.

But after attending Denison University in Ohio as an English literature major for a few years, he dropped out and traveled throughout the U.S. and Europe with only a backpack. Eventually he returned home to Pittsburgh without a degree or a job.

Because of his entrepreneurial drive, he quickly found himself in Midland, Texas, after reading a *Wall Street Journal* article about a west Texas oil boom. He drove through a sandstorm to obtain a job as a roughneck in the oilfields, circa 1980.

-continued-

He presently oversees all construction and governmental permitting activity for the waterfront high-rise condominium projects (evaluated at $1.5 billion) of Signature Communities, a major real-estate development company.

His days as a roughneck were not easy, especially when his blue-collar co-workers found out he was hired by the company's president and he was a college boy. They needled him, calling Corace a "Yankee worm." But he came to be embraced by his oil comrades.

Corace, 47, hopes his writing in the corporate thriller genre will be embraced the way John Grisham is for the legal thriller, Tom Clancy for the military-spy thriller, and Michael Crichton for science-medical thriller.

Don's adventures have taken him to West Texas, Southern California, and Naples, Florida, where he now resides with his wife of 22 years, Ammi, and their three children. For more information, consult: *www.DonCorace.com*

Carol Bruess, Ph.D.
Biography

Carol Bruess, Ph.D., is the coauthor of a new book, ***What Happy Couples Do: The Loving Little Rituals of Romance*** (Fairview Press, February 2008). Her book is based on 15 years of interviews and surveys with hundreds of couples.

She earned her Ph.D. in interpersonal communication from Ohio University, her M.A. in interpersonal communication from Ohio University, and a B.A. in graphic communication (magna cum laude) from St. Norbert College in DePere, Wisconsin.

Carol is a frequent media guest. She's appeared twice on CBS-TV's *Early Morning Show*, nine times on WCCO-TV in Minneapolis, and on PBS.

Since 1989, Carol has taught at the college level. She has served as a tenured associate professor in the department of communication studies at University of St. Thomas since 2002.

She's received numerous academic honors, including: the Faculty Service Learning Award from University of St. Thomas, member of Omicron Delta Kappa of the National Leadership Honor Society, and Judy C. Pearson Graduate Award for Research in the area of gender and family communications.

She has participated in numerous presentations at various professional conferences, including: the National Communication Association, Central States Communication Association, Speech Communication Association, International Network on Personal Relationships, National Society for Experiential Education, and Service-Learning in Communication Conference.

-continued-

Carol's first book was co-authored with Mark P. Orbe in 2005, *Contemporary Issues in Interpersonal Communication*, published by Roxbury/Oxford University Press.

Happily married to Brian for 17 years, she resides with her husband and two children in St. Paul, Minnesota. For more information, please consult: *www.WhatHappyCouplesDo.com.*

20 Story Angles
Autism Today

There Is a Clearinghouse of Information Available at *www.AutismToday.com*

A Look at How Parents Rise to the Occasion and meet the Challenges of Raising a Child with a Disability

Why Attitudes Need to Shift Toward Special Needs People—Time to Acknowledge Their Gifts, Strengths, and Unique Talents

What We Can Learn from Children with Special Needs

Back from the Dead: One Woman's Powerful Story of How She Cheated Death, Raised Two Special Needs Children, and Found Her Calling

Why Is There an Autism Epidemic? New Insights and the Latest Research on Potential Causes and Possible Cures

Does Your Child Have Autism or Aspergers Syndrome? How to Identify the Symptoms and Get Diagnosed Now

What Are the Myths and Misconceptions the Public and Even Professionals/Doctors, Teachers, Therapist Have about Autism?

The Teen Years with Autism: How to Meet the Challenges

Will Your Special Needs Child Be Able to Live as an Independent Adult?

-continued-

How Do You Raise a Family of "Normal" and Special Needs Children?

Spotlight on Children Who Rise above Their Circumstances and Show How Those Affected with Autism Can Surprise Us

How Those Living the Autism Experience See Life's Odyssey

Why Early Diagnosis/Intervention Is Crucial When It Comes to Autism—How to Identify a Potential Problem Child

No Longer in Denial: Family and Friends of Autistic Children Are Out in the Open and Not Hiding with Embarrassment

How the Autistic Are Artistic

Friend or Foe: How We Should Treat and Communicate with the Members of the Special Needs Community

What Else Should the Federal Government Do as It Relates to Autism?

Humor Is Healing: How to See the Lighter Side of Autism

Celebrating Differences: Appreciating the Gifts and Talents of Autistic People

Karen Simmons
Q & A

Karen, as a parent of six children, how do you balance your time and care for your two special needs children and four normal children? Oh my God, that's the single, biggest challenge I face, especially since my husband works 24-7. I guess I can say that I don't over-do the mothering role like many parents do. There's no "white glove test" in my house. The older kids help out with the younger, which helps tremendously. I also wholly believe in seeing ALL my children as "able" and treat them just like anyone else. The special needs ones can't use their differences as an excuse. Also, letting go of "perfection" as a model of success is most important. It's more important to enjoy the journey!

As the parent of a child with autism, what words of encouragement and guidance can you offer parents and caregivers of children with special needs? Enjoy the brilliance your child brings to the world regardless of how hard it may be to find at times. We can always choose how we want to feel about any given situation, so a parent can say "I see peace instead of this." I'm not saying it's easy to take this attitude, but it certainly can be done. This way the parent can step out of the victim role and walk calmly into the role of empowerment to do whatever it takes to make everyone's life better. I believe it's true that what you focus on expands. So by paying attention to the strengths and positive attributes these special people possess, it will enable them to feel good about themselves and perhaps develop life-skills that will enhance their lives and the lives of others. Also it's important to get to know other parents with special needs children. No one needs to do this alone and parents can share their stories of humor and challenges while supporting each other during trying times.

-continued-

What are the five myths many of us have about children with autism?

1. That autistic people are retarded
2. That autistic people can't have relationships and get married, have jobs, and go on to live normal lives.
3. That people with autism don't have any feelings and emotions
4. That "refrigerator moms" cause autism
5. That autism can't get better

What's the difference between autism and Aspergers Syndrome? There are many different views even amongst the professionals in the field on this subject. Typical autism, rather than high-functioning autism, is associated with the lack of language skills, severe behavior, and the inability to function with their peers. What is more difficult to differentiate is the high-functioning autistic and Aspergers. According to DSM4, which lists the diagnostic criteria for autism, a person with high-functioning autism has significant language delays and adaptive skills when compared to the development of their "so-called" normal peers. This diagnostic tool is rapidly being challenged and by the time DSM5 is completed, it will most certainly be a completely new and different set of criteria.

How would you advise the professional community of doctors, therapists, and educators to change their approach in how they treat and view children with autism? First I would make sure they understand exactly what the autism spectrum is and how to properly recognize and diagnose it. It is appalling in this day and age to have professionals still tell parents to come back in a year after diagnosing a young child with autism without providing intervention or direction. Also professionals have been diagnosing children incorrectly in order to obtain maximum

-continued-

funding, which can skew the figures for autism. I would also encourage them to be more open-minded as far as using biomedical interventions such as nutritional considerations and other types of alternative therapies when talking to parents of newly diagnosed children with autism. They need to understand the importance of early intervention in the life of the child so they can advocate and prescribe appropriate medical and nonmedical interventions for the child.

What should a parent keep in mind when it comes to helping the siblings of a special needs child to understand the limits—as well as the feelings—of their less-able brother or sister? In real estate, it's about location. In special needs, it's about communication, because when the special needs child has difficulty communicating their thoughts, ideas and feelings, they become quite frustrated, which can result in a behavioral meltdown. This can lead to ridicule and they can become targets for bullying. What is most important is that the siblings realize that their special needs brother or sister isn't always less abled, rather, they are differently abled. For example we focused on Jonathan reading to his older brother's fourth grade class when he was 4 years old, which was very good for his self-esteem and their relationship as brothers. Matt was very proud of his brother. It is difficult at times for siblings to see that there are actual limitations, especially in the case of an invisible disability like autism or ADHD. You must clearly explain, as far as the sibling is capable of understanding, what the disability is and what the biggest challenges are in minute detail. Role-model appropriate interactions when possible, and at the same time, teach both the special needs child and the sibling to treat each other like any other human being—with respect. They must defend their special needs sibling to the bitter end, especially when they are bullied.

-continued-

What are the symptoms of autism and when do they develop? Autism can be detected in children as young as six months but is not usually recognized until around the age of two. Some of the earliest signs include a certain gaze they have towards people while lying in their crib. They may be fascinated by a swirling fan, staring at it as if they're hypnotized. When the child is around 3 to 5 years old, typical signs of autism include spinning in circles, flapping their hands in the air, lining objects up on the floor, watching the same movie over and over, displaying an apparent lack of fear in dangerous situations, and so on.

How is an autistic person treated medically? There is really nothing medically wrong with people who have autism since it is a neurological difference in the brain's wiring. However, many people with autism have gastrointestinal disturbances that should be looked into because if they go undetected, they may result in behavioral, interactive, and learning difficulties. Sometimes medications are prescribed for children so they can attend better during school and at home. Many people have also had success using vitamins and nutritional therapy in treating their child's autism.

What causes autism and how can we reverse the epidemic that has seen us go from 1 in 10,000 in 1985 to 1 in 166 in 2005 being diagnosed with autism? The most current research suggests a probable genetic factor, which in some children can be triggered by a number of possible factors such as vaccines, heavy metal toxicity, and other prenatal conditions occurring prior to birth. Most professionals in the field believe you can't reverse autism but you can implement certain treatments and methodologies that will help the child cope and overcome many characteristics of autism. There are however, some people who believe autism can be cured, though the jury is still out on this one.

-continued-

How did you find the resources—time, strength, and money—to create Autism Today? Slow and steady wins the race! It evolved over time, starting out like all other sites, one member at a time while working from my home. I created it because when my son was diagnosed, it was close to impossible to find what I needed. So when I did carve a pathway I didn't want it to be just for one child. I wanted it to be for every child. So far, all the revenue I have generated has gone right back into the Web site to make it even better for the members and supporters. Time, well since my mission is also my passion, it seems to flow right into my life. I find the time to work on it and time finds me. My thinking of the ideas to implement happens when I'm driving in the car or even when I'm in the shower. I just keep a stack of Post-it Notes handy to write down the ideas as they pop into my head. Strength, well it isn't always easy. Sometimes I have to escape from all the distractions of my life to build up my strength just to think. I must always ascertain what my priority is and stick with it. Most importantly, as long as I hold my vision on what I am doing, it unfolds as it should, synchronistically leading me down a pathway to what the parents, professionals, people with autism, and educators truly need and want.

Karen, you nearly died giving birth to one of your children. How did that event change your perspective on life? Until I went through that experience following the birth of my sixth child, I was working in the gemology/jewelry field. My focus was selling jewelry and while I was happy doing what I was doing, I didn't feel like I had a true mission and purpose for my life aside from my children and family. After I recovered, I was drawn to become the founder of a nonprofit organization, write books, host conferences and of course, creating Autism Today. The experience helped me see the true meaning and value of life, which is to live fully and completely, learn as much as you can,

-continued-

help others along the way, and leave a legacy. My father just passed away and though he will be remembered by some, the effect of his life will not have an impact on humanity. My great-uncle George Lacy, was one of the three people who donated the granite to the Texas State Capitol in Austin. I know how he will be remembered for many years to come.

Is the federal government doing enough to support the families with special needs children? What can we do better or differently? There is a tremendous lack of interest and resources allocated through the government and other agencies towards a solution. This includes actively determining the cause of autism and implementing adequate research towards curative and helpful measures. The U.S. government will happily spend 1.9 billion dollars for a single Trident nuclear submarine in a fleet of around fifty, yet is only spending 66 million dollars on the entire special education area, which includes special teachers, training and proper equipment and supports. Much needs to be done in this area.

Let's face it; most people don't want to be you. They pray to have normal, healthy children and to avoid what you've had to go through. But now that you have lived through raising children with special needs, can you help explain to us how you are able to do it? Believe me, I prayed for healthy children too! When I first discovered the challenges I would face and that my 2 special needs children would face, I was devastated. That was a turning point in my life because at that point I could have chosen to deny there was anything wrong, or feel victimized by the situation. Instead, I chose to embrace the difficulty and make the commitment to do whatever it took to help my children and others along the way. I knew that others were facing similar problems and maybe they didn't have the support or resources to help

-continued-

their children so I decided to commit to helping them as much as I could along the way.

You also founded KEEN—Key Enrichment of Exceptional Needs. What is that? It is a nonprofit organization with the following mission: *"To enrich the life experience for those with special needs while raising awareness and understanding of their issues globally."* Every day, millions of people worldwide are diagnosed with some sort of special need. These special needs could be autism, Down syndrome, cerebral palsy or Tourette's syndrome. Some argue that the recent increase in diagnosis is due to improved technology, higher medical awareness, improper diagnosis and environmental conditions. It's so easy to think of the label and the diagnosis rather than the real person who is struggling to contend with it. These individuals have real special needs and they face real daily struggles. Our goal is to enhance the education and life experience of these special needs individuals and their guardians where funding is otherwise not available. The outcome is to empower these individuals to become productive, independent, happy and fulfilled members of society, which will dramatically decrease the tremendous cost of their care to society while improving the quality of their lives.

You speak of how we should celebrate the gifts of those who are different. How do you seek out the good, the creative, and the unique in others? Everyone who spends time with anyone can certainly find something good that they do. No matter how small it is you can focus on it and give positive reinforcement for it. Maybe it's playing a song on the piano or coloring a pretty picture or writing a poem. When I sent out an invitation for artwork submissions for my autism book, we were inundated with artwork from people on the spectrum from around the globe. I am writing an e-book called *Autism 101*. To me, the most

-continued-

important section in this e-book are the comments from those with autism, which raise their self-esteem as we are talking with them, not about them. I am also developing a site for people on the ASD spectrum called ASDCommunity.com. By doing this, we embrace people for who they are and the gifts they bring to the world.

You also use humor as a form of coping and healing. How do you help others lighten up? I tell them not to take life so seriously. Watch sitcoms instead of scary movies! I share some of the funny ways Jonathan perceives the world and some of the funny things he's done. People with autism are literal thinkers, which make some of the comments they make and the perceptions they have quite funny. Like, "Why do we toast the bride, Mom?" There's a book by Wayne Gilpin called *Laughing and Loving with Autism*, which shares my sense of humor. It's filled with funny stories parents tell about their children and is a must-read for parents of children with special needs.

What is it like to be autistic? How do they see the world and what are their typical limitations? It depends on the "autie" as Stephen Shore, a dear friend of mine who is also a person with Aspergers Syndrome, would say. They perceive the world differently than we do. Stephen bases this on his own life experiences. Of course I ask him how he knows he's different than me and he's stumped since he is also a literal thinker. People with autism vary across the autism spectrum more than the so called "neurotypicals" which is a term autistic people made up to describe us, the so-called "normal" people. They have a tendency to become very focused on their interests, which allow them to hone their skills. Perhaps some of the most brilliant minds in the world had a form of autism like Albert Einstein, Marie Curie, Carl Sagan, and many more.

-continued-

What are six things society should keep in mind in how it views, interacts with, and helps those with special needs? 1. Inclusion for all people, regardless of their strengths and weaknesses is important. 2. It takes a community to raise a special needs child. 3. Focus on the positives they possess and help their light shine. 4. Treat them like regular people as much as possible, not in a degrading manner. 5. Be careful not to overprotect or mollycoddle them. 6. Don't favor them, simply treat them with respect.

Don Corace
Offshore
Q&A

Drilling in the Arctic National Wildlife Refuge has been a controversial issue. Will its development help reduce our dependence on foreign oil? Yes, it will. Even though it will take ANWR several years to develop, the U.S. is estimated to increase its demand for oil by 50 percent over the next 20 years. We currently import between 50 to 60 percent of our domestic needs. So any domestic production would obviously reduce our dependence.

The environmental community have been staunchly opposed to opening up ANWR. Why? The whole ANWR issue over the past 15 years is a prime example of emotion over fact. There are estimated to be 9 to 16 billion barrels of oil in the ground there. Environmentalists argue that the pristine wilderness will be ruined. The facts: only a small fraction of the 19-million-acre refuge will be developed; drilling around Alaska's Prudhoe Bay proves there will not be a negative impact to wildlife; and advanced technologies reduce the size of the "footprint," and safeguard the environment. Go to a search engine, type in ANWR.ORG and read about their position. Then go to the Sierra Club and other environmental groups sites and you will see that they don't back their assertions with science and facts—just emotion.

Opponents have asserted that ANWR would only meet the energy needs of the U.S. for 4 to 6 months. Is that true? This a good example of the difference between a fund-raising slogan and fact. In order for that assertion to be correct, you have to make the assumption that the U.S. will rely only on ANWR for all of its domestic needs and we do not import any oil. How realistic is that?

-continued-

Where is the next most promising area for oil development in the United States? Right in our back yard . . . in the deep waters of the Gulf of Mexico where part of my book takes place. As I said, ANWR has reserves of between 9 and 16 billion barrels, but it will take several years to bring the production to market. Current estimates for reserves for deepwater (considered to be in 3,000 feet or deeper waters) is around 25 billion barrels.

Is that why you chose the offshore oil industry as background for your book? Yes, to me it is the most fascinating part of the energy industry.

What role is technology playing in the process today? The characters in *Offshore* and people in the offshore industry are pioneers. This is cutting-edge technology. And to me, they represent the epitome of American enterprise and ingenuity. The first offshore well was drilled near Santa Barbara in 1897 on wooden piers 450 feet from the shoreline. Now, drillships (which I describe in the book) are capable of drilling in over 12,000 feet (2 miles) of water and another 35,000 feet (5 1/2 miles) beneath the sea floor. That's the maritime equivalent of landing a man on the moon. Great technological strides have also been made over the years to better identify oil and gas reserves through seismic surveys. They have substantially increased the efficiency of drilling while safeguarding the environment. And they are able to recover more oil and gas from formations than ever before. It's pretty amazing stuff . . . and the general public has no idea.

What is *Offshore* about? The Drummond family of Houston controls one of the largest offshore drilling and exploration companies in the world. Their company is under siege by a ruthless corporate raider who will stop at nothing to take it over. The book is a fast-paced corporate thriller involving corporate

-continued-

greed, romance, and murder. It's a page-turner that entertains and educates.

Does the book depict the technology you mentioned? I only broad-brush the technology. I simply want people to ask themselves, "I didn't know that's how they drill for oil offshore." This is commercial fiction. The book is character-based with a fast-paced plot. I have an obligation to entertain readers—and if they learn something along the way, that's great. But I've been careful not to get into all the technological details because it slows the story down. My goal was to write a story that both women and men would enjoy. Women tend to like character development and romance. Men who have read the book liked the technology and action. So I think I've struck a pretty good balance.

Why did you write the book? I thought it was a story that had to be told. Offshore drilling is a fascinating industry and the general public knows very little about it. And as a former roughneck (worker on a rig) and speculator in oil and gas leases, I developed a respect for the business and the people in it—especially Texans like my fictional Drummond family. I think the industry represents American enterprise at its finest.

So, are you an advocate for the industry? I wouldn't say I am an advocate, but I do share the industry's and Bush Administration's philosophy that we must continue to explore for and develop oil and gas reserves to reduce our reliance on foreign imports. And, in doing so, we must be environmentally responsible. President Bush recently said that we rely on energy sources from countries that don't particularly like us. That's the stark reality we are faced with today and for decades ahead.

-continued-

Are we doing enough to encourage conserving energy? No, we are not. The U.S. is by far the largest oil consumer in the world. We consume a quarter of the world's daily supply, or 20 million barrels per day, yet we only comprise 5 percent of the world's population. Keep in mind, however, we are also the world's most powerful economy. With that said, there is a tax loophole for gas-guzzling SUVs. The tax code, for example, allows an owner of a $110,000 luxury Hummer to write off $106,000 of the purchase price in the first year. That just doesn't make sense and sends a bad message. Bottom line: The public needs to be educated more and we must come up with more creative solutions to encourage conservation.

Shouldn't we hold out for the development of alternative sources of energy, ones that are safer to produce, better for the environment, and maybe even less expensive than oil? It is extremely important to develop alternative energy sources that are less harmful to the environment. But the reality is that many of these technologies are not economically viable—and may not be for decades. What many people don't realize is that the energy companies, along with auto makers, have invested billions into research and development for various alternative sources such as hydrogen fuel cells and hybrid electric cars. Oil companies are also at the forefront in developing diesel fuel made from natural gas, geothermal energy, ethanol (made from corn), and even solar energy technologies.

How well is the oil industry protecting the environment? Let's face it, practically every industrial operation known impacts the environment to some degree. That's a reality. With regard to the offshore-drilling industry, there are a number of procedures to greatly reduce ocean pollution—you won't hear the environmental community applauding them, however. I recently interviewed a drilling engineer with a major oil company and he

-continued-

said the environmental community does have a good purpose. They continue to push the industry to come up with better technologies to safeguard the environment.

Do you think the environmental community unfairly targets the industry? There is no doubt the industry has made mistakes. I think, by and large, they have learned from them. They are very conscious of their image and have employed resources to improve their operations—from drilling, production, pipelining, refining, and transporting. The drilling engineer I recently interviewed, for example told me that 70 percent of his work day is spent on environmental and safety issues. Besides, the industry wants to get its act together. No one wants to consciously pollute the environment. Plus, it makes good business sense not to. I would like to add one thing. A study done by NASA concluded that nearly 80 percent of all the world's oil released into the environment arises from the use of oil, such as from car engines. They estimate it's about 140 million gallons per year. Only 9 percent of that release results from oil transportation activities, including tanker spills.

The U.S. consumes 25 percent of the world's annual usage, but only produces 45 percent of what it needs, relying on imports for the rest. Has the oil supply peaked, and if not, when will we run out of oil? Good question. But the answer is nobody knows for sure. You could put three oil forecasters in a room who look at the same data and they could come up with three radically different conclusions. There are many who say world oil production could peak in 20 years. Based on that, we need to wisely develop existing oil and gas reserves by being environmentally responsible. We need to develop alternative energy sources. And we need to rise to the challenge and develop better conservation measures.

-continued-

You point out that oil is the cheapest liquid we can purchase if we went to a supermarket. So why do people complain when gas hits $2 a gallon? It goes back to the media's portrayal of the oil industry. Maybe seeing the dollars and cents on the gas pump increase while we fill our tanks has something to do with it. When we go to a grocery shelf and buy bottled water, we only see the price—we don't fill up the bottle.

Why are gasoline prices so high? There are a number of factors that contribute to higher gasoline prices. The U.S. dollar has fallen lately which means that foreign oil sellers, who control most crude supplies, want more dollars per barrel to compensate. Current U.S. supplies also impact pricing in the oil commodities market, which oftentimes does not equate to fundamental supply and demand fundamentals. Oil traders bid up prices because of fears in the future that supplies will be low. Another factor is OPEC's willingness to stabilize prices by increasing output. Short-term disruptions such as refinery shutdowns due to accidents or terrorist attacks also impact the price of gas.

How susceptible is the oil industry to terrorist attacks? The industry is very susceptible. Many oil facilities from offshore platforms, pipelines, oil refineries, and shipping terminals are considered to be "soft" targets—not easily defensible. For example, two-thirds of all Saudi oil is processed at one facility. In addition, they have two primary oil shipping terminals which over 10% of the world's oil flows through. A terrorist attack on these locations is not a fictional scenario. Highjacking a plane from Kuwait or Dubai and crashing it into these either of these complexes could effectively take 50 percent of Saudi oil off the market for at least six months. It could bring the world's oil-addicted economies to their knees—including the United States. It could be an energy Pearl Harbor. It's frightening.

-continued-

How did you end up as a roughneck (worker) on an oil rig? I was trying to find myself after I dropped out of college and read an article in the *Wall Street Journal* about the oil boom in west Texas—specifically Midland and Odessa. I was befriended by a wildcatter by the name of A.W. Dillard, Jr. and I ended up being offered the job by Don Evans, a close friend of George W. Bush and former Secretary of Commerce.

What is it like being a roughneck? It's hard, dirty work. I grew up in Pittsburgh and my family was in the construction business. My father, who was the developer, the contractor, and the guy on the bulldozer, thought it was a privilege for me to dig ditches for him when I was a teenager. And by the way, he paid accordingly. But what he instilled in me was to learn a business from the ground up. So when I decided to give the oil industry a try, I chose to be a roughneck. It can be dangerous work. I had some minor injuries, but overall there are a lot of safety precautions. I enjoyed my experience and I enjoyed the people I worked with—and I wasn't a bad "hand," as they say in Texas oil talk.

You then went into buying and selling oil-gas leases, negotiating with ranchers on behalf of oil companies. What did you learn from that experience? My experiences from buying and selling leases was my first truly entrepreneurial endeavor. Maybe a better way to explain it was learning how to survive by my wits. I developed relationships with oil companies. I found out what their exploration departments were looking for. And then I went out and found who owned the mineral rights—in many cases ranchers, who inherently were very suspicious. I can say this: buying and selling leases taught me to be a dealmaker—and I have been honing those skills ever since.

-continued-

Why is oil a political football? The media has demonized the oil industry. The environmental community has contributed to that perception as well. As a result, politicians acting in their self-interests are reluctant to support bold measures. And frankly, I think the oil industry has to do a better job getting its message out.

What does the public not fully understand about how the oil exploration process takes place? I'm not so sure the public really cares about the oil exploration process. If they understood the risks involved and the amount of money and hard work it takes to get oil out of the ground (or sea floor) maybe they would have a better appreciation of what oil companies do.

What about how oil is drilled—what kind of risks and investments are involved? I'll address offshore deepwater drilling, which is considered to be 3,000 feet or deeper. Depending upon the water depth and how far below the seafloor a company wants to drill, drilling a well can cost from between $20 to $50 million. Costs to rent a rig run $450,000 to $500,000 per day. Deepwater drilling is a hostile, unforgiving environment. Extreme water temperatures. Strong ocean currents. Potential for blowouts. Even underwater mudslides. And a host of other things that can go wrong. I touch on some of this in the book.

The oil industry publications claim your book is the first fictionalized account of a story relating to offshore drilling. Why do you feel that no other book up to this point has been published? Because the offshore industry is very complex. But in reality, I am doing what Michael Crichton does in his books—weaving a good story around technology. One thing that may set me apart, however, is that my stories are character-based. I broad-brush the technology, but the interplay of the characters and mak-

-continued-

ing the book a quick, entertaining read comes first. I often get asked what objective I had in mind when writing the book. I respond by saying, "I want to write page-turners that entertain and educate."

Don, you've had a diverse career, from roughneck to real estate developer. You were a land speculator, lobbyist, and bank director. *Offshore* centers around the behind-the-scenes financial dealings and squabbles of a family business. Do you find this depiction rings true for any industry? Yes. And the corporate thriller genre I am creating will do exactly that. My next book will revolve around a high-rise developer in Miami who has struck a deal, despite the U.S. embargo, to build a Las Vegas on the Caribbean in Cuba. My third book will be about the mysterious investment hedge-fund business and how financiers, terrorists, and global mafias have developed alliances. I've got another dozen or more books in varying stages of development.

Is oil still filled with a lot of family businesses? Are they all like the Ewings of Dallas—or your Drummond family dynasty of Houston? That's funny that you mention the Ewings of Dallas. A reviewer recently wrote that *Offshore* will do for Houston what the TV program *Dallas* did for that city. I certainly didn't have that in mind when I wrote the book and screenplay and, frankly, the oil industry never liked how they were depicted in the series. But to answer your question: Yes, there are families like the Ewings still out there—with probably more soap-opera–like scandals than there were on the TV series.

What are three myths or misconceptions most consumers have of the oil industry? 1) We shouldn't worry about shortages of oil. It'll always be around; 2) Oil companies are evil price-fixers; and 3) The oil industry has President Bush in their hip pocket.

-continued-

Which character do you relate the most to with—if any? Why? I get asked that a lot. I suppose there's a little of me in every main character. I can probably relate the most with Clay Drummond, but I am, by no means, a womanizer, a heavy drinker, or a gambler. I can also relate quite a bit with D. L. Drummond, the family patriarch. He has many of the same hardworking, no-nonsense attributes as my late father. My father died of cancer. And D. L. has terminal cancer.

Don, can you understand why consumers consider oil a necessary evil yet can't tolerate corporate greed, sloppy environmental practice, nor understand why our government goes to war, in part, over oil? Instances of corporate greed and sloppy environmental practice have not been exclusive to the oil industry. As far as going to war, oil supply and national security go hand-in-hand. The U.S. has to protect its interests or else we will be held hostage economically. Do you want to go back to the Arab oil embargo of 1973 when we stood in line to fill our gas tanks?

You are a partner and oversee all governmental permitting and construction activity for waterfront high-rise condo projects in Naples, Florida, for Signature Communities, a major real estate development company. Those properties are valued at over $1.5 billion. Is land development similar in many respects to exploring and drilling for oil? Great question. From the standpoint of the exploration and production side of the oil industry, yes. The aptitude to develop real estate and develop oil and gas is the same. Both industries are inherently risky. There is a great deal of upfront diligence and research to determine whether a development is in a good location and can support market demand. Extensive engineering studies are done to make sure the product can be built on that location. The same thing in the oil industry. A lot of studies, specially seismic surveys and engineering

-continued-

analysis is done to determine the probability a specific formation holds economically viable amounts of oil and gas reserves.

***Offshore* centers around a corporate raider seeking to take over an oil drilling company. Are many oil companies susceptible to the same kind of dealings displayed in *Offshore*?** Yes. All the big players are publicly traded and are susceptible to corporate raiders, like my Wall Street financier character, Ramsey Croft. Companies are always trying to gobble up one another. It's Darwinian. Many of the major oil companies like ExxonMobil have already merged, but there are several independent oil companies, drilling contractors, and suppliers who are always looking to increase market share and provide better returns for their shareholders.

How did you get started? I enjoyed reading thrillers and just said to myself one day, "I can do that." But it was a little more difficult than I thought. This business is not for the faint-hearted. Even though writing is a creative process, I have approached it like many of the entrepreneurial ventures I have been involved with over the years.

Do you feel your varied business experiences have helped you become a writer? Sure. There is no formula on how to become a writer. Ernest Hemingway once said that a prerequisite was to have an unhappy childhood. I can't relate to that because I grew up in a very loving home. But the ups and downs I have had in business, and life experiences in general, is something I draw on. I am also extremely fortunate to have met my wife of 22 years, Ammi, who has always supported me. I was a husband, father, and businessman before I became a writer. She has helped me keep that in perspective—so do my three kids. Without Ammi, I would never been able to pursue my passion.

Testimonials

Praise for Books by

Karen Simmons

"*Little Rainman* shows that autism can be seen and understood by everyone. After reading this book full of miraculous pictures, I feel greater love, compassion and understanding of a situation that somehow touches us all sooner or later."—**Mark Victor Hansen, co-creator, #1 *New York Times* bestselling *Chicken Soup for the Soul* series**

"Autism demonstrates the genius in every human soul. This book is an absolutely genius idea!"—**Robert G. Allen, author of *Multiple Streams of Income* and *Nothing Down*, coauthor of *The One Minute Millionaire***

"These pictures are some of the best illustrations of what autism is. They give the reader a really good picture of how a child with autism thinks. They think with pictures in their head. I use them in my presentation and lectures to demonstrate the visual thinking process."—**Temple Grandin, autistic adult, presenter, and author of *Thinking In Pictures***

"Thank you for allowing us to share your stories with our readers. It was one of the most touching and unforgettable I have ever worked on."—**Kathy Fitzpatrick, writer for *Woman's World* magazine**

-continued-

"There are no words to express my appreciation for your creativity. I just know it is going to help many, many people. I spent two years as a fellow in child psychiatry seeing only autistic children so you can see I have great compassion for the challengers in your life . . . and how out of those challenges you are helping others."**—Gerald Jampolsky, M.D., author of the bestselling *Love Is Letting Go of Fear***

"*Little Rainman* gives a more simplistic, yet comprehensive explanation of this strange disorder than any other book we have seen. Written through the eyes of her child, Karen gives the reader a unique view of autism that explains the challenge in a very 'user friendly' manner."**—R. Wayne Gilpin, president, Future Horizons, Inc.**

INDEX

JAY CONRAD LEVINSON

Jay Conrad Levinson is the author of thirty-nine business books including the bestselling marketing series in history, *Guerrilla Marketing*. His books have sold over 15 million copies worldwide, are available in forty-nine languages, and are required reading in MDA programs worldwide.

For ten years, Jay taught guerrilla marketing at the extension division of the University of California in Berkeley. He served as Senior VP at J. Walter Thompson, and in Europe, as Creative Director of Leo Burnett Advertising, where he was part of the creative teams behind the Marlboro Man, the Pillsbury Doughboy, Allstate's "good hands," United Airlines' "friendly skies," and Sears' Diehard battery.

An acclaimed, inspirational, and witty speaker, Jay speaks and teaches all over the world. He is also the Chairman of Guerrilla Marketing International and The Guerrilla Marketing Association—a marketing support system for small business.

Jay can be contacted at *www.gmarketing.com* and *www.guerrilla marketingassociation*.

RICK FRISHMAN

Rick Frishman, the founder of Planned Television Arts (*www.plannedtvarts.com*), has been one of the leading book publicists in America for over thirty years. He works with many of the top book editors, literary agents, and publishers in America. Rick also serves as Publisher at Morgan James Publishing in New York (*www.morganjamespublishing.com*), which annually publishes over 130 nonfiction books for authors who believe in giving back—a portion of each book sold is donated to Habitat for Humanity.

Rick has appeared on hundreds of radio shows and more than a dozen television shows nationwide including *Oprah*, *Bloomberg TV*, and *Fox Business*. He has been featured in the *New York Times*, *Wall Street Journal*, *Associated Press*, *Selling Power Magazine*, *New York Post*, and scores of publications. He is the coauthor of eight books, including national bestsellers *Guerrilla Publicity* and *Networking Magic*. Along with media personality Robyn Freedman Spizman, Rick also co-wrote the popular four-book series *Author 101* and recently teamed up for their highly acclaimed book entitled *Where's Your Wow? 16 Ways to Make Your Competitors Wish They Were You!* For more information on Rick see *www.rickfrishman.com*.

Rick and his wife Robbi live in Long Island with their three children, Adam, Rachel, and Stephanie.

JILL LUBLIN

Praised as a modern-day Dale Carnegie for how to be influential, Jill Lublin authored *Get Noticed . . . Get Referrals: Build Your Client Base and Your Business by Making a Name for Yourself.* She is also the coauthor of the national bestselling books, *Networking Magic*, which rose to #1 on the Barnes and Noble charts for three weeks, and *Guerrilla Publicity*, the PR bible, which has also reached bestseller status. Jill is the founder of GoodNews Media, Inc. and hosts the TV program, *Messages of Hope*, and the nationally syndicated radio show, *Do the Dream.* She has also authored two audio programs, three DVD training videos, and a workbook.

Jill is a popular international speaker who teaches powerful publicity, networking, and how to be influential techniques. As the CEO of the strategic consulting firm, Promising Promotion, Jill has trained companies in innovative techniques to improve bottom line results. In the past twenty years, she has worked with ABC, NBC, CBS, and other national media, and knows what the media wants.

Jill has been featured in the *New York Times*, *Woman's Day*, *Fortune Small Business, Inc*, and *Entrepreneur Magazine*, and on ABC and NBC radio and television national affiliates.

Her website is: *www.JillLublin.com*.